POLITICAL ANALYSIS

Series Editors: B. Guy Peters, Jon Pierre and Gerry Stoker

Political science today is a dynamic discipline. Its substance, theory and methods have all changed radically in recent decades. It is much expanded in range and scope and in the variety of new perspectives – and new variants of old ones – that it encompasses. The sheer volume of work being published, and the increasing degree of its specialization, however, make it difficult for political scientists to maintain a clear grasp of the state of debate beyond their own particular subdisciplines.

The Political Analysis series is intended to provide a channel for different parts of the discipline to talk to one another and to new generations of students. Our aim is to publish books that provide introductions to, and exemplars of, the best work in various areas of the discipline. Written in an accessible style, they provide a 'launching-pad' for students and others seeking a clear grasp of the key methodological, theoretical and empirical issues, and the main areas of debate, in the complex and fragmented world of political science.

A particular priority is to facilitate intellectual exchange between academic communities in different parts of the world. Although frequently addressing the same intellectual issues, research agendas and literatures in North America, Europe and elsewhere have often tended to develop in relative isolation from one another. This series is designed to provide a framework for dialogue and debate which, rather than advocacy of one regional approach or another, is the key to progress.

The series reflects our view that the core values of political science should be coherent and logically constructed theory, matched by carefully constructed and exhaustive empirical investigation. The key challenge is to ensure quality and integrity in what is produced rather than to constrain diversity in methods and approaches. The series is intended as a showcase for the best of political science in all its variety, and demonstrate how nurturing that variety can further improve the discipline.

Political Analysis Series
Series Standing Order
ISBN 0–333–78694–7 hardback
ISBN 0–333–94506–9 paperback
(outside North America only)

You can receive future titles in this series as they are published by placing a standing order. Please contact your bookseller or, in the case of difficulty, write to us at the address below with your name and address, the title of the series and one of the ISBNs quoted above.

Customer Services Department, Macmillan Distribution Ltd
Houndmills, Basingstoke, Hampshire RG21 6XS, England

POLITICAL
ANALYSIS

Series Editors: B. Guy Peters, Jon Pierre and Gerry Stoker

Beyond Paradigms

Analytic Eclecticism in the Study of World Politics

Rudra Sil
and
Peter J. Katzenstein

657223865

First published 2010 by
PALGRAVE MACMILLAN

Palgrave Macmillan in the UK is an imprint of Macmillan Publishers Limited, registered in England, company number 785998, of Houndmills, Basingstoke, Hampshire RG21 6XS.

Palgrave Macmillan in the US is a division of St Martin's Press LLC, 175 Fifth Avenue, New York, NY 10010.

Palgrave Macmillan is the global academic imprint of the above companies and has companies and representatives throughout the world.

Palgrave® and Macmillan® are registered trademarks in the United States, the United Kingdom, Europe and other countries

ISBN 978-0-230-20795-0   hardback
ISBN 978-0-230-20796-7   paperback

This book is printed on paper suitable for recycling and made from fully managed and sustained forest sources. Logging, pulping and manufacturing processes are expected to conform to the environmental regulations of the country of origin.

A catalogue record for this book is available from the British Library.

A catalog record for this book is available from the Library of Congress.

10 9 8 7 6 5 4 3 2 1
19 18 17 16 15 14 13 12 11 10

Printed in China

Also by the Authors

RUDRA SIL:

Reconfiguring Institutions Across Time and Space: Syncretic Responses to Challenges of Political and Economic Transformation (New York: Palgrave Press, 2007), co-edited with Dennis Galvan.

World Order After Leninism (Seattle: University of Washington Press, 2006), co-edited with Vladimir Tismaneanu and Marc Morjé Howard.

Managing 'Modernity': Work, Community, and Authority in Late-Industrializing Japan and Russia (Ann Arbor: University of Michigan Press, 2002).

The Politics of Labor in a Global Age: Continuity and Change in Late-Industrializing and Post-Socialist Economies (New York: Oxford University Press, 2001), co-edited with Christopher Candland.

Beyond Boundaries? Disciplines, Paradigms, and Theoretical Integration in International Studies (Albany: State University of New York Press, 2000), co-edited with Eileen M. Doherty.

PETER J. KATZENSTEIN:

Civilizations in World Politics: Plural and Pluralist Perspectives (New York: Routledge, 2010), edited volume.

European Identity (New York: Cambridge University Press, 2009), co-edited with Jeffrey T. Checkel.

Rethinking Japanese Security (New York: Routledge, 2008).

Anti-Americanisms in World Politics (Ithaca: Cornell University Press, 2007), co-edited with Robert O. Keohane

Beyond Japan: East Asian Regionalism (Ithaca: Cornell University Press, 2006), co-edited with Takashi Shiraishi.

Religion in an Expanding Europe (New York: Cambridge University Press, 2006), co-edited with Timothy A. Byrnes.

World of Regions: Asia and Europe in the American Imperium (Ithaca: Cornell University Press, 2005).

Rethinking Security in East Asia: Identity, Power, and Efficiency (Stanford, CA: Stanford University Press, 2004), co-edited with J. J. Suh and Allen Carlson.

Exploration and Contestation in the Study of World Politics (Cambridge, MA: The MIT Press, 1999), co-edited with Robert O. Keohane and Stephen D. Krasner.

For Stanley Hoffmann

and

To the memories of

Karl W. Deutsch
(1912–1992)

and

Ernst B. Haas
(1924–2003)

Contents

List of figures, tables and boxes

Figures

Table

Boxes

Acknowledgments

We have incurred a large number of debts along the way. This book would not have been possible without the help of the 15 colleagues whose scholarship we discuss in Chapters 3 to 5: Alice Ba, Michael Barnett, Martha Finnemore, Ian Hurd, Nicolas Jabko, Robert Jervis, David Kang, T. V. Paul, Benjamin Schiff, Frank Schimmelfennig, Leonard Seabrooke, Timothy Sinclair, Etel Solingen, Richard Stubbs, and Cornelia Woll. Each of these scholars generously offered statements about their personal experiences with eclectic research. These statements are presented in separate one-page boxes that appear with our own review and analysis of the 15 works.

Numerous other colleagues and friends have offered insights, suggestions, and criticisms that have made this a better book. With apologies to those we may have failed to mention here, we acknowledge our gratitude to Amel Ahmed, Andrew Bennett, Jeffrey Checkel, Stephen Crowley, Michael Doherty, Charlotte Epstein, Emiliano Grossman, Peter Haas, Gunther Hellman, Adam Humphreys, Jeffrey Isaac, Patrick Thaddeus Jackson, Robert Keohane, David Laitin, James Mahoney, Bruce Mazlish, Ido Oren, Christian Reus-Smit, Srirupa Roy, Ian Shapiro, Kathleen Thelen, Veljko Vujacic, Stephen Watts, Pan Wei, Alexander Wendt, Wang Yizhou, Brigitte Young, and Ruizhuang Zhang, as well as our anonymous reviewers.

We are also grateful for the reactions we received from participants at lectures and seminars convened at various institutions, including Beijing University, the Chinese Academy of Social Sciences, Oberlin College, Oxford University, Sciences-Po, Tianjin University, University of Frankfurt, and the University of Massachusetts. Emma Clarke, Stefan Heumann, and William Petti provided invaluable research assistance.

In addition, Sil would like to thank the School of Arts and Sciences at the University of Pennsylvania, and in particular the Christopher H. Browne Center for International Politics, for providing financial support at various stages of this project.

Katzenstein would like to thank Cornell University for providing, as it has for many decades, incomparable intellectual and financial support when this project was germinating, as well as Louise and John Steffens, whose Founders' Circle Membership at the Institute for Advanced Study at Princeton University supported his work during the academic year 2009–2010.

Figure 2.1 has been adapted from Peter Katzenstein and Rudra Sil, 'Rethinking Asian Security: A Case for Analytical Eclecticism,' in J. J. Suh, Peter J. Katzenstein, and Allen Carlson, *Rethinking Security in East Asia: Identity, Power, and Efficiency* (copyright 2004 by the Board of Trustees of Leland Stanford Junior University and used with permission of Stanford University Press).

Our publisher, Steven Kennedy, gave us his enthusiastic support from the outset. We thank him also for his excellent editorial advice and suggestions, his willingness to push us to think harder about the implications of our arguments, his unfailing attention in the midst of his many other duties to important details we might have overlooked, and his confidence in our ability to meet various deadlines. We also appreciate the assistance provided by others at Palgrave Macmillan, notably Stephen Wenham and Sarah Fry. We are grateful to Susan Curran of Curran Publishing Services for overseeing the production process with efficiency and grace. And we thank Sarah Tarrow, whose exquisite editorial touch and administrative acumen once again made the preparation and submission of the final version of the manuscript appear effortless. It goes without saying that this book could not have been written without the support and encouragement we received from our better halves, Eileen and Mary.

RUDRA SIL
AND
PETER J. KATZENSTEIN

Preface

For a long time, both of us have been baffled and frustrated by emotionally charged paradigmatic debates about the nature of international relations and the growing gap between the worlds of scholarship and politics these debates revealed. At a 2003 workshop, we had ample opportunity to define and debate an alternative mode of inquiry we now refer to as 'analytic eclecticism.' Our lively discussions at that workshop and a series of jointly authored papers prepared us to write this book.

We have learned a great deal from each other and about ourselves – including about the benefits of having the trains run on time and the beauty of a sentence that runs less than six lines. We have exchanged over 2,000 e-mail messages sharing ideas, arguing points with seriousness and humor, and making countless revisions in our writings. Above all, we have enjoyed our intellectual conversations and company. Writing this book has been unmitigated fun.

The last two decades have witnessed important changes in world politics. The end of the Cold War and the disintegration of the Soviet Union in 1989–91, Al-Qaeda's 9/11 attacks and their aftermath, and the financial crisis of 2008 constitute major events with far-reaching consequences for the structure of world politics. They also present unique opportunities for learning about the limitations of the paradigms with which scholars apprehend the world. Too often, these opportunities are wasted; for too often, we pull up drawbridges protecting our paradigmatic sandcastles rather than lowering them to explore how wind and water have altered the terrain outside of the fragile walls we have built. In this book we challenge that practice. Eclecticism cultivates conversations, not only with like-minded scholars but also with others combing the same beach equipped with different intuitions and tools. Learning from unfamiliar encounters, we argue, is a wise investment, not a waste of time.

All of the normal caveats obtain about the limitations of this book. We know firsthand that scholars have strong feelings and voice strong opinions about some of the issues we raise. Nobody has the last word on questions that cut to the core of what international relations scholarship is and does. Ongoing conversations about these issues remain central to international relations, political science, and the social sciences. Making the case for analytical eclecticism in a discipline wedded strongly to paradigmatic conventions and presenting some outstanding eclectic scholarship will, we hope, further such conversations.

Indeed, our intellectual engagement with colleagues whose works we discuss in Chapters 3 to 5 has been enormously instructive. These diverse examples of eclectic scholarship have helped us refine our own thinking and reinforced our conviction that the variety of eclectic scholarly practices is the strongest defense against any future attempt at turning analytic eclecticism into yet another paradigm. That would indeed be ironic! Limitations of space and time prevented us from engaging with many other eclectic studies and scholars. And, it goes without saying, throughout our careers we have learned enormous amounts from many outstanding works of scholarship that were not eclectic in sensibility, style or approach.

We dedicate this book to three of our teachers, mentors, and friends. Stanley Hoffmann and the late Karl W. Deutsch and Ernst B. Haas were European émigrés who ranked among the finest and most distinguished scholars of international relations in the second half of the twentieth century, both in the United States and worldwide. They articulated in the 1960s what today would be considered paradigmatically different approaches to the analysis of world politics. Our students tell us that Deutsch, Haas, and Hoffmann were all wrong. It is the role of younger scholars to judge harshly past scholarship as part of the dark ages and to proclaim confidently the coming of a new dawn – a practice we remember all too well. It is the wisdom of older scholars to know better.

Deutsch, Haas, and Hoffmann were fiercely independent scholars who cared more about the world they studied than about their professional standing or shifting fashions of theory and method. Different in intellectual temperament and orientation, their writings and teachings were exemplary in the fresh articulation of research questions, the development of explanations that could travel beyond specific empirical domains, and the relevance of their findings for the world of politics and policy. Like all of us, they were wrong at times. But, they were right in many other ways. Their intellectual appetites for new and different ways of seeing the world were voracious. Their brilliant minds crossed all sorts of boundaries with ease. They never lost the skeptical admiration with which European scholars viewed American scholarship. And they remained always aware of both the limits of our theoretical models and the capaciousness of human reason.

With a twinkle in his eye, Deutsch used to tell an imaginary story of Tom Schelling and Morton Halperin, instructed by their models of coercive bargaining, both driving their cars through Harvard Square at high speed without looking right or left; after encountering each other at an intersection, they appeared heavily bandaged in class the next day. Haas exuded the image of the stern German father, offering scathing criticisms to legions of graduate students, many of whom would later become prominent scholars in their own right. To Rudy, he even wrote an irate letter after a first-semester IR seminar announcing that 'Berkeley is not the right place for you,' only to later hire him as a research assistant and serve on his dissertation committee. He had high standards, but no fixed truths. Still legendary today are the many dry asides with which Hoffmann liked to puncture the overblown claims of a supposedly universal yet embarrassingly ahistorical and American-centric science of world politics. And all three acknowledged freely the forever preliminary, contingent, and contestable nature of our claims and findings.

In today's paradigm-centered world, Deutsch's twinkles, Haas's tough love, and Hoffmann's dry wit too often have given way to nasty reviews, verbal assaults, and barely concealed snickers. The border separating paradigmatic debate from inter-paradigm warfare is thin. Even though we live in our fragile sandcastles on beaches exposed to stormy waters, often we are too certain of ourselves and too willing to take no prisoners in proclaiming victory. This book is in part a modest effort to counteract these unfortunate tendencies. As scholarly conversationalists, we fall well short of the standards of a Stanley Hoffmann, a Karl Deutsch, or an Ernie Haas. Their intellectual boldness, humility, honesty, and openness to alternative ideas, however, have been an important source of inspiration for this book.

RS AND PJK
PHILADELPHIA AND PRINCETON
JULY 2010

Chapter 1

Analytic eclecticism

In a *Washington Post* column titled 'Scholars on the sidelines,' Joseph Nye (2009) has lamented the growing gap between theory and policy in the field of international relations: 'Scholars are paying less attention to questions about how their work relates to the policy world.... Advancement comes faster for those who develop mathematical models, new methodologies or theories expressed in jargon that is unintelligible to policymakers.' Nye's fears are not unfounded. In fact, they are a stark reminder of the truth of Charles Lindblom's and David Cohen's (1979) observation made exactly three decades before: that there is a persistent chasm between what 'suppliers' of social research offer and what the prospective 'users' of this research seek. One reason for this has to do with the excessive compartmentalization of knowledge in the social sciences, and particularly in the field of international relations. Simply put, too much of social scientific research in the academe is divided across, and embedded within, discrete approaches that we often refer to as 'paradigms' or 'research traditions.' Paradigm-bound research provides powerful insights, but in the absence of complementary efforts to compare and integrate insights from multiple paradigms, the latter can become a 'hindrance to understanding,' as Albert Hirschman (1970) noted long ago.

Proponents of particular paradigms proceed on the basis of specific sets of a priori assumptions not shared by others. They pose research questions, establish boundaries for investigations, and evaluate research products in a manner that reflects these assumptions. Based on ontological and epistemological principles established by fiat, they posit clusters of theories or narratives that assign primacy to certain kinds of causal factors rather than others. In doing so, over time adherents of paradigms discover novel facts

1

and generate increasingly sophisticated arguments. But this is understood as progress only by the adherents of a given paradigm. It does not redound to progress that is recognized or appreciated, either by the discipline writ large or by those outside the academe who look to social scientists for usable knowledge. Instead, scholarly discourse risks becoming dominated by self-referential academic debates at the expense of addressing the complexities and messiness of everyday problems.

In this book, we aim to do more than show that paradigm-bound scholarship has come up short. We argue that it is possible, indeed necessary, for scholars to resist the temptation to assume that one or another research tradition is inherently superior for posing and solving all problems, and we maintain that we can and should do a better job of recognizing and delineating relationships between concepts, observations, and causal stories originally constructed in different analytic perspectives. At the same time, going 'beyond paradigms' does not mean discarding or ignoring the work being done by adherents of those paradigms. It means exploring substantive relationships and revealing hidden connections among elements of seemingly incommensurable paradigm-bound theories, with an eye to generating novel insights that bear on policy debates and practical dilemmas. This requires an alternative way of thinking about the relationships among assumptions, concepts, theories, the organization of research, and real-world problems. We call this alternative *analytic eclecticism*.[1]

We are not the first to note the shortcomings of paradigm-bound research or to make reference to eclectic approaches. However, our argument is distinctive in its effort to create a more coherent and systematic understanding of what constitutes analytic eclecticism, how it engages and integrates existing strands of scholarship, and what value it adds to academic and policy debates. This is more than a call for pluralism and tolerance. And it is more than a plea for more policy-oriented research at the expense of theory. Analytic eclecticism is about making intellectually and practically useful connections among clusters of analyses that are substantively related but normally formulated in separate paradigms. It rests on a pragmatic set of assumptions, downplays rigid epistemic commitments, and focuses on the consequences of scholarship for concrete dilemmas. It challenges the analytic boundaries derived from paradigmatic assumptions, and refuses to carve up complex social phenomena solely for the purpose of making them more tractable to a particular style of analysis. Instead, it identifies important substantive questions that have relevance for the real world, and it integrates empirical observations and causal stories that are posited in separate paradigm-bound theories or narratives. In doing so, analytic eclecticism holds forth the promise of richer explanations. It also offers a means to reduce the gap between the practical knowledge required by policymakers and everyday actors, and the research products generated by academic disciplines and subfields. Since it depends heavily on the theoretical and empirical work generated within paradigms and research traditions, analytic eclecticism does not seek to displace them. The goal is not to synthesize, subsume, or replace paradigms. It is to demonstrate the practical relevance of, and substantive connections among, theories and narratives constructed within seemingly discrete and irreconcilable approaches.

In this chapter, we first lay out what we mean by paradigms and research traditions, and consider both their usefulness and their limitations. We then offer a more explicit definition of analytic eclecticism, and elaborate on the reasons that make it a valuable complement to paradigm-bound scholarship in the social sciences. We also address the issue posed by the supposed incommensurability of theories embedded in alternative research traditions, and we distinguish analytic eclecticism from unifying synthesis and from multi-method research and triangulation. We then identify three markers we employ to identify eclectic scholarship throughout this book.

Chapter 2 conceives of eclecticism in relation to paradigms in international relations, emphasizing the complex interactions among the distribution of material capabilities (privileged by realists), the interests and efficiency gains pursued by individual and collective actors (privileged by liberals), and the ideational factors that shape how actors understand their world and their identities within it (privileged by constructivists). Chapters 3 to 5 offer illustrations of eclectic work in the fields of national and international security (Chapter 3), global political economy (Chapter 4), and various forms of global/regional governance (Chapter 5). In the Conclusion (Chapter 6), we consider the lessons to be gleaned from these examples of eclectic scholarship in international relations. We do not offer a synthetic guide to eclectic research, which would run counter to the pragmatist ethos of analytic eclecticism. Instead, we emphasize the distinctiveness and usefulness of adopting an eclectic approach to the formulation of problems, to the construction of explanations, and to the connection of theory to practice. We also consider the professional risks and trade-offs of eclectic scholarship for individuals, and argue that we should accept them in light of the limitations of paradigm-bound scholarship in reducing the gap noted by Nye (2009) between theory and policy. We also note the proliferation of parallel arguments in favor of eclectic styles of reasoning in other fields of scholarship and practice.

Paradigms and research traditions

Social science disciplines have witnessed many battles among contending approaches, each claiming to offer a superior analytic framework for making sense of core issues in various disciplines. What most consistently divides these schools of thought are not their substantive claims about specific phenomena but their metatheoretical assumptions concerning how such claims should be developed and supported. Although such foundational assumptions typically cannot be subjected to empirical tests, they influence many research tasks, including specifying whether the objective is to uncover general laws, develop deeper understandings of action in specific contexts, or encourage critique and political action; determining what aspects of phenomena are worth analyzing and how questions about these phenomena are to be posed; and establishing what types of concepts, methods, and standards are to be followed in developing answers to these questions, whether in the form of theories, models, narratives, or ethnographies.[2]

Following the seminal work of Thomas Kuhn (1962), some scholars have employed the concept of paradigms to characterize and distinguish approaches on the basis of their core foundational assumptions. Kuhn challenged Karl Popper's (1959) characterization of scientific knowledge, which treats falsification as the basis for continuous and cumulative progress. Kuhn interpreted the history of science as a sequence of discrete periods of normal science, separated by relatively short episodes of revolutionary science. A period of normal science is typically marked by the ascendance of a single dominant paradigm that determines the central research questions, the theoretical vocabulary to be employed, the range of acceptable methods, and the criteria for assessing how well a given question has been answered. When fully institutionalized, the weak links of a paradigm are no longer recognized, its foundational assumptions are no longer questioned, and its anomalies are consistently overlooked or considered beyond the purview of acceptable research endeavors. Revolutionary science occurs in those brief interludes when scientific communities, frustrated by increasing numbers of anomalies, begin to focus on new problems and take up new approaches that help resolve such anomalies. Once a new cluster of questions, assumptions, and approaches has acquired large numbers of supporters, the door is open for the emergence of a new paradigm. Significantly, paradigms are assumed to be incommensurable with one another, making it impossible to integrate or compare theories developed within each of them.

Other scholars (Elman and Elman 2003) have employed Imre Lakatos' (1970) concept of research program to map diverse strands of scholarship and assess the possibilities for progress in a given field. Responding to Kuhn's rejection of objective markers of continuous progress, Lakatos sought to make room for a more pluralistic view of coexisting scientific communities, each with its own research program. Lakatosian research programs have a number of features – a 'hard core,' a 'protective belt' of auxiliary assumptions, and positive and negative 'heuristics' – which essentially perform the same functions as Kuhn's paradigms: they protect core metatheoretical assumptions from being challenged or subjected to empirical tests. Yet Lakatos extends the 'staying power' of a theory by giving proponents the opportunity to defend or refine their theories, rather than discard a theory at the first sign of disconfirming evidence or unexplained anomalies. This possibility is related to the distinction Lakatos draws between 'progressive' and 'degenerative' research programs. Progressive programs are capable of producing new theories that can surpass the explanatory power of past theories while striving to account for previously unexplained phenomena. Degenerative programs face a growing number of anomalies, and deal with these by offering ad hoc accounts that are only loosely attached to existing theories developed in a progressive phase. A Lakatosian view of science allows us to capture the varying trajectories of contending approaches in such fields as international relations. It still assumes, however, that substantive research proceeds forward within research communities whose members agree upon core assumptions, questions, methods, and standards of evaluation. Without such a consensus, adherents of different research programs are not likely to hold common views on whether a given program is progressive or degenerating.

Whatever their utility in tracing the history of the natural sciences, both Kuhnian and Lakatosian models of scientific progress face limitations when it comes to capturing the enduring debates and intellectual shifts characteristic of international relations. The recurrent and divisive confrontations over various tenets associated with positivism are difficult to square with the notion of international relations as a 'normal' science with a single dominant paradigm. Lakatos does allow for the coexistence of research programs, but he does not envision entire disciplines marked by unending competition among rival approaches, each viewed by its proponents as 'progressive' and challenged by its opponents as 'degenerating.' Furthermore, various foundational assumptions can be weighted and prioritized quite differently by adherents of a research program; this can give rise to discrete strands of research that operate with their own 'hard cores' and 'protective belts,' as may be happening with various types of constructivism in international relations (Checkel 2006). Indeed, some of the most important foundational divides underlying inter-paradigm debates – for example, objectivism versus subjectivism, universal versus particular, agency versus structure, material versus ideational – have proven to be enduring 'fractal distinctions' (Abbott 2004, pp. 162–70) which generate and structure debates within the same paradigm or research program.[3] At the same time, certain ontological principles can be held in common by theories that originate in different paradigms – as evident in the fact that some constructivists accept the realist view of states as motivated by survival in an anarchic system, while others join liberals in emphasizing the emergence of institutionalized cooperation in international behavior (Chernoff 2007, p. 69). In short, while Kuhnian paradigms and Lakatosian research programs can be helpful in capturing some aspects of evolving debates in international relations (Elman and Elman 2003), rigid conceptions of either do not square with the complicated and contentious history of social scientific disciplines in general, and international relations scholarship in particular.

In this book, we employ a flexibly defined conception of paradigm, one that approximates the concept of *research tradition* as articulated by Larry Laudan (1977, 1996). Like Kuhn and Lakatos, Laudan recognizes the central role played by long-enduring epistemological commitments that govern the scope and content of scientific research in any given field. These commitments produce discrete research traditions, each of which consists of: '(1) a set of beliefs about what sorts of entities and processes make up the domain of inquiry; and (2) a set of epistemic and methodological norms about how the domain is to be investigated, how theories are to be tested, how data are to be collected, and the like' (Laudan 1996, p. 83). However, unlike Kuhn and Lakatos, Laudan offers no uniform model for how to track the progress or decline of successive or competing approaches. Instead, he suggests that different research traditions not only coexist, but frequently react to each other. He also observes that research traditions are not mutually exclusive when it comes to the empirical realities they interpret. Substantive theories from different research traditions can converge both in their findings and in their implications. Laudan goes as far as to acknowledge the possibility of a single scholar working in multiple research traditions even where their foundations are widely understood to be incommensurable (Laudan 1977, pp. 104–10).

Laudan thus offers us a view of social science in which intellectual history need not be neatly sequenced into a succession of Kuhnian paradigms. Moreover, at any given moment, diverse scholarly activities need not be shoehorned into one of a handful of Lakatosian research programs. Laudan's treatment of the varied and complex efforts to produce knowledge – with its attention to the possibilities of overlapping assumptions and converging substantive interpretations across research traditions – is much more realistic when it comes to mapping the diverse intellectual currents that have emerged in the field of international relations over the past half century. In acknowledging the possibility of scholars working across traditions, Laudan opens the door to the 'amalgamation' of theoretical constructs taken from diverse research traditions (1977, p. 104). We will use the terms 'paradigm' and 'research tradition' interchangeably throughout this book, and will understand both terms as referring to the latter, as characterized by Laudan.

Substantive research that is conceptualized and pursued within paradigms has much to contribute. For any given problem, before a more expansive dialogue can take place among a more heterogeneous community of scholars, it is useful to first have a more disciplined dialogue on the basis of a clearly specified set of concepts, a common theoretical language, and a common set of methods and evaluative standards predicated on a common metatheoretical perspective. Such a set of initial shared understandings allows for focused empirical research that can be more easily coded, compared, and cumulated within distinct research traditions. This process also facilitates the generation of clear, parsimonious arguments as well as rudimentary stocks of knowledge that can help to operationalize and delimit further research without having to reinvent the wheel each time. In international relations, for example, the (neo)realist paradigm provided a common theoretical language and analytic framework for focused debates concerning such phenomena as the causes of war, patterns of alliance-building, and the logic of deterrence. Similarly, neoliberal theorists adopted a distinct set of metatheoretical assumptions as their starting point in order to develop a core literature on the definition and effects of interdependence and on the different routes to institutionalized cooperation. It is also worth emphasizing that 'creative confrontations' (Lichbach 2007, p. 274) between paradigms have often spurred intellectual progress within a paradigm by motivating its adherents to refine their theories and narratives in response to challenges from others.

These sorts of intellectual benefits are not, however, a guarantee of progress for any discipline writ large. Different paradigms adopt different strategies for limiting the domain of analysis, identifying research puzzles, interpreting empirical observations, and specifying relevant causal mechanisms. Given the emphasis on parsimony in the social sciences, adherents of paradigms also tend to rely heavily on simplifications that make it easier to problematize complex social phenomena and apply their preferred concepts and tools. Those aspects of reality that are not readily problematized and analyzed within a given analytic framework are often ignored, 'blackboxed,' or treated as 'exogenous to the model.' What makes this practice problematic is that the same empirical phenomenon may be parsed in different ways for no other reason than to enable the application of assumptions, concepts, and methods associated with a given metatheoretical perspective. And because each paradigm puts forward its own distinct criteria for evaluating the theories it engenders, there is no basis for shared criteria that a discipline as a whole can employ to compare the usefulness of theories for addressing real-world phenomena. As Ian Shapiro (2005, p. 184) notes, 'if a phenomenon is characterized as it is so as to vindicate a particular theory rather than to illuminate a problem that has been independently specified, then it is unlikely to gain much purchase on what is actually going on.'

Thus, it is not surprising that there has been growing interest in alternatives to scholarship that is explicitly or implicitly designed to defend the core metatheoretical postulates of a paradigm or research tradition. Such alternatives focus on the practical utility of theories in relation to concrete problems in the real world rather than on their ability to meet the criteria established by proponents of particular paradigms. Within the context of international relations, a growing number of scholars (including those featured in Chapters 3 to 5 in this book) have chosen to bypass the paradigm wars. Instead, they address vexing issues of both scholarly and practical import through complex arguments that incorporate elements of theories or narratives originally drawn up in separate research traditions. Many of these works are also a response to the growing gap between self-contained, academic debates and broader public debates over policy and practice. What we call analytic eclecticism is intended to capture the contributions of, and provide a coherent intellectual rationale for, this relatively new movement that resists 'a priori constraints on the kinds of questions that social scientists ask of social life and on the kinds of theories they are likely to entertain' (Shapiro and Wendt 2005, p. 50).

What analytic eclecticism is and does

Simplifications based on a single theoretical lens involve trade-offs, and can produce enduring blind spots unless accompanied by complementary, countervailing efforts to 'recomplexify' problems (Scott 1995). Without such efforts, academic discourse risks becoming little more than a cluster of research activities addressing artificially segmented problems, with little thought to the implications of findings for real-world dilemmas facing political and social actors. This is where analytic eclecticism, despite its own limitations (noted below), makes its distinctive contribution as social scientists seek to contend with the complexity of social phenomena that bear on the practical dilemmas and constraints faced by decision makers and other actors in the 'real' world.

We define as eclectic *any approach that seeks to extricate, translate, and selectively integrate analytic elements – concepts, logics, mechanisms, and interpretations – of theories or narratives that have been developed within separate paradigms but that address related aspects of substantive problems that have both scholarly and practical significance.* Paradigm-bound scholarship typically focuses on questions that conform to particular metatheoretical assumptions and lend themselves to the use of particular concepts and approaches. Analytic eclecticism takes on problems as they are understood and experienced by political actors, without excessively simplifying such problems simply to fit the scholarly conventions or theoretical boundaries established by any one tradition. Paradigm-bound scholarship typically assumes the ontological and causal primacy of certain types of phenomena, mechanisms, and processes while disregarding or marginalizing others. Analytic eclecticism explores how diverse mechanisms posited in competing paradigm-bound theories might interact with each other, and how, under certain conditions, they can combine to affect outcomes that interest both scholars and practitioners. In this section, we elaborate on the rationale for eclectic scholarship, consider the challenge of incommensurability, and sharpen the definition of analytic eclecticism by stipulating what it is not.

The rationale for analytic eclecticism

Even though there is no basis for definitively establishing whether one set of a priori principles is inherently more 'correct' than others, paradigms and research traditions proceed on the basis of a distinct set of foundational principles, and frame their problems and arguments accordingly. This means that the kinds of empirical observations and causal logics offered in defense of a theoretical argument developed in one paradigm will not have the same significance for a theoretical argument developed on the basis of a different set of foundational assumptions. Certainly, one can still work within a single paradigm to reveal its full potential. However, the reasonableness of the core foundational postulates identified with competing paradigms also justifies a more eclectic search for hidden connections and complementarities among theories embedded in different paradigms. In the context of the philosophy of science, this position is analogous to one invoked by John Vasquez (2003, p. 426) in defending his use of multiple frames of appraisal:

Eclecticism is a well-known response to the quandary of having to adapt a philosophy when one finds all existing philosophies having some flaws but, at the same time, some elements worthy of adopting. This is the situation in all of the social sciences when we find ourselves confronting the fields of epistemology and philosophy of science. It is perfectly permissible to select one frame and apply it systematically, but given that there is no one single flawless frame, there is no reason that would logically prohibit the use of other frames as well.

There exists also a second and positive reason for making more space for analytic eclecticism: eclectic modes of inquiry increase the chances that students of world politics, and the ordinary actors they claim to study, might more frequently generate more useful theoretical and empirical insights. These insights can elude adherents of paradigms who view their problems through distinct lenses that are specifically designed to filter out certain 'inconvenient' facts to enable a more focused analysis. The very features that enable proponents of a paradigm to delimit the objects of their research entail that the research will not speak to a range of potentially relevant phenomena, processes, and mechanisms. This is precisely why analytic eclecticism is a vitally important complement to paradigmatic scholarship: it forgoes the simplifications required by paradigmatic boundaries and permits a more comprehensive assessment of the practical relevance and relative significance of findings generated within multiple paradigms.

This line of argument harkens back to Hirschman's (1970, p. 341) observation that experienced politicians, whose intuitions are more likely to take into account 'a variety of forces at work,' frequently offer more useful conjectures and forecasts in a given situation than do adherents of paradigms, who necessarily ignore some of these forces and run the risk of a high degree of error in their efforts to explain phenomena and forecast large-scale transformations. Paradigms may be 'useful for the apprehending of many elements' in the unfolding of significant transformations; but, for Hirschman (1970, p. 343), proponents of specific paradigms have little to offer to actors seeking to engineer social change:

> The architect of social change can never have a reliable blueprint. Not only is each house he builds different from

any other that was built before, but it also necessarily uses new construction materials and even experiments with untested principles of stress and structure. Therefore what can be most usefully conveyed by the builders of one house is an understanding of the experience that made it all possible to build under these trying circumstances.

Echoing Hirschman's position, Philip Tetlock (2005, p. 214) contends that a single analytic framework 'confers the benefits of closure and parsimony but desensitizes us to nuance, complexity, contingency, and the possibility that our theory is wrong.' Utilizing differently calibrated tests of judgmental accuracy in a wide variety of settings, Tetlock's study of decision making demonstrates that grossly inaccurate forecasts are more common when experts employ a single parsimonious approach and rely excessively upon broad abstractions 'to organize messy facts and to distinguish the possible from the impossible' (Tetlock 2005, p. 88). Conversely, better forecasts are more likely when experts rely on various kinds of knowledge and information to improvise ad hoc solutions in a rapidly changing world. Adapting the famous reference from Isaiah Berlin's work, Tetlock suggests that, all other things being equal, 'eclectic foxes' tend to do better than 'intellectually aggressive hedgehogs.' What distinguishes the cognitive style of foxes and enables them to gain higher forecasting skill scores is their refusal 'to be anchored down by theory-laden abstractions,' along with their readiness 'to blend opposing hedgehog arguments' (Tetlock 2005, p. 91).

Analytic eclecticism represents such an effort at blending, a means for scholars to guard against the risks of excessive reliance on a single analytic perspective. This is particularly true when it comes to understanding intersections and interactions among multiple social processes in different domains of social reality. Peter Hall (2003, p. 387) notes that the ontologies guiding the study of politics are increasingly characterized by 'more extensive endogeneity and the ubiquity of complex interaction effects.' Accordingly, analytic eclecticism refuses to exclude certain aspects of social phenomena from the framework of analysis simply for the purpose of satisfying boundary conditions and scholarly conventions linked to a priori paradigmatic assumptions. Instead, it trains its sights on the connections and interactions among a wide range of causal forces normally analyzed in isolation from one another. This does not guarantee consensus on forecasts or prescriptions that can assist policymakers and lay actors. It does, however, encourage a wider, more open-ended conversation about how the different causal forces identified by proponents of different paradigms might coexist as part of a more complex, yet usable analytic framework that helps in making sense of concrete social phenomena.

Analytic eclecticism is also a response to what Shapiro (2005, p. 2) refers to as 'the flight from reality' among academics, that is the growing gap between theoretical debates within the academe and demands for policy relevance and practicality outside it. We are not suggesting here that all academic scholarship be reorganized so as to cater to the existing agendas of policymakers. Indeed, as Anne Norton (2004) cautions, problem-oriented scholarship can end up enlisting scholars in the unreflective service of those exercising power. In this it often reinforces acceptance of particular worldviews and uniform modes of inquiry at the expense of critical thinking in relation to existing policy agendas and practices. At the same time there exists a very real danger of scholarship getting overly preoccupied with purely academic disputes that are hermetically blocked off from public discourse and policy debates about important issues of interest to both scholars and practitioners. Analytic eclecticism is part of a wider effort to restore 'the balance between detachment and engagement, between withdrawal behind the monastic walls of the university and the joys and dangers of mixing with the profane world outside' (Wallace 1996, p. 304).

The not insurmountable challenge of incommensurability

Trafficking in theories drawn from competing paradigms has its hazards. Most significant is the possible incommensurability across theories drawn from different paradigms. The incommensurability thesis has its roots in early twentieth-century philosophy, in the work of Pierre Duhem (1954) among others. In contemporary discussions, it is most famously associated with arguments of Paul Feyerabend (1962) and Thomas Kuhn (1962). The thesis makes a straightforward claim. Because they are formulated on the basis of distinct ontologies and epistemological assumptions, the specific concepts, terms, and standards used in one theoretical approach are not interchangeable with those used in another. There can be no equivalence, either in the meaning of concepts used in different paradigms, or in the standards established by those paradigms to evaluate or compare theories. Theories cannot be validated or refuted on the basis of any one set of empirical observations. Simply put, there exists no agreed-upon understanding about the significance of specific observations or about the testing protocols followed by proponents of different theories.

The incommensurability thesis could be interpreted in such a way as to render futile any effort to integrate the concepts, analytic principles, and theoretical propositions formulated across different research traditions. As James Johnson (2002) notes, danger lurks when we move between research traditions founded on competing ontological and epistemological principles. Specifically, unrecognized conceptual problems are likely to subvert the explanatory objectives of a theory when we use its conceptual vocabulary unreflectively in a fundamentally different analytic framework. Moreover, there is the danger that attempts at integrating theories from different paradigms may superficially homogenize fundamentally incompatible perspectives at a higher level of abstraction without enhancing our ability to understand complex phenomena on the ground (Harvey and Cobb 2003, p. 146). The problem of incommensurability thus poses an important challenge for eclectic analyses. For two reasons, however, we do not believe that the problem is insurmountable.

First, the incommensurability thesis is most compelling when it comes to uniform criteria for evaluating diverse theories; it is much less constraining when it comes to integrating elements from these theories. Donald Davidson (1974) and Hilary Putnam (1981) have both noted that the incommensurability thesis would be valid only if it were completely impossible to translate terms expressed in the language of one theoretical scheme into the language of another. Putnam (1981, p. 115; see also Oberheim 2006, p. 28) argues: '[I]f the thesis were really true, then we could not translate other languages – or even past stages of our own language.' Others have suggested that a 'hard' version of the incommensurability thesis entails a narrow vision of science in which various theories are treated solely as mutually exclusive explanatory systems, when in reality key elements or terms within certain theories can be adjusted and incorporated into others (Hattiangadi 1977; Wisdom 1974).[4] In fact, Feyerabend himself was primarily concerned with the idea of neutral testing protocols that could be invoked to compare different types of theories; he neither viewed incommensurability as implying untranslatability, nor assumed that translatability was a precondition for theory comparison (Oberheim 2006). The incommensurability thesis does pose a serious problem for the notion of objective criteria for *evaluating* theories drawn from different paradigms. When it comes to combining elements from different theories, however, the challenge is not as severe as is frequently assumed.

Second, within the context of the social sciences, it is worth noting that theories concerning substantive questions must ultimately rely on empirical referents to operationalize concepts, variables, and mechanisms. These referents provide a means for adjusting and integrating features of theories originally embedded in different paradigms. By focusing on the substantive indicators employed to apply concepts, it becomes possible to reconceptualize and partially combine specific causal links drawn from different paradigm-bound theories. Alternatively, as Craig Parsons (2007, p. 3) notes, it is possible to break down competing explanatory logics into modules in such a way that they become compatible at a higher level of abstraction, 'such that we could imagine a world in which all were operating while we debate how much variants of each contributed to any given action.' It thus becomes possible to temporarily separate foundational metatheoretical postulates from specific substantive claims or interpretations. This, in turn, opens the door to direct comparison between, and greater integration of, analytic elements drawn from casual stories embedded in different paradigms so long as these stories concer similar or related phenomena.[5]

These observations suggest that the problem of incommensurability is a relative one. Even within a single paradigm, the same term can be defined and used differently by different scholars offering different causal stories. Admittedly, the challenge is greater when traversing paradigms. But it is not insurmountable as long as proper care is taken to consider the premises upon which specific analytic components are operationalized. It is possible to ensure that concepts and analytic principles are properly understood in their original conceptual frameworks, and to adjust or translate these terms by considering how they are operationalized in the relevant empirical contexts by proponents of various paradigms. This does not guarantee theoretical coherence or conceptual equivalence in all cases, but it does point to possibilities for limiting the problem of incommensurability.

Clarification: What analytic eclecticism is not

Analytic eclecticism is not intended as a means to hedge one's bets to cope with uncertainty, as Göran Therborn (2005, pp. 25–6) has suggested. We view eclecticism as focused on seeking the best answer for a problem at any given time, on the basis of relevant insights drawn from existing theories and narratives. We also see it as courageous in that it requires scholars to engage in research without the 'protective belts' and 'negative heuristics' (Lakatos 1970) that often shield scholars operating within the confines of a research program. In addition, eclectic scholars have to engage quite diverse cognitive styles while coping with wide-ranging challenges from those who have greater commitment to, and more command over, specific theoretical elements.

Analytic eclecticism is not predicated upon the idea that incorporating elements from diverse theories will necessarily provide a single 'correct' answer. A commitment to an eclectic approach leaves ample room for disagreement about the significance of particular configurations and the relative weights of various causal forces in relation to a specified problem. The point is not to insist on consensus on substantive issues by mechanically staking out an intermediate position between starkly opposed perspectives. Rather, it is to ensure that communities of scholars do not speak past each other when they simplify complex phenomena and slice up real-world problems in line with their preferred theoretical vocabularies and analytic boundaries.

Analytic eclecticism does not imply that 'anything goes.' In fact, the general definition of eclecticism as well as its utility in a specific context depends on the recognition that paradigm-bound research has generated plentiful evidence about the causal significance of various mechanisms and processes operating in some domain of the social world. In other words, analytic eclecticism requires us not only to appreciate the theories and narratives developed within different paradigms, but also to make the wager that they contain important causal insights that need to be taken seriously in any effort to make sense of complex social phenomena. It is entirely possible, indeed likely, that these insights might never have emerged without the concerted efforts of researchers operating on the basis of paradigmatic assumptions and boundaries. The value-added of analytic eclecticism lies not in bypassing paradigm-bound scholarship or giving license to explore each and every imaginable factor, but in recognizing, connecting, and utilizing the insights generated by paradigm-bound scholarship concerning the combined significance of various factors when domains of social analysis are no longer artificially segregated. Both logically and temporally, analytic eclecticism follows paradigmatically organized efforts to develop insights and arguments about segments of social phenomena. As Parsons (2007, p. 43) notes, 'There is no solid middle ground without poles, no useful eclecticism without distinct things to mix.'

Analytic eclecticism is not theoretical synthesis. It is true that what we regard as 'eclecticism' is sometimes referred to casually as 'synthesis.' Gunther Hellmann (2003, p. 149) speaks of a 'pragmatic fusion of synthesis and dialogue' in promoting open-ended communication and combinatorial problem solving, both of which we associate with eclecticism. We view analytic eclecticism as a flexible approach that needs to be tailored to a given problem and to existing debates over aspects of this problem. As such, it categorically rejects the idea of a unified synthesis that can provide a common theoretical foundation for various sorts of problem. Genuine theoretical synthesis requires something very rare and extraordinary: a marked departure from the core ontological and epistemological assumptions associated with contending research traditions, followed by a convergence upon a new set of foundational assumptions that will bound and guide research on all kinds of substantive issues and problems. Without such a convergence, efforts at synthesis are likely to remain, at best, intellectually hegemonic projects that end up marginalizing the contributions produced by existing paradigms (Lichbach 2003).

Andrew Moravcsik (2003) offers a dissenting view. He recognizes that theories operate on the basis of different ontologies, but he views theoretical synthesis as both possible and desirable so long as elements of a synthetic argument are disaggregated and tested with specific methods. We share the pragmatic spirit of Moravcsik's argument, which downplays epistemic principles. However, we are not certain that it constitutes a move towards genuine 'synthesis' as the term is normally understood. Moravcsik implies that synthesis is additive, with each element constituting an independent proposition and subjected to a specific type of test. However, different methods of theory testing are predicated on different epistemological assumptions linked to Popperian, Hempelian, and Lakatosian views on the role of empirical observations in the development of theory. In contemporary social science, while some are content with an exclusive focus on statistical tests, others are more concerned with internal logical consistency than with the results of any one particular form of external empirical validation. Moreover, the testing of different components of a 'synthetic' theory would require scholars to put the emphasis right back on the separate causal claims, drawing attention away from the complex interaction effects at play within a given context or problem. Eclectic work does need to be assessed in relation to available evidence and alternative arguments. Such work cannot, however, be evaluated solely on the basis of separate tests applied to discrete components; it is also necessary to consider the originality and utility of the whole as it relates to both existing scholarly debates and concrete issues of interest to policymakers or other practitioners.

Finally, analytic eclecticism is not coterminous with multi-method research or methodological triangulation (Jick 1979; Tarrow 1995; Lieberman 2005; Capoccia 2006). To be sure, analytic eclecticism benefits from the pluralistic impulse associated with multi-method research. Moreover, attempts to investigate the interaction between macro-level phenomena, micro-level decision making and context-specific processes will benefit from attention to findings generated through different kinds of approaches. Analytic eclecticism thus requires a broad understanding of the particular strengths, limitations, and trade-offs across different methodological perspectives. Yet it is important not to conflate analytic eclecticism with multi-method research. Analytic eclecticism is focused on the theoretical constructs that we deploy to capture the complexity of important social problems. The combinatorial logic of analytic eclecticism depends not on the multiplicity of methods but on the multiplicity of connections between different mechanisms and logics normally analyzed in isolation in separate research traditions. In principle, such a project can be advanced by the flexible application of a single method – be it game theory, regression analysis, case studies, or ethnography – so long as the problem and the emergent causal story take into account elements drawn from theories developed in separate paradigms.

Recognizing analytic eclecticism

Eclecticism can be pursued at many levels, ranging from the negotiation of competing strands of analysis within a paradigm to a more holistic search for interactions among theoretical principles found across disciplines as diverse as biology and sociology. In the particular context of international relations, we distinguish analytic eclecticism from paradigm-driven research on the basis of three markers. These are related to the manner in which problems are recognized and articulated, the complexity of the explanatory strategy and causal story, and the extent of pragmatic engagement with concrete real-world dilemmas and conditions (see Table 1.1).

Table 1.1   *The markers of eclectic scholarship*

- Open-ended problem formulation encompassing complexity of phenomena, not intended to advance or fill gaps in paradigm-bound scholarship.

- Middle-range causal account incorporating complex interactions among multiple mechanisms and logics drawn from more than one paradigm.

- Findings and arguments that pragmatically engage both academic debates and the practical dilemmas of policymakers/practitioners.

First, analytic eclecticism features the articulation of problems that reflect, rather than simplify, the complexity and multi-dimensionality of social phenomena of interest to both scholars and practitioners. Research questions within paradigm-bound projects tend to be formulated to test theories derived from that paradigm, to fill in gaps thought to exist among theories constructed within the paradigm, or to explore anomalies or new phenomena that these theories have yet to account for. That is not to say that adherents of paradigms are not concerned about concrete social phenomena or policy debates. However, the fact remains that the kinds of question privileged in paradigm-bound research rely on a set of cognitive structures – concepts, foundational assumptions, and analytic principles – to delimit and simplify complex social phenomena. Such simplification can be fruitful and is often unavoidable in light of practical research constraints, especially in relation to phenomena on which there is little existing research. It is also true that 'scientists always choose or sample a part of reality to serve as the object of investigation' (Lichbach 2003, p. 135). However, the *extent* to which and the *manner* in which social phenomena are simplified in the articulation of research questions matter greatly in the evolution of our understanding. As Shapiro (2005, p. 184) argues: 'If the problems posited are idiosyncratic artifacts of the researcher's theoretical priors, then they will seem tendentious, if not downright misleading, to everyone except those who are wedded to her priors.' This is an especially serious limitation when research focused on such problems is in a position to influence the beliefs and actions of policymakers and thus have consequences beyond the confines of the academe.

Eclectic scholarship requires us to transgress paradigmatic boundaries. An eclectic approach seeks to identify and understand problems that, while of interest to scholars, bear at least implicitly on concrete challenges facing social and political actors. Because they subsume or combine substantively related aspects of questions that have been constituted within the analytic boundaries of competing paradigms, such problems are likely to have greater scope and complexity than conventional research questions. Analytic eclecticism thus does not exist in direct competition with research traditions. It does not seek to develop better answers to questions already identified by specific research traditions. Its value-added lies instead in expanding the scope and complexity of questions so as to facilitate a more open-ended analysis that can incorporate the insights of different paradigm-bound theories and relate them to the concerns of policymakers and ordinary actors.

A second distinguishing feature of analytic eclecticism is its attention to the multiplicity, heterogeneity, and interaction of causal mechanisms and processes that generate phenomena of interest to scholars and practitioners. Elsewhere (Sil and Katzenstein 2010), we have reviewed how current treatments of mechanisms differ on whether they are intrinsically unobservable entities, whether they must recur across a given range of spatio-temporal contexts, and whether their operation must be mediated by the cognition and behavior of individuals. Here, we simply note that different conceptions of mechanisms reflect fundamental differences in ontology and epistemology, which incline paradigm-bound theories to focus on particular domains of reality and to privilege causal forces whose effects are most obvious in those domains. This may be appropriate for tackling narrowly defined questions that are posed to illuminate certain aspects of social reality. But for the kinds of

Figure 1.1   *Eclecticism and the agency/structure and material/ideational divides*

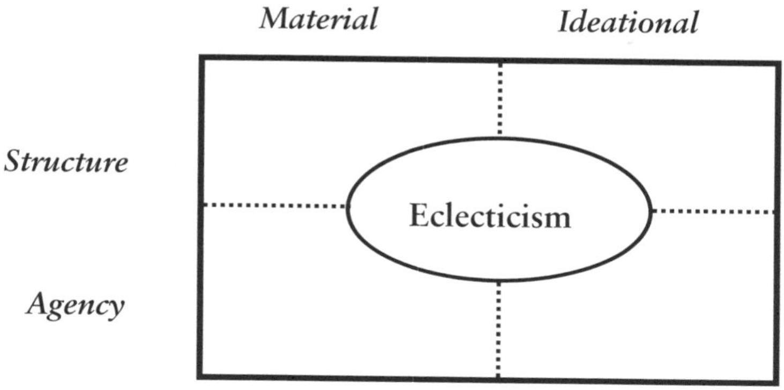

Source: adapted from Sil (2000a, p. 360); see also Wendt (1999, p. 32).

open-ended problems on which eclectic scholarship trains its sights, we argue that a more expansive and flexible view of causality is indispensable for revealing those hidden relationships and complex interaction effects that tend to elude paradigm-bound research.

In practical terms, this requires careful attention to processes that cut across different levels of analysis and transcend the divide presumed to exist between observable material factors and unobservable cognitive or ideational ones. For the substantive questions on which analytic eclecticism is intended to shed light, assumptions concerning the ontological primacy of agency/structure or of material/ideational domains of social reality cannot be converted into a priori causal primacy of either agents or structures, and of either material or ideational factors (see Figure 1.1). Eclectic research considers the different ways in which individual and collective actors in world politics form and pursue their material and ideal preferences within given environments. It also draws attention to the manner in which external environments influence actors' understandings of their interests, capabilities, opportunities, and constraints. And it considers the extent to which the material and ideational components of these environments are reproduced or transformed as a result of those actors' varying preferences and varying abilities to act upon those preferences.

This also implies that eclectic research will typically produce neither universal theories nor idiographic narratives, but something approximating what Robert Merton (1968) famously referred to as 'theories of the middle range.' Middle-range theories are specifically constructed to shed light on specific sets of empirical phenomena; as such, they do not aspire to offer a general model or universal theory that can be readily adapted to investigate other kinds of phenomena. At the same time, even the most idiosyncratic 'middle-range' analysis differs from a historical narrative in that it seeks to offer a causal story that can account for a range of outcomes across a limited set of comparable contexts. In addition, it incorporates cause–effect linkages that can, in principle, recur with some degree of frequency within contexts that possess certain conditions or characteristics relevant to the problem or phenomenon under investigation.

Finally, analytic eclecticism encourages the construction of theories or narratives that generate 'pragmatic engagement' with the social conditions within which prevailing ideas about world politics have emerged (Haas and Haas 2009, p. 101). Eclectic research is thus, at least in principle, cast in terms that explicitly or implicitly allow for the extraction of useful insights that can enrich policy debates and normative discussions beyond the academe. The point is not merely to articulate a new argument for the sake of novelty; nor is it simply to carve out a line of analysis that defies classification under an existing set of contending paradigms. It is also to explore how insights generated by paradigm-bound research may be used for the purpose of developing a causal story that captures the complexity, contingency, and messiness of the environment within which actors must identify and solve problems. Even when it is not offering explicit policy prescriptions, eclectic scholarship should have some clear implications for some set of policy debates or salient normative concerns that enmesh leaders, public intellectuals, and other actors in a given political setting. In the absence of a concern for framing one's research in such a way, eclectic scholarship will fare no better than paradigm-bound scholarship in terms of confirming Nye's fear that 'academic theorizing will say more and more about less and less.' Chapter 2 elaborates on this point in the context of the 'pragmatist turn' in international relations scholarship.

Certainly, this is not the first time that scholars have criticized paradigmatic boundaries (e.g. Hirschman 1970), promoted middle-range theorizing (e.g. Merton 1968), encouraged problem-driven research grounded in the real world (e.g. Shapiro 2005), or called for a narrower gap between social-scientific research and public policy (e.g. Lindblom and Cohen 1979; Nye 2009). Our conceptualization of eclectic scholarship is distinctive in that it seeks to bridge *all* of these concerns, linking a pragmatist orientation towards the production of useful knowledge to problem-driven research aimed at a better understanding of real-world phenomena and to mid-range causal accounts that draw upon mechanisms and processes normally analyzed in isolation within separate paradigms. In contrast to past efforts to casually defend eclectic approaches (Evans 1995a), we have offered a clear rationale for analytic eclecticism, emphasizing its distinctive value-added in light of existing theoretical contributions and research practices. In addition, we have developed a set of criteria that are reasonably flexible and yet useful for consistently identifying eclecticism as a distinct, recognizable style of research as evident in the shared attributes of the varied scholarship showcased in Chapters 3 to 5. We view this style of research not as a substitute for but as a necessary complement to paradigm-bound research. As such, analytic eclecticism is in a position to open up new channels for communication among adherents of contending paradigms. It also increases the potential for creative experimentation with different combinations of concepts, mechanisms, logics, and interpretations in relation to substantive problems. And, in doing so, it increases the chances that scholars will be able to collectively generate more novel and more useful answers to questions that are of both theoretical and practical significance.

Chapter 2

Eclecticism, pragmatism, and paradigms in international relations

Since its inception in the early twentieth century, the field of international relations has been divided by enduring and evolving fault lines between proponents of realism and idealism, of behaviorism and traditionalism, of neoliberalism and neorealism, and of rationalism and constructivism. Beginning with the publication of Kuhn's (1962) book on scientific revolutions, it has been fashionable to think of these contending schools of thought as paradigms. In fact, recent surveys conducted by the Project on Teaching, Research, and International Practice (TRIP) indicate that the vast majority of scholars worldwide continue to view international relations scholarship as dominated by paradigmatic analysis. In the 2006 survey of 1,112 scholars in the United States and Canada, respondents indicated that over 80 percent of the international relations literature is devoted to scholarly studies based on one paradigm or another (Maliniak et al. 2007, p. 16). This pattern continued to be evident in the 2008 survey, which included responses from 2,724 scholars from the United States and nine other countries. American respondents estimated that non-paradigmatic scholarship accounted for just 11 percent of the literature, while estimates from respondents in other countries ranged anywhere from 6 percent of the literature in South Africa to 13 percent in Ireland (Jordan et al. 2009, p. 41). The prevalence of paradigms is evident in teaching as well: in the 2008 survey, respondents estimated that 73 percent of course readings in international relations courses taught worldwide represented paradigmatic work of one sort or another, with two-thirds of that work coming from the triad of realism, liberalism, and constructivism (Jordan et al. 2009, p. 18).

For the purpose of distinguishing eclectic scholarship in contemporary international relations, we rely in this chapter on the familiar triad of constructivism, liberalism, and realism. It goes without saying that other paradigms have acquired significance, at times for long periods, in various countries. Marxism and the English School, for example, continue to be influential outside of the United States. Furthermore, there exist important variations within and across paradigms. Nevertheless, the TRIP surveys confirm that currently constructivism, liberalism, and realism are the most established and most visible contenders for paradigmatic dominance.[1] These three labels capture meaningful differences in the ways in which scholars identify themselves and in the cognitive structures that shape how they pose and approach the problems they seek to solve. Thus, it is in the context of debates between realists, liberals, and constructivists that we find it most useful to elaborate on the significance of analytic eclecticism for the study of world politics.

We are self-conscious in not using capitals to delineate analytic eclecticism. Eclecticism is not meant to constitute a discrete new 'ism' to replace or subsume all other 'isms' in the field of international relations. It is, however, a useful heuristic for capturing the common requirements of metatheoretical flexibility and theoretical multilingualism necessary for substantive analyses that are not embedded in any one paradigm. In fact, there are indications of at least some growing interest in such analyses among a sizable minority of international relations scholars worldwide. It is worth noting, for example, that 36 percent of the American respondents in the 2008 TRIP survey (and about the same percentage of respondents worldwide) indicated that their own work did *not* fall within one of the major international relations paradigms.[2] This figure is noticeably larger than in previous years (Jordan et al. 2009, pp. 9, 33). This increased receptiveness to non-paradigmatic scholarship makes it all the more necessary to think carefully and systematically about what kinds of metatheoretical reformulations and research strategies are most likely to produce useful, coherent eclectic alternatives to theories put forward by the established paradigms.

The next section considers the implications for inter-paradigm debates of the proliferation of discrete clusters of theories within a paradigm, and of the substantive convergence sometimes seen among theories embedded in contending paradigms. The following section considers what an eclectic approach brings to the study of world politics, highlighting statements from prominent scholars who identify with a given paradigm but anticipate the need for complementary eclectic modes of analysis. The final section identifies important points of connection between analytic eclecticism and the ethos of pragmatism, a philosophical perspective that has been on the margins of American international relations but is now beginning to gain some ground.

The limits of the inter-paradigm debate

For heuristic purposes, Figure 2.1 depicts constructivism, liberalism, and realism as three sides of a triangle. Eclectic scholarship explores points of connection between at least two, and preferably all three, of the sides.[3] The three paradigms are typically distinguished based on certain core assumptions about the nature of international life, for example in the priority given to identities and norms, to interests and efficiency gains, or to the distribution of material capabilities. Because these paradigms are so well known, we do not offer a comprehensive overview of each of them. Rather, our discussion emphasizes two related points that are significant for the case we make for analytic eclecticism. First, each of the major paradigms encompasses discrete strands that can be distinguished in terms of the relative priorities assigned to different ontological, epistemological, and substantive assumptions normally associated with that paradigm. The resulting heterogeneity of approaches *within* paradigms suggests that they may not be as coherent, uniform, and rigid as often assumed. Second, because
of their internal heterogeneity, each of the paradigms has produced a fairly wide range of substantive arguments, some of which converge with arguments developed in other paradigms on particular issues and policies. This may not herald the end of inter-paradigm debates, as some have hoped (Waever 1996). It does, however, point to the possibility of relaxing some of the more restrictive metatheoretical postulates and theoretical assumptions typically employed to delimit and distinguish paradigms. If so, this would pave the way for a greater acceptance of eclectic modes of inquiry.

Figure 2.1 *The triad of major international relations paradigms*

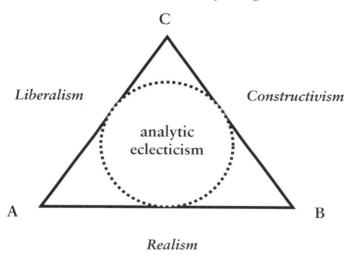

C

Liberalism   Constructivism

analytic
eclecticism

A   B

Realism

Source: adapted from Sil and Katzenstein (2004). Reproduced with the permission of Stanford University Press.

The emergence of diversity within paradigms

For much of the twentieth century, realism was the dominant paradigm in international relations scholarship. After a period of decline immediately following the Cold War, realism appears to have entered a phase of 'renewal' (Frankel 1996). Realists view the most critical outcomes in world politics – war and peace among states – as driven primarily by the balance of power among states operating in an anarchic system based on the principle of self-help. In such an environment, what matters most are relative gains in the distribution of material capabilities, measured largely in terms of resources required to defend one's borders and inflict harm on other states. Given the objective character of these measurements, realists see no need for the emphasis constructivists place on the ontological priority of intersubjective constructions. Contra liberals, they see patterns of cooperation, however institutionalized, as reflecting either the mutual interests of alliance members or a fleeting convergence of interests around issues of 'low' politics rather than the 'high' politics of war and peace.

Over time, important distinctions have emerged within the realist paradigm. The most significant move featured a departure from the classical realism of Hans Morgenthau – which emphasized state-craft based on a balance-of-power logic – in favor of a focus on structural processes and outcomes at the level of the international system. Neorealists, or structural realists, view states in the international system as analogous to firms in the marketplace. Thus, they treat the distribution of material capabilities among the great powers in the system in zero-sum terms; the extent to which there exists a balance of power is directly related to the persistence or disruption of equilibrium in the system (Waltz 1979). Among structural realists, there is a significant divide between offensive and defensive variants, which stress, respectively, states' readiness to engage in conflict in the quest for greater power (Mearsheimer 2001) and states' preoccupation with their own security (Waltz 1979). Recent neorealists have turned their attention to the emulation of successful military practices and innovations, something never fully developed by earlier realists but clearly implied by the logic of competition under anarchy (Resende-Santos 2007). An increasingly prominent neoclassical variant of realism (Rose 1998) has sought to integrate classical realism's emphasis on statecraft with neorealism's focus on the structure of an anarchic international system. This approach is concerned with how individual actors' preferences and perceptions, as well as the character and internal political dynamics of states, mediate system effects on the content of grand strategies and specific foreign policy choices in various international environments (Lobell, Ripsman, and Taliaferro 2009; Schweller 2006; see also Finel 2001/02). Neoclassical realists differ from other realists in the importance they attach to the role of emotions, identities, and interests of individual actors (Lobell et al. 2009). These differences are significant in that they anticipate the possibility of interfacing with approaches drawn from constructivism and liberalism that stress, respectively, the role of ideas, norms, and identities, and the significance of information and coordination in institutions.

Liberal theories take issue with realists' skepticism concerning the prospects for cooperation in a fundamentally anarchic world (Mearsheimer 1994/95), and instead stress the potential for enlightened self-interest and progressive change. While liberalism may be traced back to Wilsonianism, the spectacular failure of the liberal international order between the two world wars prompted most 'new liberals' (Moravcsik 1997) to move away from idealism toward a rationalist conception of state interests. This is illustrated well by Keohane and Nye's (1977) landmark study of 'complex interdependence' and its implications for states' prioritization of various types of interests. Liberals accept the realist view of the anarchic nature of the international system but allow for a wider range of conditions, particularly in an interdependent world, under which absolute gains motivate cooperative state behavior even in the absence of a hegemon (Keohane 1984). Thus, what distinguishes neoliberals from realists is not ontology or epistemology so much as the designation of the central problems to be investigated. This, in turn, reflects competing assumptions about the preference-ordering of states (whether they seek absolute or relative gains) and the causal impact of international institutions (whether, in the interest of all states, they introduce a greater degree of transparency, reciprocity, and predictability).

The past two decades have witnessed the emergence of discrete strands of liberalism that differ in their view of the variability of state interests and the extent to which these are influenced or constrained by institutions, ideas, and transnational factors. One prominent strand discounts the configuration of international institutions in favor of evolving state preferences that are embedded in states' domestic and transnational social environments (Moravcsik 1997). In a similar vein, commercial liberalism focuses on how the shifting structure of the global economy alters the position of particular assets in international markets as well as patterns of distributional conflict within and between states. This prompts domestic economic actors to reformulate their interests and to pressure governments to adjust or maintain their policies on free trade, exchange rates, and other aspects of economic exchange (Alt and Gilligan 1994; Frieden 1991; Milner 1988; Moravcsik 2008). Neoliberal institutionalists emphasize the significance of extensive investments that powerful states have made in a whole range of multilateral institutions. These represent equilibrium outcomes of strategic interactions and payoff structures in relation to various sorts of cooperation problems. Institutions serve the interests of states by reducing transaction costs, providing information, making commitments more credible, and encouraging reciprocity (Keohane and Martin 1995; Krasner 1983; Martin 1992). Some neoliberals take seriously the role of ideas and beliefs in connection with international institutions (Goldstein and Keohane 1993). However, they treat ideas, not as forces that can independently alter the core interests of actors, but rather as focal points for coordinating policies. These and other variants of liberalism differ from a more normative strand of liberal theory that harkens back to Wilsonian idealism in its emphasis on the role of a community of liberal democratic states in designing a rule-centered world order based on international laws and institutions (Hoffmann 2000; Ikenberry and Slaughter 2006; see also Simpson 2008).

Constructivism is defined less in terms of specific assumptions about the nature of states and their environments, and more in terms of its ontology. It holds to the premise that social constructs that are not directly observable – most commonly collective norms and identities – have a powerful effect on how actors in particular contexts perceive, understand, negotiate, and reproduce the social structures they inhabit (Wendt 1999). Constructivists may be open to both the realist precondition of international anarchy and the liberal emphasis on the possibilities for negotiated cooperation. They emphasize, however, the ontological priority of unobservable identities and norms. These emergent identities and norms are 'constructed' by actors in the context of long-term processes of social interaction, but they also mediate how actors perceive, create, and respond to emergent features of world politics. Such a view of international relations requires, at the individual level, 'a conception of actors who are not only strategically but also discursively competent' (Ruggie 1998, p. 21). This perspective also enables constructivism to highlight the significance of generative or transformative processes such as deliberation, persuasion, and socialization, which, for better or worse, can lead to the transformation of identities and preferences (Johnston 2001; Wendt 1999).

As with realism and liberalism, constructivism has also seen the crystallization of discrete strands that represent different foundational orientations. 'Conventional' constructivists adopt a more positivist orientation when it comes to issues of epistemology and methodology (Hopf 1998; Checkel 2004). They are comfortable proceeding on the basis of a 'naturalist' form of positivism (Dessler 1999; Wendt 1999), and can commit themselves to contingent explanatory propositions in which ideational variables play a central role. Post-positivist alternatives to conventional constructivism adopt a constitutive epistemology (Hopf 1998), seeking to understand and/or critique, rather than trace the causes or effects of, ideational constructions. An 'interpretivist' variant, which has been more popular in Europe (Checkel 2004), seeks to reconstruct identities through the analysis of discourse. It seeks to understand rather than discover the causes and consequences of norms and identities as reflected in discourse. Critical constructivism has a markedly more normative orientation (Price and Reus-Smit 1998; Checkel 2004), rejecting the neutrality professed by conventional constructivists and seeking to expose the naturalized power relationships that lie behind myths and social practices (Hopf 1998). Finally, some scholars have built on Pierre Bourdieu's sociology of practice by highlighting 'the logic of habit' (Hopf 2009). This approach focuses on the importance of dispositions and self-evident understandings as illustrated, for example, in the impact of everyday diplomatic practice on foreign affairs (Pouliot 2010).

Points of convergence across paradigms

The emergence of discrete variants within each of the major paradigms suggests that paradigmatic fault lines are less impermeable than is frequently assumed, and the problems of inter-paradigm incommensurability correspondingly less daunting than they first appear (Jackson and Nexon 2009; see also Moravcsik 2008). Because they encompass a number of ontological and epistemological principles that are not uniformly ordered and weighted within each paradigm, the metatheoretical postulates of competing paradigms can be reformulated or reprioritized to permit some convergence on substantive arguments and prescriptions. This is precisely what we see happening in recent discussions tracking the convergence of certain strands of realism and liberalism (around corner A in Figure 2.1), of constructivism and realism (around corner B), and of constructivism and liberalism (around corner C).[4]

The realist assumption that a state's material interests and resources are unproblematic is not inconsistent with the neoliberal premise that states are self-interested rational actors motivated by material gains. This overlap permits some convergence in substantive analyses (at corner A in Figure 2.1) around issues that realists may assign to the domain of 'low' politics but consider worth investigating nonetheless. Moreover, in terms of fundamental issues of ontology, the gap between neorealists and neoliberals is certainly not as significant as that between both of these traditions and constructivism. In fact, it may be in response to the emergence of constructivism as a distinct tradition that strands of neorealism and neoliberalism have converged upon a 'neo-neo synthesis' (Waever 1996, p. 163). This synthesis, often referred to as 'rationalist' (Katzenstein 1996; Katzenstein, Keohane, and Krasner 1999) or 'neo-utilitarian' (Ruggie 1998), is predicated on the shared premise of the centrality of state interests and rational state behavior, in combination with a common positivist search for explanations of states' behavioral regularities within an objective international reality that transcends specific contexts (Keohane 1989, esp. p. 165). While not all realists and liberals see this underlying rationalism as important enough to warrant ignoring all other principles that have long distinguished the two camps, the appeal of this synthesis among many proponents of neorealism and neoliberalism points to the possibility of a convergence in substantive theories generated by the two paradigms.

Yet this synthesis has not overrun the field of international relations precisely because, in different intellectual contexts, other points of convergence have also emerged. One such point (at corner B in Figure 2.1) involves a 'realist-constructivism' as articulated in the work of Samuel Barkin (2003, 2004, 2010), among others. Realist constructivists (Barkin 2010; see also Nau 2002) acknowledge that, in addition to their respective emphases on material and ideational factors, realists and constructivists diverge on whether actors are following the logic of consequences or the logic of appropriateness. However, the gap between the two paradigms is frequently overstated, as specific strands of each can converge in their analysis of different forms and expressions of power in specific contexts (Barkin 2003, 2010). Norm-guided behavior can emerge from material interests, and rational action can be oriented towards socially constructed ideals. Patrick Jackson and Daniel Nexon (2004) offer a somewhat different view of the convergence of realism and constructivism, emphasizing a post-structuralist grounding that discards the emphasis on human nature and international anarchy in favor of a focus on the forms of power within all social structures. A more structured version of realist constructivism views the social construction of domestic group identities and practices as mediating the perceptions of international anarchy and mitigating its negative effects on the possibilities for cooperation (Sterling-Folker 2002, pp. 101–4). These different formulations of realist constructivism vary in the ontological status they assign to power and anarchy; they share, however, a focus on the operation of power in various domains of international life.

Finally, there is a range of possibilities (at corner C in Figure 2.1) where constructivism and liberalism converge. Classical liberalism, in particular, shares with constructivism an emphasis on how the interplay of ideas, shared knowledge, emergent legal principles and multilateral institutions can reshape actors' identities and preferences, and engender reciprocal understandings and levels of cooperation that cannot be reduced to fixed state interests (Haas 2001; Reus-Smit 2001). For some liberals and constructivists, this commonality is so significant that they choose to transcend fundamental differences in ontology and gravitate towards a liberal-constructivist orientation along the lines outlined by Jackson and Nexon (2009). Indeed, some proponents of realist constructivism characterize conventional constructivism as an alternative reconstruction of liberal idealism (Barkin 2003). The rationalist features that permit a convergence between neoliberal and neorealist approaches (at corner A) are discounted in this broader view of liberal theory; the focus is less on actor preferences and strategic rationality, and more on the complex processes leading to the emergence of cooperation in specific contexts. In relation to these processes, conventional constructivism and classical liberalism can be treated as complementary rather than competing (Sterling-Folker 2000). Some constructivists (Steele 2007) see this move as undermining the distinctive foundations of constructivism and diluting its ability to challenge mainstream realist and liberal theories. However, if we choose to relax paradigmatic commitments in favor of practical assumptions that can guide problem-focused substantive research, then there is reason to take seriously the idea of some common ground between specific strands of liberalism and constructivism, at least for certain questions.

The significance of these various points of convergence becomes even clearer when we consider that adherents of any given paradigm are capable of developing theories to support quite varied, even diametrically opposed, policy prescriptions. This also implies that scholars identifying with different paradigms can converge in their support for, or opposition to, particular policies. This point is demonstrated in Fred Chernoff's (2007, pp. 75–7) effort to lay out the various rationales that potentially support either a more aggressive or a more cooperative approach in US policies towards Iraq, North Korea, and China. Concerning Iraq, for example, opposition to unilateral invasion was backed by liberal arguments about the long-term value of multilateralism and institutionalized cooperation, and by constructivist arguments emphasizing the emergence of a social basis for sustained cooperation through long-term engagement. The Bush administration invoked realist principles justifying unilateral invasion on the grounds that Iraq's nuclear weapons program posed a serious and imminent threat, as well as liberal ones asserting that the invasion would uncover the roots of a vigorous democratic politics. At the same time, many realists joined liberals and constructivists in opposing the invasion, based on doubts about the extent of the threat posed by Iraq.

Similarly, in relation to North Korea, a policy of isolation and containment could be supported by rationalist theories drawing on both realism and liberalism to emphasize the dangers of rewarding bad behavior. On the other side, a 'sunshine policy' aimed at easing North Korea's insecurity and building confidence through incremental concessions could be justified through constructivist arguments about how actors' identities change, liberal arguments about how engagement can spur demands for political reform, and realist arguments about the increased restraint likely to be shown by states possessing nuclear deterrents. As Chernoff (2007, p. 153) puts it, 'There is no inherent reason why one of the foundational-philosophical positions is locked into supporting one particular substantive theory above others.'

In advancing the case for greater analytic eclecticism in international relations, it is worth underlining the obvious. Although they are based on competing epistemic commitments, paradigms and research traditions are not usually so rigid as to produce uniform research products that predictably converge on substantive interpretations, explanations, or prescriptions. In engaging particular problems, it is entirely possible for constructivists, liberals, and realists to disagree amongst themselves, while some types of realists, liberals, and constructivists may be able to converge on substantive characterizations of, and prescriptions for, a particular problem in international life. Such convergence points to the possibility and utility of eclecticism in the study of world politics.

What eclecticism can contribute

As noted in Chapter 1, paradigms have an enduring quality and confer certain important advantages. Paradigms and the theoretical languages they employ enable more focused and fluent conversations about problems that are considered significant. They offer criteria for assessing the quality of scholarship, and help scholars to cultivate recognizable professional identities while facilitating the psychological and institutional support of fellow adherents. In addition, the debates among paradigms create the conditions for developing sharper, more refined analyses. All of this contributes to the professionalization of international relations research, and partly explains the findings about the continuing prevalence of paradigmatic analysis in the TRIP surveys (Jordan et al. 2009; Maliniak et al. 2007).

The boundaries between paradigms, however, also produce an excessive compartmentalization in international relations scholarship. They obscure conceptual and empirical points of connection between analyses constructed in competing research traditions and presented in different theoretical vocabularies.[5] Moreover, the host of intellectual, financial, institutional, and psychological investments that go into building and sustaining a paradigm militate against addressing important aspects of problems that are not easily represented in the conceptual apparatus it favors. And the focus on intra-paradigm progress and inter-paradigm debates detracts from attention to practical real-world dilemmas while widening the chasm between academia and the world of policy and practice. This chasm is particularly disappointing in view of the fact that the field of international relations originally emerged out of 'reflections on policy, and out of the desire to influence policy, or to improve the practice of policy' (Wallace 1996, p. 302).

Analytic eclecticism is essentially a countervailing effort to overcome these limitations inherent in paradigm-bound research in international relations. Eclectic scholarship is designed to highlight the substantive intersections and practical relevance of theories originally constructed within separate paradigms. Rather than 'stigmatizing as eclectic whatever approach to the current problems in international politics does not fit along the established axes of scholarly enlightenment' (Hellmann 2003, p. 149), the academe could then recognize the virtues of scholarship that can serve to expand the channels of communication among separate research communities, and to generate recombinant analytic frameworks that incorporate concepts, logics, interpretations, and mechanisms from various paradigms. Since no one paradigm is universally recognized by the discipline as having a monopoly on intellectual progress, 'the best case for progress in the understanding of social life lies in ... the expanding fund of insights and understandings derived from a wide variety of theoretical inspirations' (Rule 1997, p. 18).

The specific attributes of a given intellectual environment obviously affect what counts as 'mainstream' scholarship and what constitutes an eclectic mode of inquiry. As noted above, analytic eclecticism is conceptualized in this book in relation to realism, liberalism, and constructivism, since these are the most prevalent approaches in the United States and worldwide. In other countries, however, a number of other paradigms enjoy equal or greater visibility in international relations debates (Jordan et al. 2009; Maliniak et al. 2007). For example, the English school, feminism, post-modernism, and Marxism all have a much broader following in Britain, Canada, and Australia than in the United States. On the European continent, hermeneutic and interpretive approaches are much more a part of the 'mainstream' than in the United States. In China and Russia, Marxism continues to offer a suitable analytical frame in some circles. And in various other countries and regions, distinctive cultural templates and intellectual traditions frequently inflect scholarly analyses of world politics (Acharya and Buzan 2010; Lemke 2003; Tickner 2003; Tickner and Waever 2009). Moreover, in contrast to the United States, rationalist perspectives in those countries and regions occupy a less central place in scholarly debates, and do not influence as significantly the prevailing research protocols or evidentiary requirements. In such settings, although the general logic of eclecticism still applies, what constitutes eclectic research practice would have to be redefined.

Eclecticism can also be recast at a more general level, beyond the field of international relations. For example, it can take the form of analytic frameworks seeking to bridge comparative politics and international relations (Caporaso 1997) and of interdisciplinary research seeking to draw together insights from economics, psychology, sociology, and geography (Sil and Doherty 2000; Wallerstein et al. 1996). At an even higher level of generality, eclecticism can take the form of efforts to translate or combine concepts and processes originally posited within very different kinds of scholarly projects in the natural sciences, social sciences, and humanities (Kagan 2009). Here, advances in neuroscience, evolutionary biology, and the study of chaos and complexity point to new mechanisms potentially affecting international processes and outcomes. In short, eclecticism is a general strategy for developing complex problem-focused arguments that cut across, and draw creatively from, artificially segmented bodies of scholarship. The specific contours of this strategy depend on the relevant intellectual context.

In the context of contemporary international relations, analytic eclecticism is minimally operationalized as analysis that extricates and recombines elements of theories embedded in the three major paradigms – realism, liberalism, and constructivism – in the process of building complex middle-range causal stories that bear on important matters of policy and practice. Eclectic modes of analysis trace the dialectical and evolving relationship between individual and collective actors in world politics, on the one hand, and the material and ideational structures that constitute the contexts within which these actors form and pursue their preferences. This requires attention to two sets of factors: first, the manner in which external environments shape actors' understandings of their interests, the constraints and opportunities they face, and their capabilities; and second, the manner in which environments are reproduced or transformed as a result of those actors' varying preferences and capacities. An eclectic approach also assumes the existence of complex interactions among the distribution of material capabilities (typically emphasized in realism), the gains pursued by self-interested individual and collective actors (typically emphasized by liberals), and the role of ideas, norms, and identities in framing actors' understanding of the world and of their roles within it (privileged by constructivists). Put differently, eclectic analysis seeks to cut across and draw connections between processes that are normally cast at different levels of analysis, and are often confined to either material or ideational dimensions of social reality (see Figure 1.1 in the previous chapter).

The anticipation of eclecticism

While the label of analytic eclecticism and the specific definition we offer may be original, it is not difficult to find examples of scholars, including prominent scholars frequently identified with an established paradigm, who have acknowledged the limitations of paradigmatic work. No less a realist than Morgenthau noted long ago the limitations of scholarship confined to a single theoretical perspective. Most theories of international relations, he argued (1967, p. 247), offer 'a respectable protective shield' behind which members of the academic community engage in theoretical pursuits while bypassing controversies relevant to the policies and prospects for survival of entire nations. In his classic book, *Man, the State and War*, Kenneth Waltz (1959, pp. 229–30) also highlights the necessity of considering numerous causal forces operating at multiple levels of analysis:

> The prescriptions directly derived from a single image [of international relations] are incomplete because they are based upon partial analyses. The partial quality of each image sets up a tension that drives one toward inclusion of the others. … One is led to search for the inclusive nexus of causes.

While Waltz's later (1979) work focuses at the level of the system, his earlier openness to the multiplicity of causal factors located at different levels is recaptured in neoclassical realist commentaries emphasizing the importance of opening up the 'black box' of the unit level (Finel 2001/02; see also Waltz 1967).

In the context of political economy, Robert Gilpin's (1975, 1987) attempts to grapple systematically with competing perspectives led him to draw upon liberal, realist, and Marxist analytic principles in order to shed light on different facets of international political economy. In his more recent work, characterized as a 'state-realist' approach to political economy, Gilpin (2001) goes on to challenge the stark separation of constructivism and realism. He notes:

> Ideas are obviously important, but the world is composed of many economic, technological, and other powerful constraints that limit the wisdom and practicality of certain ideas and social constructions. Any theory that seeks to understand the world must … seek to integrate both ideas and material forces. (Gilpin 2001, p. 20)

A leading figure in the neoliberal camp, Robert Keohane, also acknowledges the importance of approaching problems from multiple vantage points, as is evident in his analysis of cooperation without a hegemon. Keohane (1984, p. 39) accepts the realist theory of hegemonic stability as 'a useful, if somewhat simplistic starting point.' But he then goes on to construct a framework of analysis that not only combines elements of realist and liberal theory, but also borrows extensively from Antonio Gramsci's theory of hegemony as well as the work of Karl Kautsky (Keohane 1984, pp. 43–5). Keohane (1986), as well as John Ruggie (1986), although generally considered critics of neorealism, do not discard Waltz's structural realism. Instead, they view it as an essential and valuable foundation for the building of more complex frameworks, in which Waltz's notion of structure coexists with other non-systemic factors that can better capture the effects of growing interdependence and the dynamics of system change.

A strong proponent of liberalism, Andrew Moravcsik (2008), has also called for de-emphasizing theoretical parsimony and ontological consistency in order to facilitate synthetic analyses featuring causal factors drawn from different theories. Moravcsik (2003, p. 132) notes:

> The complexity of most large events in world politics precludes plausible unicausal explanations. The outbreak of World Wars I and II, the emergence of international human rights norms, and the evolution of the European Union, for example, are surely important enough events to merit comprehensive explanation even at the expense of theoretical parsimony.

For this reason, Moravcsik (2003, p. 136) has called for empirically grounded 'midrange theories of concrete phenomena' that are not constrained by prior assumptions about the 'metatheoretical, ontological or philosophical status of social science.'

Stanley Hoffmann (1995, 2000) has been increasingly convinced that liberalism is in crisis and in desperate need of rethinking. Hoffmann attacks liberal theory's tendency to bypass ethical considerations and to overvalue the significance of convergent state interests and economic interdependence for international harmony. Anticipating some of the arguments of liberal-constructivists, Hoffmann (1995, 2000) emphasizes the need for a serious reformulation of liberalism that might incorporate ethical considerations in supporting a stronger role for international institutions to regulate 'what may soon be seen as a transnational Frankenstein monster' (Hoffmann 1995, p. 177).

Generally identified with defensive realism, Jack Snyder (2002, p. 34) has also argued recently for a more holistic and multi-dimensional conception of systems than the one realists have generally employed: 'No single part of a system suffices to define the system and its behavior. Even anarchy itself, though it may load the dice probabilistically in favor of war, does not predetermine action in the system.' This does not imply, however, a defection to the constructivist camp. In fact, Snyder describes constructivism as 'one-dimensional,' insisting that a more useful approach would be to 'integrate material, institutional, and cultural aspects of social change, drawing on the insights of theories of complex systems' (Snyder 2002, p. 9).

Nina Tannenwald (2005) has sought to expand the boundaries of constructivism by suggesting that ideas operate through mechanisms (such as learning and socialization) whose effects can vary depending on material conditions and constraints (such as interests and resources). Tannenwald breaks down the concept of 'ideas' into discrete elements (ideological, normative, and causal beliefs as well as policy prescriptions), recognizing the different ways in which each of these elements interact with material factors. She emphasizes that material conditions and constraints are often constituted by prior ideas that, in turn, take shape within particular material environments even if they subsequently have long-term independent effects. Tannenwald's move is aimed at defining and defending 'constitutive explanation' in constructivist research. Yet, like Snyder, she effectively opens the door to an eclectic approach.

A more general case for moving beyond paradigm-bound research in international relations is evident in the critique of the field offered by Steven Bernstein, Richard Ned Lebow, Janice Stein, and Steven Weber (2000). For them, international relations theory has been inordinately influenced by a model of science drawn from physics, a field featuring closed systems in which strict boundary conditions can be specified and consistently maintained in order to reveal law-like relationships between variables. In the construction of useful theories of international relations, this is neither feasible, nor effective. The authors argue:

> Even the most robust generalizations or laws we can state –
> war is more likely between neighboring states, weaker

> states are less likely to attack stronger states – are close to trivial, have important exceptions, and for the most part stand outside any consistent body of theory. (Bernstein et al. 2000, p. 44)

A more appropriate model, they argue, would be evolutionary biology, which features a more open-ended system in which specific mutation and interaction processes cannot be foreseen in light of uncertainty regarding contingencies. Under these conditions, a practically useful approach is oriented not towards point predictions based on rigid theoretical principles, but rather towards scenarios that require 'the identification and connection of chains of contingencies that could shape the future' (Bernstein et al. 2000, p. 53). In the context of international relations, Bernstein et al. (2000, p. 57) point out that while competing theories emphasize different drivers and behavioral expectations, they frequently 'acknowledge the importance – sometimes determining – of elements outside their theory.' This suggests that international relations theories are likely to do better when they take into account the wide-ranging causal factors from diverse paradigms, then demonstrate how these factors affect one another or combine to generate certain outcomes under certain conditions.

We could easily expand this list of calls for more complex theoretical frameworks extending beyond the boundaries of prevailing paradigms. Instead, our purpose is better served by considering studies of specific problems that, explicitly or implicitly, illustrate the potential value of analytic eclecticism. We undertake this task in Chapters 3 to 5, which address concrete problems related respectively to issues of conflict and security, political economy, and governance in regional, international, and global settings.

A note on labels

We view here as 'eclectic' the arguments of some scholars who may not generally think of their work in such terms. Indeed, many scholars tend to identify with a recognizable paradigm even while engaging in pragmatic, middle-range theorizing that incorporates a wide range of mechanisms and factors in the same way that we expect self-consciously eclectic scholars to do. This is especially true in the case of constructivism. Chronologically, it is the last member of the 'triad' to arrive on the scene, and so must contend with well-developed arguments embedded in well-established paradigms. Analytically, it sees as one of its missions the incorporation of 'omitted variables' that are considered fundamental in other social science disciplines but were tangential to the realist–liberal debate that until recently dominated the field of international relations. That is, in an environment dominated by contending rationalist perspectives, it is not surprising that a scholar seeking to bring in the role of norms and identities would choose to self-identify as a 'constructivist' solely for the purpose of targeting an audience that does not a priori discount ideational factors.[6]

Given these circumstances, when a scholar characterizes their work as 'constructivist' primarily for the purpose of demonstrating how ideas matter – a proposition now acknowledged by many realists and liberals – we are not deterred from classifying that work as analytically eclectic so long as it roughly matches the three identifying markers of eclecticism noted at the end of Chapter 1 (see Table 1.1). This is, in fact, the case with a number of the authors we discuss below, such as Finnemore (2003) in Chapter 3, Jabko (2006) in Chapter 4, and Ba (2009) in Chapter 5. What is not consistent with eclecticism is a program aimed at a total reorganization of international relations in which the 'social construction' thesis is deployed so as to privilege ideational mechanisms, subsume other mechanisms, and dismiss the significance of previous work that ignores or rejects the primacy of ideas. In this regard, we concur with Gilpin (2001, pp. 19–20) when he writes:

> Although constructivism is an important corrective to some strands of realism and the individualist rational-choice methodology of neoclassical economics, the implicit assumption of constructivism that we should abandon our knowledge of international politics and start afresh from a tabula rasa wiped clean by constructivism is not compelling.

A meaningful and consistent line can thus be drawn between the 'practical' (or weak) identification with constructivism, or with any paradigm for that matter, and a 'programmatic' (or strong) identification that compels a scholar to follows specific epistemic commitments linked to fixed analytic boundaries and rigid research protocols. Constructivists – as well as realists and liberals – who are not programmatically committed to the epistemological and causal primacy of particular analytical factors operating within a particular empirical domain and at a particular level of analysis may produce eclectic research. This, however, is not likely to be the case when problems are defined in such a manner as to explicitly correspond to the analytic boundaries of a paradigm; when the research is designed to vindicate existing theories or fill in gaps within paradigm-bound scholarship; or when substantive arguments are premised on an analytic framework that assumes the significance of certain mechanisms and chooses to discount others. In other circumstances, however, it is entirely possible for a scholar to nominally self-identify with a paradigm when in fact their scholarship is eclectic in design and substance. Similarly, a scholar may opt to frame an argument as eclectic when in fact that argument is little more than a refinement of an existing paradigm-bound theory. In the end, whatever label others may apply to a given research product, any scholarly work that meets the three criteria outlined at the end of Chapter 1 (see Table 1.1) – open-ended problem formulation, a complex causal story featuring mechanisms from multiple paradigms, and pragmatic engagement with issues of policy and practice – qualifies here as analytically eclectic.

Analytic eclecticism and the pragmatist turn[7]

Positivists, while disagreeing on certain ontological and epistemological issues,[8] share a view of social science in which patterns of human behavior are presumed to reflect objective laws or law-like regularities. These laws and regularities exist above and beyond the subjective orientations of actors and observers, and can be approximated with increasingly greater accuracy through the cumulation of theory and the application of increasingly more sophisticated research techniques (Laudan 1996, p. 21). Although subjectivist approaches, too, vary in terms of specific assumptions, objectives, and methods,[9] they evince a common skepticism about the possibility of inferring generalizations on the basis of human behavior that is meaningful only within particular contexts. Instead, they commit to a context-bound understanding of the 'meaning-making' (Yanow 2006) efforts of actors as they make sense of their roles and identities within their immediate social environments. In light of significant and persistent differences on the most fundamental questions concerning the aims and processes of scholarly inquiry, we set aside the 'epistemological absolutism' (Sil 2000b) of both hard-core positivists and committed subjectivists. We opt instead for a pragmatist conception of inquiry.

Pragmatism can be traced back to the late nineteenth- and early twentieth-century writings of American philosophers such as Charles Pierce, William James, and John Dewey, among others. Challenging the Kantian tradition that continued to guide European philosophy, American pragmatists held that 'philosophy should concern itself with the messiness' of human meaning and practice (Kaag 2009, p. 63). After the two World Wars, pragmatism experienced a period of marginalization precipitated largely by the behavioral revolution and the dominance of analytic philosophy. In the last three decades, however, pragmatism has been revived and carried forward by Richard Rorty (1982, 1999) and other philosophers (e.g. Bernstein 1983, 1992; Putnam 1981, 2002) who have offered nuanced critiques of positivism without surrendering to the stark relativism embraced by many post-modernists. The history of pragmatism reveals some sharp divisions as well as significant change over time (Festenstein 1997; Joas 1993). Nevertheless, far from representing a residual category, pragmatism can meaningfully be identified as a coherent and reasonable perspective on what kinds of knowledge are worth pursuing, in what manner, and with what aims.

Despite originating in the United States, pragmatism appears to have had very little effect on contemporary American international relations debates (Bauer and Brighi 2009a). This is particularly surprising in light of the fact that some of the key figures in the early development of American international relations, notably Morgenthau and Reinhold Niebuhr, engaged regularly with pragmatist arguments (Bauer and Brighi 2009b, p. 165). Some rare exceptions notwithstanding (Gould and Onuf 2009; Haas and Haas 2009), contemporary international relations scholars in the United States have not followed up on this engagement. Our efforts to make more space for analytic eclecticism in the study of world politics are related to our view that pragmatism offers a reasonable, flexible, and useful alternative to rigid (if implicit) epistemic commitments which frequently drive and are reinforced by inter-paradigm debates. To that end, we have distilled four broad pragmatist notions concerning the nature of social inquiry that have influenced our conceptualization of eclectic scholarship.

One is an aversion to excessively abstract or rigid foundational principles in favor of a focus on the consequences of truth claims in a given context. Following James (1997, p. 94), pragmatists seek to bypass unresolvable metaphysical disputes and instead 'try and interpret each notion by tracing its respective consequences' in concrete situations. For Dewey, the complexity of social life and the heterogeneity of social contexts suggest that covering laws or general theories are little more than fleeting efforts to exert 'control' over the real world (Cochran 2002, p. 527). Moreover, as Gunther Hellmann (2003) puts it, practically useful knowledge cannot wait for the emergence of a definitive consensus on what constitutes a 'final' truth. Instead, pragmatism encourages a spirit of fallibilism, while engaging diverse sources and contending narratives for the purpose of identifying 'facts' that can tentatively be deployed to cope with specific problems (Isacoff 2009). For international relations, a pragmatist perspective implies that competing perspectives need to be reformulated in order to facilitate novel efforts to constitute and solve a problem (Owen 2002).

A second useful pragmatist principle concerns the adaptation of elements of knowledge in relation to novel experiences and changing circumstances. As Dewey (1916, cited from Menand 1997, p. xxiii) put it: 'We take a piece of acquired knowledge into a concrete situation, and the results we get constitute a new piece of knowledge, which we carry over into our next encounter with our environment.' Far from being a 'vulgar rejection of theory,' this emphasis on practices and problematic situations suggests that 'theory is the outcome of our interaction with and in the world and, as such, is imbued with actually existing practices' (Bauer and Brighi 2009b, p. 162). Theoretical knowledge claims, however they are produced and defended, need to be reasonably close to the experiences of real-world actors in order to be reconsidered and reformulated in light of these experiences. Insofar as they accept causal analysis, pragmatists are more likely to be open to middle-range accounts than to universal laws or general theoretical models – given that pragmatist philosophy aims to 'clip the wings of abstract concepts in order to ground philosophy in the particularities of everyday life' (Kaag 2009, p. 70). At the same time, the door remains open to engaging existing paradigms, since, 'in the very identification of potential causal factors, we are creatively arranging the ambiguous material of the world in dialogue with the scholarly traditions within which we locate ourselves' (Jackson 2009, p. 658).

A third relevant theme has to do with the emphasis on dialogue and inclusiveness in the process of social inquiry. Pragmatists view the production of knowledge as fundamentally a social and discursive activity (Friedrichs and Kratochwil 2009) in that scholarly activities and boundaries are not seen as separate from or privileged over a more fluid and open process of deliberation among all who are interested in a given problem (Menand 1997; Joas 1993; Rorty 1982). Pragmatists certainly recognize that research communities inevitably establish their own rules, methods, and boundaries. However, they place greater emphasis on a wider community of inquirers in which expanded participation and open deliberation are counted upon to legitimize whatever consensus emerges in relation to specific problems (Bohman 1999; Brunkhorst 2002). In the context of international relations, this implies that scholars 'should be wary of intellectual gatekeepers and avoid division into theoretical feuds, but should rather provide a forum for honest and fair intellectual exchange' (Bauer and Brighi 2009b, p. 161). Significantly, expanded participation and open deliberation are not merely procedures to improve the quality of knowledge about international affairs; they also enhance the prospects of consensual norms that can help legitimize institutions governing international affairs (Buchanan and Keohane 2006).

A fourth pragmatist theme, concerning ontology, is largely informed by the work of George Herbert Mead (1934). Mead offered an extensive account of the social and psychological processes through which the evolution of the 'mind' depends on its relationship with meanings shared with other 'minds' in a given social environment: the 'self' is constructed and reconstructed in continuous dialogue with others in that environment. Not surprisingly, this feature of pragmatism has been invoked in support of quite different intellectual perspectives in contemporary scholarship. Some stress the role of rational, intelligent, communicative agents in the dialectical engagement between self and society, suggesting a strong connection between rational choice theory and pragmatist inquiry (Knight and Johnson 1999). For others, Mead's symbolic interactionism draws attention to processes of collective identity formation in relation to actors' identities, actions, and social environments (Wendt 1999). Still others emphasize the role institutions can play in generating collective learning and perhaps even a new consensual discourse (Haas and Haas 2009, p. 134). Each of these formulations stresses a different element of Mead's social psychology: the importance of actors capable of bringing reason to bear in their dealings with society; the processes through which actors' self-conceptions emerge out of a dialectical interaction with society; and the role of institutionalized meaning in transforming pragmatist inquiry into consensus. Collectively, these elements also provide a potential basis for eclectic scholarship. They suggest a more open-ended approach to the question of how and why, in certain contexts, some agents maintain or redefine, and others accept or resist, existing material and ideational structures (Sil 2000a).[10]

This distillation of pragmatist notions relevant to eclectic scholarship may seem overly simplistic to seasoned pragmatists. Nonetheless, it reveals the ways in which analytic eclecticism can fruitfully mediate the dialogue between pragmatist inquiry and paradigm-bound research in international relations. Like pragmatism, analytic eclecticism bypasses excessively rigid metatheoretical postulates in favor of open-ended efforts to frame and address socially important problems facing actors in the social world. Like pragmatism, analytic eclecticism emphasizes creativity in adapting and recombining elements of theoretical knowledge produced by separate research communities in light of diverse experiences in given contexts. Like pragmatism, analytic eclecticism eschews rigid boundaries and hierarchies in the production of knowledge, encouraging reflection and deliberation among all who show interest in aspects of a given problem. And like pragmatism, analytic eclecticism wagers that most outcomes of interest to both scholars and practitioners require attention to the manner in which the material and ideal interests of actors are constituted in relation to their cognitive dispositions, their collective beliefs, and their institutional and social environments.

In the absence of common ground on core issues of ontology and epistemology, eclectic approaches founded on pragmatist principles offer some hope of ongoing engagement with adherents of multiple paradigms, as well as with those who are looking to the academe for usable insights. The result, we realize, may not constitute progress in the sense of facilitating better research design, continuous refinements in a given theory, or more sophisticated techniques of modeling and testing. There is, however, the potential for a different, non-linear kind of 'progress' related to how elements of knowledge produced through paradigms may be creatively reframed, recombined, and redeployed to advance our tentative understandings of interesting and problematic phenomena in the social world. As Ernst Haas and Peter Haas (2009, p. 114) note:

> If agreement is impossible, all ought to be able to make their peace with the looser notion of causality urged by pragmatists, as it is accepting of overdetermination and interactive outcomes. ... In that case fundamentals are not reconciled, but interesting phenomena are confirmed intersubjectively. Trends in international relations may be fruitfully explored and the causal understanding of the interplay between forces typically analyzed by discrete schools is advanced.

This is precisely why the accommodation of analytic eclecticism stands to benefit the field of international relations as a whole. Eclectic scholarship does not require that paradigms be disbanded or their scholarly output discarded. It does, however, require that scholars leave behind the rigid metatheoretical principles upon which paradigms rely in their quest for parsimony and theory cumulation. Analytic eclecticism seeks to expand the opportunities for engaging relevant theories produced by competing paradigms, and for creatively utilizing elements from these theories to generate useful insights about complex social phenomena. The following three chapters offer a sample of scholarly analyses pointing to modest steps now being taken towards this sort of progress in the field of international relations.

Chapter 3

War and peace, security and insecurity

For millennia, wars have been an intrinsic aspect of human existence. But wars also change. In the past, they were fought between empires and tribes, villages and kingdoms. In the modern era they have been fought largely by sovereign states. During the Cold War military strategists came to regard crisis, particularly in the relations between the two nuclear superpowers, as the functional equivalent of war. The 1990s certainly saw its share of collective violence, but there were virtually no traditional wars between sovereign states. And in the wake of 9/11, President George W. Bush sought to rally the American nation to wage 'war' on a more nebulous enemy – terror. This was a call to arms, but without the 'blood, sweat and tears' that Churchill had asked for at the onset of the Second World War.

In recent years, conceptions of war and security have evolved further. Americans are still told that the country is at war and that their security is at risk. But the enemy in the war and the nature of the threat vary greatly. A global pandemic, the H1N1 virus (or swine flu) killed more than a thousand Americans in 2009. In July 2009, a US Department of Defense report concluded that in the coming decades, climate change will raise profound strategic problems for the United States: the effects of violent storms, floods, droughts, and pandemics may force US military interventions in far-flung areas of the world (Broder 2009). US national intelligence chief Dennis Blair testified before Congress in February 2009 that not only was the financial crisis of 2008–09 the most serious in decades, it would also intensify security risks for the United States. Citing the prospects of growing instability in many governments and the weakened position of allies, Blair warned: 'The longer it takes for the recovery to begin, the greater the likelihood of serious damage to US strategic interests.'[1]

49

Because of these changes, the study of war and peace, security and insecurity, no longer falls within the narrow domain of military science and security studies. Increasingly, there is an awareness of the relevance of other fields such as comparative politics, sociology, criminology, economics, science and technology studies, gender studies, and anthropology, as well as a host of hard sciences dealing with issues of technology, global warming, and biodiversity. This explosion of disciplinary interests in various aspects of security studies is invigorating the field. It presents an intellectual opening for newcomers. And it is a challenge for traditional security specialists who are often expected to master new approaches and materials. The expanding definitions of 'war,' 'crisis,' and 'security' since the end of the Cold War bring with them intellectual opportunities and difficulties. They enhance awareness of connections among phenomena previously thought to be unrelated; but they also raise the risk of excessive 'concept stretching' (Sartori 1970) to the point of obfuscating our understanding of interstate disputes and conflicts. This has implications for the nature of dialogues, both among scholars studying war and security issues, and among policymakers in various parts of the world.

Worldwide, these conceptual ambiguities are generating different theoretical approaches. For example, Europeans conceived of 9/11 not in terms of a new kind of war, but as a problem of law enforcement. If this was a war, it would have to be fought and won by judges, police, intelligence services, and undercover agents. Confronted with the serious threat posed by large Muslim immigrant communities and a radicalized fringe of Islamicists, European scholars and policymakers embraced the notion of 'human security,' not as a substitute for but as a complement to the traditional concept of 'national security.' From a European perspective, the conceptual foundation for both policy and theory could no longer be accommodated fully by the traditional concept of national security. But for President Bush and most Americans, this was not so. Challenged to the core by an attack as traumatic as Pearl Harbor, Americans turned, almost instinctively, to the military as the most suitable instrument for defending the nation in the midst of a new war with a new enemy.

However, the biggest and most decisive break with the traditional analysis of war and security issues came not with 9/11, the spread of ethnic conflict, the threat of a pandemic, or even the financial collapse of 2008–09, but with the fall of the Berlin Wall in

November of 1989 and the collapse of the Soviet Union two years later. The end of the Cold War was a revolutionary discontinuity in the structure of world politics, more far reaching than the important new challenges that would emerge in its wake. Students of national and international security were caught flat-footed. None had intimated that anything as momentous was or could be in the offing. The effect on the discipline of international relations and security studies was comparable to that of the sinking of the *Titanic* on the field of naval engineering. The categories of analysis on which security studies could rely were simply inadequate for the purpose of analyzing the breathtaking developments of those dramatic years.

While these momentous changes were occurring, academics were fully absorbed by the latest round of a debate that had occurred many times before – between variants of (neo)realism and (neo)liberalism. The disjunction between revolutionary upheaval in world politics and abstract academic debate could not have been greater, as neither realism nor liberalism was intellectually well equipped to deal with the kinds of changes rapidly unfolding in the real world. Reflecting on the scholarship published in the premier journal *International Security* during the years 1989–94, Hugh Gusterson (1995, p. 6) concluded that 'old stories have been bent to new times rather than questioned or cast away.' Only one article, written by a historian, pointed to the elephant in the room: how reigning paradigms of international relations could have been so unobservant and so unable to anticipate such a dramatic transformation in world politics. The field of national and international security studies slept right through a revolution that fundamentally altered the structure of the international system.

Structural realism, in particular, remained focused on a parsimonious theory cast solely at the systemic level (Waltz 1979). Waltz self-consciously took economics as the model for his theory of international relations. Economic markets and the international system, Waltz argued, have structural characteristics that are defined by competition among units and the emergence of power constellations – monopoly or unipolarity, duopoly or bipolarity, and oligopoly or multipolarity. Economics offers a precise and deductive logic that, for Waltz, is an obvious analogue for understanding the relationships among states in an anarchic environment. In moving the discipline toward a rigorous social science, Waltz broke with an older generation of classical realists.

Most notable was Morgenthau (1970), who had decried the mind-less scientism and empiricism of American social science by anticipating the behavioral revolution of the 1950s and 1960s and the subsequent rise of a quantitative style of international relations scholarship. But Morgenthau's brand of realism offered little more than a proliferation of explanatory constructs and no sharply defined problem. Waltz consistently argued that a sparse, systemic theory of international relations is not geared towards analyzing everything, including the foreign policy choices of states, but meant to explain only one big thing: the recurrence of balancing in world politics. That one big thing was determined solely by the distribution of material capabilities. According to Waltz (1979, p. 95), the Soviet Union – and with it the bipolar world – would last at least until late in the twenty-first century. The implication was that if bipolarity were to break down, chances were excellent that nobody would be around to ask why.

The indeterminate conclusions of Waltz's theory have left many realists unsatisfied. In the words of Stanley Hoffmann (2006, p. 6),

> realism's assumption that the choice of states is between balancing and bandwagoning is certainly parsimonious, but it is also a bit miserly. ... In its neorealist or 'structural' realist form, the theory discards domestic factors and transnational phenomena, makes little or insufficient room for the role of ideas, and displays a certain poverty in its conceptions of change.

Thus, by relaxing some of Waltz's assumptions and through numerous adaptations, realists of various stripes have returned to Morgenthau's less precise but more capacious approach. This gave them license to examine factors such as perceptions of the offense–defense balance, proximity of threats, states' intentions, domestic politics, and individual motives (Bennett and Elman 2006; Walt 2003).

A key aspect of this shift is evident in the increasing attention being paid to the balance of threat rather than the balance of capabilities. This important reformulation has opened the door to a host of other questions and possibilities not previously considered by neorealists. The very concept of threat, defined by Walt (1987) as capability plus intention, implicitly draws attention to the role of perceptions and beliefs held by various actors. Intentionality is inherently a broader and more subjective concept than is capability. If material resources were as decisive as neorealists believe, then countries like Canada and Great Britain should be viewed as posing more of a threat to the United States than Cuba does. Since this is clearly wrong, the intentional component of threats must be at least partly constructed within particular historical or regional contexts. It can greatly magnify or dilute the perceived significance of material capabilities. An effort to make sense of his data on alliance formation in the Middle East, Walt's conception of threat-balancing is not only a refinement of Waltz's structural realism, but unintentionally paves the way for a more fundamental reformulation that allows realism to be coupled with a very different social theory of how actors perceive and respond to threats (Barnett 1996, pp. 403–13; see also Barnett 2003).

Whether addressing capabilities or threats, realist scholars became increasingly interested not only in the presence of the balance of power in the international system writ large, as Waltz was, but also in its particular direction within more narrowly circumscribed contexts. At the end of the Cold War, for example, would Europeans balance against a larger united Germany as Europe's leading power, or against the United States as the remaining superpower? With China rising, would the states of East Asia balance against China or bandwagon with China against the United States? Since Waltz's theory by its very nature operates only at the systemic level and is indeterminate on the choices of states, it is not designed to provide an answer to these important questions. Waltz (1996, 1999) continued to draw a stark distinction between systemic theories and foreign policy analysis, insisting on the primacy of balancing based on material capabilities even in a highly interdependent system. His students and followers, however, sought to make realism more relevant to the practical exigencies of foreign policy. To do so, they found it necessary to sacrifice parsimony to get more purchase on the substantive problem at hand, and thus to open up for investigation many of the 'blackboxed' assumptions on which structural realism had been founded. For some, this is evidence of realism's degeneration as a research program (Vasquez 1997). To others it is testimony to its progressive character (Walt 1997). For us, what is most significant is the gradual relaxation of the analytic boundaries of the neorealist paradigm, and the resulting possibilities for building new bridges toward other analytical perspectives dealing with such variables as state institutions, domestic political pressures, ideas and identities, cognitive factors, and the role of non-state actors and transnational politics (Elman 1996; Finel 2001/02; Lepgold and Lamborn 2001; Rose 1998; Vasquez and Elman 2003).

Often made without either acknowledgement or awareness of the important theoretical departures they entailed, these adjustments led realist scholars after the end of the Cold War to rediscover topics such as nationalism and ethnicity. Internal characteristics of states, Waltz had argued, were irrelevant to the analysis of balancing. But realists intent on understanding the collapse of an old international order and the emergence of a new one were increasingly prepared to sacrifice the elegant logic of systemic analysis in order to better address real world problems. Furthermore, eager to move beyond Europe, where their theory had been disproven so spectacularly, some realists shifted their attention to the balance of power in Asia – and pointed to the instabilities and wars that, supposedly, were just around the corner there (Friedberg 1993/94). In these analyses, the geographic shift of focus frequently proved more dramatic than the analytical one. Domestic politics and transnational relations typically remained underexamined. Instead of reassessing or refurbishing their paradigm, many realists simply reapplied their core concepts and logics in an often poorly understood context. Nevertheless, the stretched boundaries of the realist paradigm and the intellectual sensibilities of a younger cohort of realist scholars have combined to create more space for eclectic styles of analysis than was possible at the height of the Cold War.

Liberalism has been the second protagonist in a longstanding paradigmatic debate among scholars over war and peace, security and insecurity. As is true of realism, liberal theory has several different variants. Neoliberal institutionalism, sometimes called structural liberalism, operates at the international level, while other variants focus at the domestic level. Neoliberal institutionalism (Keohane 1984; Baldwin 1993) shares with neorealism the basic presupposition of an anarchical international system comprised of competing unitary actors. Like neorealism, it takes the interests of those actors as given. In contrast to realism, neoliberal institutionalism argues that international institutions can alleviate the security dilemma that states confront in the international system through the reduction of information uncertainties. What is true of international trade or financial organizations, such as the World Trade Organization (WTO) or International Monetary Fund (IMF), also holds for international security organizations such as the North Atlantic Treaty Organization (NATO) (Haftendorn, Keohane, and Wallander 1999). Such adaptations, however, did not constitute a fundamental challenge to neorealism. They were even consistent with many of the assumptions concerning alliance formation and balancing behavior in systemic neorealist theories. In fact, by accepting core neorealist premises on the basic character of the international system, neoliberal institutionalists helped to consolidate a widely shared view about the character of international politics and how to study it. This is perhaps one reason that the end of the Cold War and the collapse of the Soviet bloc were no more anticipated by neoliberal institutionalists than by realists or neorealists.

Other variants of liberalism operate at the domestic level. While the specific formulations vary, they share an underlying common logic that Andrew Moravcsik (1997) has articulated very clearly. State preferences are shaped neither by relative capabilities as in neorealism, nor by the institutional and informational characteristics of international organization, as in neoliberalism. Instead, they are influenced by self-interested individuals or private groups within domestic society. Governments or other public actors come to represent the interests of some subset of societal interests and act purposefully to achieve these interests in world politics. Liberal states are thus constituted by representative institutions and practices that transmit societal interests to state actors and institutions, thus shaping fundamental state preferences. Since societies vary greatly in the range and distribution of interests, so do the preferences of states in different contexts and arenas. State behavior is not determined solely by the sum total of institutionally mediated societal interests, however. It is also the result of policy interdependence of different states. From this perspective, the alignment or misalignment of states' preferences in the international arena with the underlying distribution of societal interests in each state – or what Robert Putnam (1988) referred to as the dynamics of 'two-level games' – is the ultimate basis for the extent of cooperation in security affairs.

Based on these foundational assumptions, two other variants of neoliberal theories have emerged: republican and commercial liberalism. Republican liberalism focuses on the representative institutions – parties, elections, and bureaucracies – that link society to the state and determine which social preferences become politically privileged. One central proposition of this approach emphasizes the peace-inducing effects of democratic institutions, asserting that the rule of law, franchise, and a free press make democracies more transparent and thus less prone to war than are autocracies. Social interests are represented with varying degrees of accuracy. To the extent that institutions reflect broadly based individual or group preferences, liberal polities will refrain from bellicose foreign policies. In imperfectly representative regimes, concentrated groups can band together in support of such policies, and audience costs for doing so are comparatively low. In general, the interests of dominant social and political coalitions get primary access to representative institutions and thus have the greatest effect on policy. Recent scholarship, however, also reflects growing awareness of the possibility and significance of audience costs in autocratic regimes (Weeks 2008), which requires, at a minimum, a significant relaxation of the assumptions behind which institutional features of regimes affect their propensity towards conflict or cooperation.

Commercial liberalism analyzes the likelihood of conflict by considering the effects of domestic and transnational actors on state behavior. Changes in the domestic and global economy alter the costs and benefits of economic cross-border exchange, influencing the interests of powerful actors and generating political pressure for governments to follow specific policies in line with those interests. Incentives for specific policies and distributional conflicts generate patterns of policy that are more or less cooperative and lead to more or less openness. Economic interdependence by itself is indeterminate. The eventual political outcome depends on the pattern of policy, itself shaped by domestic and transnational conflicts among winners and losers. Commercial liberalism holds that economic interdependence breeds peace by mobilizing constituencies that lose by war. The issue is not transparency or audience costs, as in republican liberalism, but rather the preferences of powerful financial interests in stable conditions that enable the maximization of gain. As Jonathan Kirshner (2007) has shown compellingly, for reasons of self-interest rather than pacifism, bankers are a force for peace not war; war brings social and economic instabilities, budget deficits, and inflation – all factors that undercut the value of money. Yet despite the power of finance, wars continue to break out. Commercial liberalism suggests an important mechanism that is often overlooked in security studies: the role of financial groups in influencing policy. But it cannot, by itself, project the likelihood of war or peace based on the preferences of any one group, however powerful it may be.

The end of the Cold War has also created more space for sociological or constructivist approaches to issues of war and security (Onuf 1989; Wendt 1999; Kratochwil 1989). Although a powerful intellectual current in Europe (Hoffmann 1986), constructivism was until the 1990s quite marginal in the United States. As with realism and liberalism, constructivism features a number of schools of thought and can be applied at both the international and the domestic levels. Unlike realism and liberalism, which normally take identities or preferences to be exogenous, constructivism problematizes the relationship between identities and preferences, as well as their origins. And unlike neoliberal institutionalism, it directly challenges a core realist premise about the nature of the international system. Anarchy, for Wendt (1992), is nothing more than 'what states make of it.' That is, it is not an objective but an intersubjective fact, a powerful social myth that carries different meanings for different actors (Hopf 1998; Wendt 1992). This has enormous significance for whether and how states understand the regional and international arenas of which they are a part; what specific criteria they use to identify allies and enemies; and whether and how they perceive threats to their security. In other words constructivists analyze what realists and liberals take for granted; they treat the international system as at best a heuristic device for capturing the security environment as various actors perceive it. Consequently, as Johnston (1998) argued in his analysis of Chinese strategic culture, even strategies that appear to be driven by realist logics can be constructed on the basis of particular historical contexts and cultural traditions.

In addition, constructivism analyzes two topics neglected by realism and liberalism: the content and sources of state identities (Checkel 1998). Indeed, its most significant theoretical contribution in the arena of security studies has been to highlight the relevance of actor identity to enduring rivalries or collective security arrangements that do not fit neatly with predictions based on realist or liberal premises. This shift in analytical focus has allowed constructivist scholars to see considerable significance in security regimes, such as the Concert System of great powers in Europe after 1815, and in security communities that institutionalize dependable expectations of peaceful change, as in the European Union or the

Association of Southeast Asian Nations (ASEAN). Such regimes and communities provide a context that shapes norms of proper conduct prescribing what actors should and should not do. Even after a particular security community has broken down, its legacies frequently shape actors' identities and their interests within their respective regional contexts.

Yet another strand of constructivism stresses the role of dispositions that emerge among security practitioners and influence the prospects for conflict resolution. Self-evident understandings arising out of the practice of diplomacy are driven more by the 'logic of habit' (Hopf 2009) than by reasons of consequences or appropriateness. Sometimes they pave the way for the non-violent resolution of conflicts, and at other times they reinforce tensions stemming from incongruities between actors' dispositions and the positions they represent (Pouliot 2010). Focusing on regulative and constitutive norms, as well as on the effects of practice and habit, constructivist scholarship seeks to extend the causal chain that leads states to identify enemies and threats, initiate disputes, or participate in measures to enhance collective security. At the same time, constructivist approaches are limited in how efficiently they explain the remarkably similar calculations that very different states often undertake when facing similar distributions of power.

During the two decades from 1990 to 2010, changes in the real world have compelled scholars to broaden their paradigmatic vistas. As the dominant intellectual perspective in security studies during most of the twentieth century, in recent years realism has increasingly sought to relax its analytic boundaries and investigate core assumptions in order to make itself relevant to policy issues and substantive dilemmas facing actors in the post-Cold War era. Liberalism, in its multiple variants, has pointed to the relationships between domestic and transnational actors and institutions insofar as these provide a deeper understanding of the conditions under which states are inclined to initiate disputes or seek peace. And constructivism, as a latecomer to the debate, has had little choice but to take note of the longstanding traditions of realism and liberalism in seeking to make its contributions to the study of war and security. Thus, its primary point of impact has been at the levels of ontology and epistemology: by problematizing such fundamental concepts as 'anarchy' and 'interest,' constructivists have created space for analyzing the effects of collective identities and norms on state behavior in historical and regional contexts. Collectively, these intellectual shifts within various paradigms have created movement towards more eclectic approaches which draw on causal mechanisms and processes from multiple analytical perspectives.

The studies discussed in this chapter tend to do well on the three criteria we use to distinguish analytic eclecticism in international relations scholarship. Most of the works considered below address questions about war and security that are of greater scope than the more narrowly circumscribed inquiries that drive research within each of the contending paradigms. They also tend to occupy a middle ground between excessively abstract generalizations and overly detailed descriptive accounts. They specify and seek to show interconnections between mechanisms or causal logics drawn from various paradigms. And they give us insights that not only challenge existing debates within international relations scholarship but also potentially contribute to rethinking policy on crucial issues. None of the works necessarily scores high on all of the three criteria we use to distinguish analytic eclecticism, but each does reasonably well across most of them. And they all score high on the most significant criterion: constructing complex causal stories that incorporate mechanisms and processes from theories embedded in at least two of the major paradigms. This chapter discusses exemplars of analytic eclecticism addressing issues of peace among all of the world's major powers (Jervis 2005), military intervention (Finnemore 2003), the spread of nuclear weapons (Solingen 2007), the tradition of the non-use of nuclear weapons (Paul 2009), and the implications of China's rise for regional stability (Kang 2007).[2]

Robert Jervis, *American Foreign Policy in a New Era* (2005)

'Current world politics,' writes Jervis (2005, p. 1) on the first page of his book, 'challenges many of our theories because it is new in fundamental ways.' The last page of the book concludes that, as a result of the Bush doctrine, '[w]e are headed for a difficult world, one that is not likely to fit any of our ideologies or simple theories' (p. 138). While pessimistic, the latter prediction is not simply a sweeping polemical statement. It derives from Jervis's reconsideration of the contours of the present international environment and of its implications for the foreign policies of the United States and its allies and adversaries. The book is in effect a 'hybrid' effort (p. 5), combining scholarly analysis of the complex set of conditions that have shaped the contours of post-9/11 international relations with a critical re-evaluation of American foreign policy. The book has implications for both policy debate and public discourse. Jervis is clear at the outset that he opposes the Bush administration's approach to the post-9/11 world. But he does not let this opposition influence his framing of the problems or his balanced efforts to produce a deeper understanding of the nature of the international order by selectively combining explanatory factors drawn from various perspectives. Without completely relinquishing his realist footing, Jervis makes a bold move in the direction of eclecticism.

The book is focused on the United States' foreign policies in the post-Cold War era. It is predicated on the assumption that international relations are now characterized by a number of related features that make them distinct from any era in the past. Most significantly, a potentially revolutionary transformation has taken place in the international system: a distinctive kind of security community has emerged, consisting of the most powerful developed states in the world – the United States, Japan, and the more influential countries in western Europe. These nations no longer fear the breakout of armed conflict among them. Although today this state of affairs is almost taken for granted, Jervis points out that it is 'an enormous, indeed revolutionary, change from the past' (p. 1). Threatening, planning, waging, and seeking to avoid war has been a central aspect of great power politics for centuries. Although smaller security communities had emerged in the past, for example in Scandinavia, they never included all of the most powerful states in the international system. For Jervis, the current security community constitutes 'proof by existence of the possibility of uncoerced peace without central authority' (p. 35).

Jervis does not discount the potential significance of China and Russia in world affairs, acknowledging that these two countries may indeed come into conflict. However, while recognizing that some may regard China and Russia as great powers, Jervis emphasizes that they are not yet to be counted among the most developed great powers: they lack key attributes such as stable internal regimes, advanced forms of technology and economic organization, the capacity to project power beyond their surrounding regions, and the ability to serve as models that are emulated by others. Among established great powers, this new era of enduring peace represents a novel development that requires scholars and policymakers to adjust their assumptions about the nature of international affairs. For Jervis, this is a spectacular change, and the most striking discontinuity that the history of international politics has provided (p. 13).

A related change is American primacy – the result of the disintegration of the Soviet Union, the failure of the European Union to unite and form a cohesive unitary actor, and the inability of any state to seriously challenge the United States for several decades to come. In material capabilities and influence, in the ability to establish the framework for global debates, and in the capacity, if not always willingness, to provide public goods, the extent of the dominance enjoyed by the United States is very large and possibly unprecedented. And yet, Jervis contends, American behavior 'tracks in important ways with what very powerful states have done in the past, and … it is likely to prove self-defeating' (p. 2).

Jervis also identifies a third major change, the threat of terrorism and the American response it has generated. He does not see this change as an enduring or revolutionary transformation. While terrorist attacks certainly require analyses that extend beyond the scope of theories focused on normal interstate relations, Jervis views existing theories of international politics and foreign policy as useful in capturing the behavior of states in response to terrorism. However, the other two changes – the security community among great powers and the extent of American dominance – are unprecedented and require fundamentally different modes of analysis.

Having identified the novel features of the post-Cold War international order, Jervis proceeds to ask two sets of substantive questions. First, does the emergent security community of great powers end security threats to its members, particularly the United States? And second, what factors explain the emergence of this security community, and how long will it endure? The very framing of these questions requires a relaxation of the boundaries of existing paradigms in international relations. To conceptualize a security community of great powers, we must go beyond the traditional assumptions of (neo)realism. Yet the composition and significance of the community rest on members' power and capabilities relative to others. Moreover, analyzing security threats and foreign policy against this backdrop points inevitably and directly to a range of concrete prescriptions concerning how the relevant actors should act in the new environment. Jervis's questions thus have implications for both the conduct and the analysis of international affairs (p. 13).

The answer to the first question is a resounding 'no.' The existence of a security community only suggests that the most developed great powers do not regard each other as threats. However, terrorist groups, rogue states, and potentially Russia or China continue to pose security threats to these states. But even those most afraid of these potential threats do not see these powers as ready to attack the United States, Europe, or Japan without direct provocation. And neither Russia nor China has done anything to indicate that they seek to replace the United States as the world's primary power. The assertiveness in their policies – and the tensions it engenders – centers on their demands for limited spheres of influence that would be closed to the United States. Certainly, there is American opposition to those demands, and this opposition may increase tensions in particular regional theaters. But this does not suggest a challenge to American primacy in the global arena writ large. In any case, none of these challenges, including the threat of terrorism, is having as deep an impact on the entire fabric of world politics and American foreign policy as did the possibility of great power clashes in the past. Although less capable powers seek to carve out their own spheres of influence, the struggle for international primacy among the great powers of the world is no longer a favored sport.

The second question concerns the origins and future prospects of this security community. Based on the history of the last two decades, there is ample reason to believe that discord and disagreement can intensify, as it did over the US attack of Iraq, and persist over long periods. But there is no indication that the fear of military conflict among the developed great powers will reappear in the foreseeable future. American policies that seek to maintain US advantage over Europe and Japan are not driven by security fears or uncertainties but by the expectation that political rivalries among the three great powers could impede the management of global problems. Yet Jervis heeds the counsel never to say 'never.' There are any number of future contingencies – linked to the fragility of prosperity and democracy, or drastic climate change, to name but two scenarios – that might shake to its foundations the assumptions and expectations we currently take for granted. Yet it seems improbable that factors endogenous to international politics that have traditionally led to disputes and rivalries among states will eliminate the kind of security community that has evolved among the developed major powers.

The durability of the security community is thus a function of the factors that explain its emergence. Noting that no single theory can independently explain the dynamics of the new security community, Jervis relies on the overlapping features of, and intersections among, core explanatory factors posited in each of the three paradigms, even though they proceed from different metatheoretical assumptions (p. 16). To do this effectively, he considers carefully the core arguments and limitations of each paradigm within the context of the post-Cold War era.

Constructivists generally favor ideational over material factors: ideas, images of self and other, and conceptions of appropriate or habitual conduct. Rather than isolate precise causal links among these factors, constructivists highlight a virtuous cycle linking practices, beliefs, and expectations, which are seen as mutually constitutive. They also reject the notion that ideational factors are merely a reflection or consequence of the materialist factors typically emphasized in realist or liberal explanations. Of particular significance to the emergence and durability of the security community is 'the norm of nonviolence and the shared identities that have led the advanced democracies to assume the role of each other's friend through the interaction of behavior and expectations' (p. 16). Mass publics in the great powers have experienced a socialization process that encourages the peaceful resolution of conflicts and makes traditional, virulent nationalism the exception rather than the rule. The fact that all members of the security community are democracies is significant for constructivists, not so much for reasons of transparency or accountability (typically emphasized in liberal accounts of the democratic peace) but for the emergence of a common identity linked to similarity in regimes and political practices (p. 17). Learning has also played a role, generating a cognitive shift among leaders in a security community as they adopt cooperative methods for conflict resolution (p. 18). However, Jervis also notes that the spread of democracy – along with a turn away from violence, conquest, honor, and glory – over the long run could make it less distinctive and therefore less useful as a basis for collective identity. Moreover, some constructivist claims underplay the importance of human agency and overplay the importance of oversocialized individuals. Thus, Jervis's discussion underscores the fact that ideational factors such as identities, norms, and learning are important but not determining elements in a fully satisfying explanation of the emergence of the security community.

Liberal explanations point to the pacifying effects of three factors: democracy, economic interdependence, and joint membership in international organizations. The observation that democracies rarely if ever fight one another has become one of the most robust and central findings of democratic peace theory. Although the devil resides here in the statistical detail, and the controversy over the theory is ongoing, there is an emergent scholarly consensus on the core logics emphasized in this literature: a constitutionally imposed dispersion of power that acts as a break on a rush to war; democratic norms that require the settlement of disputes by peaceful means and with respect for law; unrestricted flow of information that encourages public debate and better elite decision making; and electoral and coalitional constraints on rash decision makers who seek to maintain themselves in power by winning contested elections. These causal arguments, Jervis argues, are thoughtful and often ingenious but not always adequate for explaining the novel security community forged by great powers. For example, these arguments lead to the expectation that democracies should not only behave in a peaceful manner in their relations with each other, but should not seek to overthrow or fight the governments of non-democracies – expectations that are demonstrably wrong empirically. The dispersal of power and the accountability of leaders, which are supposed to make democracies more judicious and selective in fighting wars, also make leaders of non-democracies cautious. And it is not clear how the posited causal effect actually operates in multilateral rather than bilateral settings, as each country must assess the behavior and expectations of all others. Liberalism points to some important mechanisms. But in and of themselves, these mechanisms do not adequately explain the security community among great powers (pp. 19–20).

Economic interdependence and international organizations are also regularly cited by liberals as forces that incline countries towards the peaceful resolution of conflicts. Individuals, groups, firms, sectors, and regions get politically invested in the advantageous benefits they derive from rising trade and investment, and thus become powerful lobbies for peaceful and good relations with other countries. While consumption politics is a fact of life, in crisis situations it can be replaced by another kind of politics. It is far from certain that the coalition of those benefiting from trade and investment will always prevail over countervailing political forces. International organizations enhance information flows, ease problem solving, increase the stake in cooperation, and reinforce the risk of isolation. These are all important mechanisms that may have significant effects in particular circumstances. Jervis does question, however, the magnitude of this effect when circumstances are so variable. Furthermore, liberal arguments downplay the possibility that the division of relative gains will exacerbate conflict in situations of high interdependence, as it did before the First World War. In addition, economic interdependence and cooperation in international organizations may be the effects rather than the causes of some underlying and more fundamental set of factors in the international system.

Finally, traditional realist explanations about the role of external threats in forging cooperation do not explain the new security community. The Soviet threat was very important in helping create a security community among the United States, Europe, and Japan. But it is implausible to argue that Russia, China, or any other state has posed a similar threat since the end of the Cold War. Terrorism certainly poses new threats; however, there exists great disagreement on how best to combat it. A more promising realist argument sees the security community as a mere byproduct of American dominance in a unipolar system. America's defense budget is larger than that of the rest of the world combined. America's allies do not fear being attacked by each other, nor do they have the ability to carry out a sustained military campaign against each other. Still another sensible realist explanation concerns the pacifying effects of nuclear weapons, which have made war among great powers 'a feckless option' (p. 25). Neither of these arguments, however, can satisfactorily explain the distinctive aspects of the present security community. American hegemony is certainly dominant, but other major powers, rather than being coerced by it, simply seek to harness or constrain it. The argument about nuclear deterrence, while useful in explaining the absence of a major war, does not preclude hostility or attempts at coercion. Furthermore, it fails to account for the formation of a full-blown security community among great powers.

Jervis's discussion of the strengths and limitations of theories embedded in the constructivist, liberal, and realist traditions is nuanced and insightful. Going well beyond critical reviews, his main goal is to disembed the most compelling factors from each explanatory framework, identify areas of overlap, and build what he calls a 'synthetic interactive explanation.' In the terminology of this book, his is a coherent, eclectic argument. Among the factors Jervis views as most interesting and important are the belief that territorial conquest is difficult and unnecessary; the recognition of the costs of war, particularly in the nuclear age; and, rooted in the spread of democracy, shifts in identity that reflect a sharp decline in militarism and nationalism and a growing value compatibility among the most advanced major powers. The significance of these shifts depends on ongoing historical processes. For example, the evolution of the international economy has produced dissociation between territoriality and national prosperity, increasing the costs of territorial acquisition. Similarly, the high degree of cooperation among the core members of the security community is partly a function of enduring Cold War legacies. States were socialized during the Cold War to behave as 'partners' and set aside their normal grievances to deal with a powerful adversary. In sum, the destructiveness of war, the benefits of peace, and a change in values are interactive and mutually reinforcing processes of change.

Finally, it is worth noting that Jervis does not treat his analysis as a purely academic exercise. He is also concerned about its implications for adjusting American foreign policy. Updating policy to deal with new threats, such as terrorism, will remain ineffective as long as it remains predicated on dated conceptions of national interest that no longer reflect the distinctiveness of the present international environment. In particular, Jervis cautions that unilateral actions by the United States, particularly since 9/11, have begun to undermine the trust of members of the security community. He also notes that members of the security community seek to check American hegemony by adopting new styles of balancing behavior. Rather than military challenges, 'soft' balancing involves subtle, coordinated efforts to socialize and entrap the United States to keep its behavior 'within acceptable bounds' (p. 31). For Jervis, this dynamic is indicative of the novelty of the new international system rather than a mere reflection of the different preferences of different policymakers. The durability of the security community is such that states 'need not moderate their scorn of each other in fear that harsh words and limited conflict might lead to a permanent break, let alone armed hostilities' (p. 104). Whether or not one concurs with Jervis' analysis, embedded in the scenarios he sketches for the future are policy prescriptions that illustrate his eclecticism and invite a more open-ended discussion among scholars and policymakers about US foreign policy in a new and evolving international order.

Box 3.1
Robert Jervis – Engaging the 'isms' without being confined by them

American Foreign Policy in a New Era (Jervis 2005) is eclectic for two reasons. First, I wrote the chapters at different times and for different purposes. Second, and more importantly, each was focused on a particular problem. For example, I drafted the second chapter in November 2001 to understand how 9/11 had changed the world. I wrote the third chapter a year later, while the United States was preparing to overthrow Saddam. I thought this policy was extremely foolish. The occupation would be long and bloody, and even if he gained weapons of mass destruction, Saddam would not be able to do much to harm to the United States and its allies. I wrote 'Understanding the Bush Doctrine' (Jervis 2005, ch. 4) to come to grips with the question, troubling especially for realists, of why a country would adopt a policy that clashed fundamentally with realist precepts. In each chapter, eclecticism was intended to unravel different puzzles. These different puzzles involved different dynamics and naturally led to the deployment of a variety of analytical approaches.

Although I wanted to be parsimonious, it was more important to me to get the answer right. This was particularly true of the first chapter, which I expanded from my Presidential Address to the American Political Science Association. As John Mueller and others had argued, we had failed to consider a revolutionary change in world politics: leading states no longer contemplate fighting each other. Here I explicitly deployed arguments from the 'isms.' None of them could account by itself for the phenomenon. I then tried combinations of elements drawn from all of them; yet here, and elsewhere, I sought to discipline my thinking by asking what alternative schools of thought would lead me to expect, and by looking for evidence that would help me to sort out alternative explanations. In exploring the cause of American policy after 9/11, I thus tried to separate arguments that stressed Bush's personality and worldview from those that pointed to enduring factors within the United States, and from arguments that in turn distinguished factors common to all great powers. I argued that in damning or praising Bush, most analysts gave insufficient weight to the third set of factors, which had also been present in the actions of many other states during the past few centuries. I thus found engagements with the 'isms' to be productive as long as I resisted the pressure to be confined by them.

Martha Finnemore, *The Purpose of Intervention* (2003)

Finnemore's book examines changing international notions about the use and justification of military intervention. For Finnemore, intervention provides a valuable lens for analyzing the purpose of force 'because it establishes boundary conditions for two central institutions of international life, sovereignty and war' (p. 7). Intervention refers to the deployment of military personnel across recognized state borders to shape the political authority structure of the target state, a distinctive type of the use of force that is generally defended with reference to some set of standards of proper conduct (p. 2). Since the conceptual labels attached to what we today understand to be intervention have changed greatly over time and in different places, Finnemore does not simply observe an event and ask 'is this an intervention?' She instead proceeds inductively by looking at the associated practices, and inquires into what they are, how they were understood, and how their patterns have changed over time. That is, she problematizes as part of her investigation the issue of what has counted as an intervention in a given historical context and what normative arguments have been invoked to justify acts of intervention in that context.

Finnemore finds that historical changes in the pattern of intervention are not determined by new military technologies or shifts in the material balance of capabilities, as dominant arguments in security studies suggest. Instead, she argues, while the fact and scale of intervention may not have varied much, state understandings of the purposes that justify the use of force have changed significantly over time, reflecting evolving notions of legitimacy and authority in the international state system. Finnemore does not find it surprising that understandings about military intervention may vary across different states and over time, but she is interested in identifying and explaining global changes in the patterns of military intervention. Some forms of intervention have disappeared altogether. New ones have emerged. But, as Finnemore puts it: 'In all cases, states as a group have rejected intervention for some purpose or have altered their understandings about how or why intervention is done, with the result that the behavior of states has changed across the system' (p. 3).

The main objective of Finnemore's book is to chart these global shifts and to generate novel hypotheses to explain them. To do so, she analyzes the array of possible explanations identifiable in existing theoretical literatures, in conjunction with detailed studies of processes of historical change. This approach – what John Ruggie (1998) called 'narrative explanatory protocol' – combines descriptive accounts of the sequence of events with the configuration of these events to emphasize aspects that are most pertinent to the question. The logic of analysis is neither purely inductive nor purely deductive, but rather a dialectical combination of both. Referred to as 'abduction' (p. 13) by Charles Pierce, one of the leading founders of pragmatist thought, this approach is not designed to yield general law-like statements or point predictions that can be subjected to standardized tests. Rather, against the null hypothesis of the constancy of state interests, Finnemore sets as her immediate objective the demonstration that state purposes change over time. Ultimately, she is interested in identifying the mechanisms that are most responsible for this change (p. 14).

Finnemore applies her approach to three different cases. For Finnemore, 'cases' are not specific interventions but shifts in the overall 'pattern of global intervention behavior' (p. 11). The first case examines economic interventions undertaken, especially by Britain and France, to collect economic debts owed by the government of one state to nationals of another, here typically British and French bondholders. Widespread in the nineteenth century, this practice ceased in the early twentieth century. Possible explanations include the rise of American power and changing conditions in the international economy. Unfortunately, there is little evidence to support the causal importance of these material factors. A more significant and defensible account for the shift is the growing importance of international law as a profession and the increasing presence of international lawyers at conferences and treaty negotiations, causing international arbitration to be regarded increasingly as both morally superior and economically more efficient than military intervention.

A second case is humanitarian military intervention. While a common practice for the last two centuries, there have been significant changes in terms of who is being protected and how a state intervenes. Today, non-White and non-Christian populations have a claim that they simply did not enjoy in the nineteenth century. Furthermore, contemporary interventions are conducted multilaterally and on behalf of an international organization, not so much to share the material burdens of intervention as for reasons of legitimacy.

A third case study focuses on military interventions in states that are thought to pose a threat to the international society of states. Here, too, the practice has been longstanding and widespread. But the modalities and justifications of interventions have changed depending on the broader international order states were defending in history – the balance of power system, a concert system, a spheres-of-influence system, or the current American-centered system. This case study, furthermore, establishes that the international order was less consistently aligned with the material distribution of capabilities than with the modalities with which interventions were carried out (pp. 3–4).

This book is exemplary in bringing together different explanations. Students of military intervention operate conventionally based on logics loosely derived from *Realpolitik*. To serve their geostrategic and economic interests, strong states always have intervened and always will intervene in weak ones. Yet states also use force for other reasons, as in the case of humanitarian intervention. In fact, the cases Finnemore investigates are not easily explained by realist formulations. For any set of state interests dictating intervention, it is easy to come up with a different specification of interests that is consistent with observed outcomes. It is more interesting to determine what state interests are, and which interests are served by interventions. Focusing on broader patterns of intervention across different international systems and issue areas, and examining the substance of the debates that accompany such interventions, leads Finnemore to an appreciation of coordinated shifts in perceptions of interests across all or most states.

Legal scholars and constructivists will be challenged by Finnemore's analysis of how changes in rules, interests, and understandings have occurred, not independently from power and interests but deeply implicated by them. The most interesting part of this analysis is how one set of rules serving the self-interest of strong states that can actively organize military interventions has been replaced by a different set of rules that serve the interest of the very same states, but constrain their actions in different ways. What is theoretically interesting is not the presence of state interests but their enormous plasticity. Historical context and contingency matter, as does purposive agency. In all three cases, Finnemore discovers what she calls 'strategic social construction' (p. 5), whereby actors set out rationally and self-consciously to alter the perceptions and values of others. In the hands of leaders like William Gladstone or Klemens Metternich, sometimes the tools of persuasion worked, and sometimes they failed. But their efforts at strategic social construction had much to do with subsequent changes in the normative fabric of world politics. Thus, an analysis of the techniques of persuasion and their effects enables Finnemore to examine how historical context and strategic agency interact with psychology and diplomacy.

Finnemore's argument also speaks to the concerns of those interested in normative theory and ethics. Interventions contradict such foundational notions of international law as sovereignty, as well as such core ethical components of the international community as self-determination. They thus cannot help but raise extended normative discussions about what is right and good in international life. In all of Finnemore's cases, an inherent tension arises between clashing norms or values: between the sanctity of contracts and state sovereignty; between normative imperatives for humanitarian intervention to protect the lives of innocents and the duty to protect the lives of one's own citizens in uniform; and between the pursuit of self-determination and the risk it can pose to the peace and security of the international community. In these clashing normative and moral claims, some claims grow weaker over time, such as glory achieved through military pursuits, while others grow stronger, such as human rights, which now rival the power of sovereignty and self-determination norms. Normative conflicts over intervention do not diminish. But the processes through which normative conflicts change alter the use of military force.

Across her cases and analytical perspectives, Finnemore comes to an understanding of a very basic point. Most of contemporary international relations scholarship contrasts two sets of competing perspectives, which stress utility and instrumental rationality on the one hand, and legitimacy and substantive rationality on the other. Across her three very different cases, Finnemore's research amply documents that utility and legitimacy are indelibly intertwined. 'Separating the two or treating them as competing explanations,' she writes, 'is not only difficult but probably misguided, since it misses the potentially more interesting question of how the two are intertwined and interdependent' (Finnemore 2003, p. 16). Over time, new forms of intervention became more effective or useful, not simply because of the availability of new methods to intervene but because the very definition of utility changed, not in material but in social and normative terms.

Finnemore is able to identify three broad empirical trends that are apparent across her cases. First, there is the malleability of state interests. Throughout history, states with greater military capacities, typically Western great powers, have frequently exercised disproportionate influence over the rules governing the international system. What is most interesting is the manner in which the interests of strong states change, and how this change subsequently alters the 'normative landscape' (p. 18) on which intervention rules are developed and applied. Second, there is evidence of a normative shift over time in the value attached to war for its own sake, at least relative to the value attached to more general norms such as sovereign equality and humanitarian protection. Although, ironically, the shift in norms has not actually reduced the use of force, it is significant that there have been 'very real shifts in the goals people fight for, the ways they use force, and the perceived imperatives those changes create for military action' (p. 19). Finally, there is the growing importance of rational-legal authority (in the Weberian sense) in governing the use of force. Much more attention is now paid to specific legal understandings as well as the rules or norms established by international organizations. Even in the case of humanitarian intervention, appeals based on preventing acts of 'barbarism,' because it was the 'civilized' thing to do, are now combined with appeals that incorporate international legal obligations and reference to decisions of various international tribunals, commissions, and other legal authorities (pp. 21–2).

To understand these shifts, Finnemore relies on the interaction of a range of collective-level and individual-level mechanisms. At the collective level, there is the obvious significance of coercion, at best a necessary condition for changing social purposes. There are also the roles played by international institutions and law, which serve to codify new social purposes, and by epistemic communities and social movements, which play critical roles in altering and institutionalizing the values and goals of a society. At the individual level, there are the processes of persuasion and communicative action that enable particular individuals to be effective in persuading or responsive to various acts of persuasion. Understanding these processes requires attention to social psychology, which stresses a number of conditions under which persuasion is more likely to

Box 3.2
Martha Finnemore – Let yourself be surprised

Good hypotheses are hard to find. As a graduate student I was trained to test hypotheses. The dirty secret no one told me was that most of the dominant 'paradigms' of our field are simply not fine-grained enough to provide hypotheses about problems that analysts and citizens care about. Thus, *The Purpose of Intervention* (Finnemore 2003), like all my work, is about discovering or generating hypotheses as much as testing them.

I backed into this book through the humanitarian intervention case. The international relations literature lacked plausible hypotheses to explain the rash of interventions we saw in Somalia, Bosnia, Cambodia, and Kosovo in the 1990s, places of minimal geostrategic or economic interest to intervening states. Humanitariansm as a motive was dismissed by the field, yet media coverage, public opinion, and decision-maker statements all focused on this motive and justification. I was intrigued. I decided to take political actors at their word and explore how humanitarian concerns could shape interventions.

History proved to be my friend. I naively assumed that these interventions were new, but quickly found that states have been doing such interventions for at least two centuries. Suddenly I had additional cases, but making sense of them was a challenge. They certainly did not let me invent some sweeping theory of humanitarian action, but they did allow me to make some limited, contingent generalizations about basic contours of change in a field preoccupied with stasis and equilibrium.

Actually, history was my friend in all these cases. In each one there were big surprises in the evidence. Perhaps the most interesting (to me) was the finding that intervention itself is a relatively recent notion, created in a particular context (post-1815 Europe) to serve particular ends of strong states, as I have argued in my book (page 10, footnote 7). I did not know what to make of this finding initially. I fretted about it and wrestled to make cases fit my framework. Oddly, admitting defeat and taking the anomalies on board turned out to be a great strategy. It let me incorporate the construction of intervention itself into my argument and provided historical material to do this.

If this translates into advice, it would be something like: 'let yourself be surprised by your evidence.' Explanations of most social phenomena are more interesting than we can imagine a priori. Consequently, our existing hypotheses are usually less interesting than the explanations we are able to construct with a fuller appreciation of our evidence.

succeed (for example, under conditions of uncertainty, or when the persuader is an authoritative member of a dominant in-group to which others want to belong). Finnemore also argues that affective mechanisms play a role in that 'empathy' or 'liking' of familiar individuals, which can be cultivated over increased social interaction among a group of individuals, can increase the likelihood of changes in perception or cognition among others. Finally, there is the process through which social influence changes public behavior without a corresponding change in private beliefs, yet generates cognitive dissonance and creates inclinations towards the internalization of values that are consistent with public behavior. Thus, Finnemore's eclectic framework not only stresses the combined significance of material and ideational factors, but also posits a number of processes featuring the interplay of collective-level and individual-level mechanisms (pp. 142–61).

The changes Finnemore documents have an aura of obviousness about them. Specifically, it may strike the contemporary observer as obvious that military intervention to collect debts, intervention intended to protect only White Christians, and unilateral intervention in weaker states are, respectively, wasteful, racist and illegitimate. One of Finnemore's main aims is to puncture this sense of obviousness by showing that at a different time and place, what now strikes us as wasteful, racist, or illegitimate was considered efficient, non-racist, and legitimate. What now is considered obvious, at an earlier time was deeply contested or rejected, and for perfectly logical and well-articulated reasons. In bypassing the boundary conditions typically observed by proponents of standard realist or constructivist accounts, Finnemore is able to problematize the obvious. There is much to be gained, for both scholars and policymakers, by considering why some set of norms and some uses of force were considered entirely plausible in one historical era but not in another. This perhaps is the book's most striking and enduring contribution.

Etel Solingen, *Nuclear Logics* (2007)

Solingen's (2007) book starts off with a deceptively simple and undeniably important question: Why have some states sought to acquire nuclear weapons while others have chosen to renounce them? The question is obviously relevant to policy, but policy studies have not taken advantage of debates in international relations theory to explore the issue systematically. International relations scholars have devoted much attention to nuclear deterrence and superpower nuclear interaction, but have not viewed the motivations for pursuing or renouncing nuclear weapons as a topic that can aid in theorizing. Solingen's book is conceived of as an effort to bridge that gap (p. ix).

The book also develops the most undertheorized aspect in explaining nuclear choice: the role of domestic politics, particularly the logic of the political survival of leaders and regimes. Much of the existing literature in international relations, in Solingen's view, has fallen victim to what Henry Brady and David Collier (2004) refer to as an 'omitted variable' problem: by neglecting domestic politics, it has misjudged the relative explanatory power of existing theories and overestimated the causal significance of certain logics, particularly the balance of power logic stressed in realist accounts. Without an approach that considers domestic politics carefully, it is difficult to understand why different leaders in the same state may adopt different nuclear preferences, or why the same state's preferences may vary over time as domestic political contexts change (p. x). At the same time, attention to domestic politics does not lead to the exclusion of causal factors stressed in other analytic perspectives. Solingen articulates these with care, submits them to careful scrutiny, and uses them, where necessary, to arrive at a satisfactory answer to her question. Solingen is eager to give her favored perspective more of a hearing than it has received to date, but she does not insist that it can or should displace all others. In fact, Solingen is explicit that the explanation and comparison of states' nuclear preferences requires incorporating multiple logics drawn not only from different brands of international relations theories – specifically neorealism, neoliberalism, and constructivism – but also from various models of domestic politics. In brief, for Solingen, a better understanding of contrasting nuclear preferences 'requires theoretical recalibration and a closer examination of competing and complementary perspectives to avoid overestimation of some theories and underestimation of others' (p. 6).

Solingen's core empirical puzzle focuses on nine countries that collectively capture two distinct regional patterns. Since the 1970s, the Middle East has largely moved toward nuclearization, while East Asia has moved in the opposite direction. In the years since China built a bomb in 1964, only North Korea has crossed the nuclear threshold (in 2006). In the Middle East, Israel had acquired a nuclear capability by the late 1960s. Iraq, Libya (until 2004), Egypt (before 1971), and possibly Iran and Syria in recent years have tried to do the same, with Saudi Arabia and Algeria as putative long-term aspirants. How are we to understand these different trajectories in the Middle East and East Asia? Are they likely to continue into the future? To what extent do various factors – ranging from globalization and the international distribution of power to the role of international institutions and the establishment of democracy – affect nuclear choices in these two regions? These questions have immediate policy relevance, and they offer an interesting puzzle that speaks to wider theoretical debates over international security. Solingen's formulation of the questions does not prematurely close off doors to particular mechanisms or levels of analysis. In fact, it invites a careful consideration of different logics and mechanisms drawn from different analytic perspectives. Moreover, by employing a focused, controlled comparison of nine cases from two different regions, Solingen avoids exceptionalist arguments shaped by a focus on a single country or area of the world. The two regions are comparable in their initial background conditions and their concentration of nuclear aspirants. At the same time, contextualized comparisons within regions provide a basis for evaluating the strength of regional properties in accounting for distinct regional pathways (pp. 8–10).

For Solingen, each of the major theoretical paradigms in international relations points to important logics that work well in explaining aspects of some important cases. Yet, none adequately explains decisions to pursue or forgo nuclear weapons (p. 11). Neorealism enjoys a particularly important place in studies of nuclear decisions and outcomes, focusing on state security as shaped by the balance of power and the logic of the security dilemma. In an anarchic world, states can rely only on self-help, and their acquisition of nuclear weapons will induce other states to do the same. Exploiting the vulnerabilities of rival states, deploying threats to maximum effect, and avoiding unnecessary concessions are behaviors that are induced by the structure of the international system. As the ultimate weapon, nuclear bombs are imputed by self-help perspectives to be guarantors of state survival. Among the early nuclear weapon states, this logic probably worked in some cases but competed with other considerations such as prestige.

Solingen's focus, however, is on cases unfolding after the inception of the Non-Proliferation Treaty (NPT). Here, Solingen argues, the structural logic is even less compelling, suffering from acute underdetermination and unfalsifiability at worst, and conceptual contradictions at best. While some states facing existential vulnerabilities, such as Israel and Pakistan, have nuclearized, others with similar vulnerabilities have not, including Taiwan, Egypt, Vietnam, Singapore, South Korea, and Japan. Neither hegemonic protection nor coercion, Solingen argues, can account for so many anomalies. At bottom, the principle of self-help points to wide-ranging options from acquisition to renunciation of nuclear weapons, raising the problem of underdetermination. Furthermore, while the Middle East and East Asia shared a multipolar and hierarchical structure that should have generated a similar outcome in both cases, during the last 30 years the two regions evolved very differently, toward and away from nuclearization. Multipolarity should have led to nuclearization in both cases, but did so only in the Middle East. Moreover, states with lower levels of external threat chose to pursue nuclear weapons, while others with more intense security dilemmas abstained. Thus, following Betts (2000), Solingen argues that a neorealist explanation focusing on structural insecurity can offer valuable insights into nuclear decision making in some cases, but is insufficient for explaining the full range of empirically observed outcomes (pp. 12–13).

Neoliberal institutionalism focuses on how international institutions advance states' rational interests by supplying information about others' capabilities and intentions, and by monitoring and enforcing compliance with agreements. The Non-Proliferation Regime (NPR), with the NPT at its heart, created a two-tiered system of five recognized nuclear weapons states and an overwhelming majority of states that have renounced nuclear weapons in exchange for access to civilian nuclear technology. Even some proponents of the NPR concede that we do not yet have systematic empirical confirmation that most states relinquished the nuclear option because of the information and monitoring built into the NPR. Furthermore, counterfactual reasoning gives little credence to the idea that absent the NPT, Japan or South Korea, for example, would have pursued nuclear weapons, or that these countries desisted from nuclearization primarily because of the existence of the treaty (p. 14). In addition, the NPT was ineffective in stopping Middle Eastern countries from moving toward nuclearization.

Solingen discusses a range of conceptual, methodological, and empirical difficulties of rationalist institutional perspectives that place them at a disadvantage in the domain of national security (p. 15). Yet she credits the NPR with, among other things, raising the political costs for acquiring sensitive nuclear technologies and equipment and changing the context within which states formulated decisions regarding nuclear weapons. Neoliberal institutionalism is thus an undeniable part of a more complex understanding of the different nuclear logics in the Middle East and in East Asia.

A constructivist approach highlights the evolution of anti-nuclear norms since the bombing of Hiroshima and Nagasaki. The NPR, it could be argued, acted as an agent of socialization that spread the regulatory and constitutive non-nuclear norms (meanings, shared beliefs, common purpose, learning, and knowledge about history) that are embedded in the NPT. Nuclear weapons are perceived to be unique in terms of their capacity for inflicting massive casualties on a horrendous scale. But while this fact may account for the emergence of non-use norms, it is far from clear that a similarly strong non-acquisition norm exists. Moreover, the logic of deterrence suggests that acquisition de facto circumvents use. Even in East Asia, where most states have not pursued nuclear weapons, there is less than compelling evidence for the role of anti-acquisition norms when considered alongside other factors including external coercion, alliances, or domestic politics. This is true even in the case of Japan, which is a most likely candidate for the normative explanation. Furthermore, competing norms are at play, as acquisition of nuclear weapons is sometimes imbued with the prestige associated with joining the ranks of major powers. Finally, as is true of neorealism, the normative argument makes a general claim that simply cannot be reconciled with the empirical record and the varying nuclear logics that have governed the Middle East and East Asia. At the same time, although the non-acquisition norm seems neither universally strong nor a necessary or sufficient condition for explaining differences in nuclear policy in these cases, norms-based approaches can be valuable when complemented with appropriate theories of domestic politics (p. 16).

The distinctiveness of Solingen's analysis lies in her suggestion that movement toward or away from nuclearization is driven, to a greater extent than is normally recognized, by different approaches to 'domestic political survival' (pp. 17–20). External changes undermining or reinforcing the security of the state are much less important than internal changes in the political coalition supporting or undermining the regime and its general approach to political and economic objectives. This explanation is underdeveloped in the literature on nuclear policy because leaders avoid publicly admitting narrow self-serving considerations of survival for themselves, their parties, or their regimes in making nuclear decisions. If we look beyond leaders' public statements, however, there is considerable evidence that domestic political considerations played a key role in guiding decisions to acquire or forgo nuclear weapons.

As developed and argued in a previous book (Solingen 1998), regimes are ruled by either outward- or inward-looking coalitions, two ideal-types that Solingen deploys for heuristic purposes. Outward-looking regimes rest their legitimacy on securing economic prosperity through export-led growth, a strategy of global integration, and an emphasis on the benefits of internationalization. Inward-looking coalitions rely on import-substitution models for economic growth, relative autarky, and extreme nationalism. These different grand strategies point to distinct incentives for regimes with regard to nuclear decisions. Typically, staunch opponents of internationalization are more prone to emphasize national self-reliance and thus to support acquisition of nuclear weapons than are their more outward-looking counterparts, who tend to seek out multilateral solutions to their security problems.

Significantly, introducing domestic political survival as a variable 'does not imply that other variables are rendered irrelevant, but rather that we are better able to understand their relative impact on nuclear choices' (p. 18). Domestic models, in other words, improve our understanding of the actual effects of structural security dilemmas, norms, and institutions on the choice to pursue or eschew nuclear weapons in particular countries. The relative causal weight of these other variables in explaining specific choices will depend very substantially on domestic political calculations. This implies that normally domestic orientations neither determine nor provide sufficient conditions for the observable outcomes. The causal effect of domestic models is influenced by the relative incidence of compatible models in the region and by temporal sequences in the acquisition of nuclear weapons (that is, precursor nuclear weapons programs may be politically easier to abandon than actual weapons, as prospect theory might suggest) (p. 286). Thus, domestic politics models serve as 'filters' (pp. 53, 285) through which regimes define and pursue security.

Japan is, in some ways, the poster child and exhibit number one for the book's central claim (pp. 57–81). Consistent with Solingen's central argument, denuclearization was part of the 'Yoshida line,' Japan's grand strategy of the last half-century which prioritized economic development in a liberalizing global economy over all other objectives. The US nuclear guarantee, Japan's Peace Constitution, and the nuclear allergy of the Japanese all reinforced the pragmatism and economic orientation of the Yoshida line. The NPT certainly generated intense political debates in Japan. But since the general policy was in place prior to the signing of the NPT, it too was of minor importance. The operative model of political survival in postwar Japan favored the pursuit of domestic legitimacy and electoral support through export-led economic growth, and a total rejection of Japan's autarkic and militarized policy of the 1930s. The resulting calculus, reiterated by successive generations of political leaders, emphasized the benefits of civilian nuclear technologies for economic growth, and remained aware of the costs of pursuing nuclear weapons for advancing regional or international objectives. The Yoshida line provided the underlying necessary condition for Japan's non-nuclear status, 'the glue that kept the anti-nuclear package together' (p. 80). The US–Japan security arrangement certainly made it easier to uphold that status. It provided the political basis for Japan's outward-looking approach, and outweighed discrete calculations based on the logic of Japan's security dilemma, the constraints imposed by international institutions, or anti-nuclear norms.

Solingen's book is self-conscious in seeking to avoid the trap of becoming so deeply embedded in any one paradigm that it is impossible to look at the world and its problems with fresh eyes. Her eclectic stance prefers instead to 'look at the problem kaleidoscopically ... from various angles, hoping to generate new insights' (p. 249). Her cross-regional comparison sketches different conceptual paths to explain movement toward or away from nuclearization; sidesteps the disadvantages of monocausal explanations; and points to the utility of integrating the insights of international relations and comparative politics in the analysis of nuclear proliferation. In some cases, to be sure, Solingen finds alternative causal pathways leading to similar predictions and outcomes, which can make it difficult to come to a definitive assessment of the weight of specific factors. But in many cases she is able to establish compellingly that particular causal factors highlighted by neorealist analysis have been overvalued, and others dealing with domestic politics have been neglected unduly. In all of the cases she examines, Solingen manages to make a compelling case that the effects of mechanisms posited by a given international relations paradigm are characterized more accurately if filtered by an analysis of the domestic political contexts. Her conclusions are thus highly germane to current scholarship on nuclear policies (Potter and Mukhatzhanova 2008).

As with many of the other studies we code as analytically eclectic, Solingen's book is pragmatic in its orientation. Her concluding chapter relates her findings to future scenarios and draws out some policy implications. She makes good use of an aspect of the study that in the world of punditry is often held against careful scholarship. Rather than regarding what she calls the 'runaway nature of events' (p. x) as a liability that will date her book before it is published, Solingen regards it as facilitating a useful natural experiment to assess the explanatory power of various theories. Her domestic political survival approach allows us to anticipate future denuclearization choices of internationalizing coalitions, and nuclear choices of inward-looking coalitions. Solingen also sketches out four scenarios, two of which support her argument and two of which would be incompatible with it. Where internationalizing coalitions pursue denuclearization or inward-looking coalitions pursue nuclearization, the argument is rendered more convincing; where internationalizing coalitions pursue nuclearization or inward-looking regimes promote denuclearization, her argument would be disconfirmed, or at least undermined (p. 287).

Although it is not possible to translate her conclusions into a set of precise recommendations, there are some clear policy implications that follow from Solingen's analysis. Because they are so well known and, as her study demonstrates, quite deficient, she makes relatively short shrift of the paradigms – structural realism, neoliberal institutionalism, and constructivist emphasis on anti-nuclear norms – that have dominated policy discourse to date. No single approach, she argues, 'opens the gate to the holy grail of denuclearization' (p. 289). Each approach confronts the conundrum that causally important variables are not always the ones that policymakers can influence in the short term. Thus, Solingen develops four broadly gauged policy prescriptions aimed at promoting denuclearization, which require

Box 3.3
Etel Solingen – Logics in the plural

I set out to examine the demand-side for nuclear weapons fully anticipating that different theories would shed light on different angles of the problem. Indeed, some colleagues suggested the title *Nuclear Logic* – in the singular – as a sharper (and more marketable) alternative. It would have highlighted the indisputable centrality of a single logic – presumably my own. Yet, since I know of virtually no arena in the social world ruled by an uncontested single logic, the plural *Nuclear Logics* (Solingen 2007) promised more truth in advertisement. I also anticipated that the omitted variable the book introduces – the distinctive 'models of political survival' leaders adopt – would, without great difficulty, accommodate, condition, or subsume accounts based solely on relative power, norms, and institutional incentives. I deployed these models – ideal-typical constructs – as filters that condition and modify the values and relative weight of other variables.

Subfields in the discipline are often under the grip of a single dominant but often limiting conceptual approach. *Nuclear Logics*' main puzzle could easily have been forced into such a straitjacket. Instead I chose to capture a more complex political reality by providing (1) a more realistic answer to the demand for nuclear weapons than structural realism can provide even in its home court – high security; (2) a core argument about different models of political survival that enable the analyst to weave together diverse strands drawn from a variety of theoretical principles; (3) a clear focus on the (primarily) political-economy preferences of domestic coalitions as agents, without neglecting the international 'world-time' context in which these preferences are formed; (4) a reconstruction of processes and mechanisms that is transferable across widely different cases and regions; (5) an analysis that highlights the real-world consequences of competing truth claims, and invites dialogue across paradigms to facilitate consensual knowledge; and, finally, (6) engagement with a practical dilemma in real-world politics.

What did I learn from the reaction of other scholars to my book? Based on wide-ranging rejoinders – both critical and supportive – to *Nuclear Logics*, it appears that the discipline has become more receptive to questions about and alternatives to paradigmatic conventions. Indeed, the tide appears to have turned decisively on the particular issue at hand. A promising research agenda attentive to complex systemic effects, reputation, domestic veto-points, dynamics of global economy, and regime survival is replacing analytically impoverished, policy-deficient, and grossly inaccurate forecasts by stale 'normal science' about why states seek to acquire nuclear weapons.

disaggregating the domestic context of the policy choices of states with nuclear aspirations: (a) reward and strengthen supporters of internationalizing models of development; (b) strip autarkic or inward-looking regimes of the means to concentrate power; (c) craft packages of sanctions and inducements that are sensitive to differences between energy-rich and energy-poor targets; and (d) where available, use democracy as an ally for denuclearization. Solingen also points to Libya's experience, as well as to the intensification of debates over Iran's nuclear policies, to emphasize the role that coordinated multilateral pressure can play in altering the odds of political survival of various domestic political actors in inward-looking regimes (pp. 293–9). Thus, in addition to providing a clear framework for tracking future scenarios across regimes and regions, Solingen's analysis aims to explicitly engage policy debates surrounding nuclear proliferation.

T.V. Paul, *The Tradition of Non-Use of Nuclear Weapons* (2009)

Paul focuses not on the choice to pursue or eschew nuclear weapons, but on an emergent tradition of non-use of nuclear weapons following the dropping of atomic bombs over Hiroshima and Nagasaki in August 1945. A tradition is a time-honored practice that has become an 'accustomed obligation' (p. 1). During the Cold War, the informal norm of non-use along with mutual deterrence preserved the peace among the superpowers and prevented the spread of nuclear weapons. Because non-use served the strategic interests of the United States and the Soviet Union, the two superpowers helped to invent a tradition of non-use to legitimize their monopoly over these weapons. So strong is this tradition that nuclear states have on occasion fought and lost wars against non-nuclear-weapon states. The general puzzle that motivates Paul is the question of why the tradition of non-use arose and why it persists. Related to this are several interrelated specific questions that probe the reasons of nuclear states, both old and new, to eschew use: the calculations of non-nuclear states that fight wars against nuclear states; the relevance of reputational concerns for theories of deterrence and compellence; the effect of non-use on the non-proliferation regime and specifically the NPT; the fragility and resilience of the norm; and the global interests, if any, that the tradition of non-use serves.

The eclectic spirit of Paul's approach is evident in his explicit aims. While he recognizes the coherence that paradigms can provide within a discipline, Paul fears that they 'limit the prospects for answering pressing policy issues or intellectual puzzles that do not have black-or-white answers' (p. 3). Moreover, efforts to make causal analysis fit under the rubric of a given paradigm result in the omission of important nuances that ought to be a part of a useful explanation of the phenomenon under study. Thus, Paul is self-conscious in adopting a puzzle-driven approach and in seeking to advance an 'intermediate' – what we call 'middle range' – rather than a 'grand' theory.

The argument Paul offers is also self-consciously eclectic, challenging the rationalist accounts of realists as well as the ideational accounts of constructivists. Most realists have not paid much attention to the issue of nuclear non-use. To the extent that they have, they are skeptical that such a tradition actually exists (for example, Gray 2000). Instead, realists explain the actual non-use of nuclear weapons based on three factors: mutual or extended deterrence, tactical or strategic unsuitability, and power politics considerations such as the fear of uncontrollable escalation dynamics in a given theater of confrontation. Nuclear weapons have not been used against non-nuclear states for narrow instrumental reasons rather than because they were stigmatized or came with reputational costs. Such reasons include, among others, fear of retaliation, lack of military utility, dearth of good targets, the ready availability of conventional weapons to destroy targets, and the complications that attend the contamination of the battlefield by nuclear weapons. More nuanced realist treatments (Sagan 2004; Martin 2004) add political considerations such as anxieties over negative consequences for other national goals, for the viability of long-term great power relationships, and for the robustness of the deterrent value of nuclear weapons. But even in these more nuanced views, there is no consideration of how morality, ethics, law, or culture might influence calculations of nuclear non-use. The latter are part of power considerations and relationships, and operate under a broad realist logic (p. 16).

This line of reasoning, Paul argues, is flawed, and for the obvious reason that the tradition of non-use undeniably exists despite the fact that *Realpolitik*-oriented leaders such as Eisenhower, Dulles, Nixon, and Kissinger ultimately chose not to use nuclear weapons after actively considering them. The historical record shows that their calculus of decision was influenced by more than the weapons' possible tactical or strategic unsuitability. Furthermore, a realist argument has difficulty answering a series of crucial questions that it ought to be able to explain. Why, for example, would states invest heavily in the expansion and modernization of their nuclear arsenal while at the same time choosing not to use it after the two initial explosions? Why did nuclear powers suffer humiliating and costly defeats – the United States in Vietnam, the Soviet Union in Afghanistan – at the hands of non-nuclear powers without resorting to the ultimate weapon to escape defeat? In both wars, tactical nuclear weapons were considered usable and could probably have decapitated the guerilla movements the two superpowers were confronting. Finally, the historical record indicates that political leaders were motivated by more than crude *Realpolitik* calculations. For them, nuclear weapons were not simply another kind of weapon. These weapons were perceived as having uniquely destructive features that placed them beyond the normal calculus of how to win a war. The *Realpolitik* argument simply denies by fiat the possibility that policymakers in fact shared such perceptions (p. 18).

Constructivist treatments of nuclear non-use highlight ideational and cultural factors, viewing the tradition of non-use as a taboo on the use of nuclear weapons because actors themselves refer to it as such. Nina Tannenwald (2007; see also Price and Tannenwald 1996) emphasizes that this taboo cannot be adequately explained through an analysis of materialist and rationalist factors. Instead, it is the result of two processes. One features regime characteristics – such as the political constraints associated with democracies or with national interest and identity – that give rise to prohibitionary norms with regard to nuclear use. In addition, non-linear evolutionary processes strengthen the norm and create a taboo because of the iterative behavior of nuclear states, the efforts of social groups and international organizations to stigmatize nuclear weapons, the moral concerns of individual political leaders, and the acceptance of the taboo by their successors. Constructivists argue that these processes have the effect of embedding deterrence doctrine and practice in a broader normative framework that includes both regulative and constitutive norms that have stabilized the practice of non-use and imposed restraints on the self-help behavior of states (p. 17).

Paul argues that constructivists undervalue material factors, such as the sheer destructive power of nuclear weapons and the self-interest of states, while overstating the significance of ideas or national culture. Even when they gesture towards the importance of combining material and non-material factors, constructivists ultimately place more causal weight on the latter and fail to see how the two sets of factors are interrelated. Furthermore, for Paul the causal weight of constitutive norms is small. In the concept of self-interest, he argues that the 'self' is much less important than the 'interest.' In addition, because previous constructivist work has focused mainly on the United States, the role of other states in the creation of the initial tradition of non-use or weak taboo has not been fully explored. During the Cold War, US and Soviet interests were well served by non-use practice, as both were bidding for support from Third World countries and had a joint interest in maintaining a firm grip on the possible proliferation of nuclear weapons beyond the club of existing nuclear weapon states. Furthermore, by declaring their no-first-use policies, both the Soviet Union and China contributed greatly to the invigoration of the tradition of non-use. That tradition also owes a lot to the United States' European allies, which steadfastly opposed the United States when it was actively contemplating the use of nuclear weapons in Korea. Domestic structures and national political culture, while important, are causally not as significant as constructivists claim. Finally, for Paul, the use of the term 'taboo' implies a norm that is more robust and unchanging than is actually the case. Instead, Paul sees non-use as an evolving tradition, the strength of which at any given time depends on shifting material factors such as changing technologies and political constraints.

Paul's alternative approach depends on distinguishing an evolving 'tradition' from a full-blown, robust 'taboo,' something that, needless to say, has not existed in the case of nuclear weapons.[3] States have doctrines, strategies, targeting plans, and launch-on-warning protocols that suggest a high level of readiness, at least for deterrence purposes. A robust taboo poses an absolute constraint that determines actors' choices in all contexts. In contrast, a tradition or a weak taboo must continually be maintained, and its impact needs to be established in a given setting. At the same time, a tradition does emerge as the result of a long-term process, and it can be strengthened over time (pp. 5–7). Paul's eclectic explanation for the emergence of a tradition of nuclear non-use self-consciously draws together rationalist/materialist and normative/ideational mechanisms. The former are manifested in what March and Olsen (1998) call the logic of consequences, while the latter are reflected in what they characterize as the logic of appropriateness. The two logics play different roles at different points in the complex causal sequence that Paul lays out in showing how recognition of the uniquely destructive power of nuclear weapons eventually leads to the crystallization of a widely held normative prohibition, which has become progressively more robust over time.

The emergence of the tradition of non-use has its roots in the widespread realization that nuclear weapons are fundamentally different from conventional weapons. Quite early on, it was recognized that the 'destabilizing and absolute character of nuclear weapons has limited their strategic utility' (p. 37). However, there is also the recognition by nuclear states of the positive strategic value of non-use of nuclear weapons. Not only did non-use reinforce the logic of peace through mutual deterrence, it also had the effect of enhancing security by supporting non-proliferation efforts (which would be undermined if nuclear weapons states ever used their nuclear weapons against non-nuclear states). The logic of consequences is invoked here to track the practical-military implications of nuclear weapons use and non-use.

The significance of the logic of consequences is not limited to the material sphere. It is also evident in the attention paid by nuclear states and their leaders to the reputational costs of nuclear use. These costs are incurred at multiple levels. They result in the loss of political control and influence, both for individual leaders of nuclear states and for states in relation to the international system writ large. The images of leaders and states that actually used nuclear weapons in a conflict with non-nuclear states would be severely compromised. Paul also distinguishes between 'deterrence reputation' and 'non-use reputation' (pp. 30–1). The former, influenced more by realism, has to do with the credibility of retaliatory threats as well as the communication of these threats and the capability to carry them out. While it is easy for a nuclear state to communicate resolve to another nuclear state, it is very difficult to do so to a non-nuclear state, especially if the stakes do not involve the survival of the nuclear state. Moreover, explicit threats involving nuclear weapons in a crisis are difficult to leverage, since there are costs to the actor's reputation and credibility if the threats are not actually carried out. Non-use reputation, viewed through the lens of neoliberal institutionalism, is driven by a concern over the future behavior of other potential nuclear states. When concerns over strategic interactions are extended over time, the shadow of the future encourages reciprocity in non-use. As a result, nuclear states are effectively self-deterred (p. 31).

Up to this point, Paul's explanation emphasizes how the logic of consequences shapes calculations in crises and thus helps bring about the tradition of non-use. But unless one pays attention to how actors reinvent and modify the tradition, this explanation does not help much to make sense of the uninterrupted strengthening of the tradition over time in an era of technological change. Changes in technology that increased the destructive potential of nuclear weapons, as in the transition from the atomic to the hydrogen bomb, probably strengthened the tradition of non-use early on. In subsequent decades, lowering the destructive potential through the deployment of 'usable' mini-nuclear weapons probably weakened it. The long-term resilience of the tradition of non-use represents the most puzzling aspect of the question Paul seeks to answer. Here, Paul's argument adds another layer of complexity. The costs of using nuclear weapons (which follow the logic of consequences) interact with the development of ideas about responsible state behavior (which follow the logic of appropriateness).

Of particular significance is the role of various 'norm intermediaries' such as the Federation of Atomic Scientists, peace movements, military strategists, and leaders of developing countries. They invoke the logic of appropriateness in different ways to magnify the reputational costs associated with the actual use of nuclear weapons and thus help generate a more robust prohibitionary norm (pp. 32–5). Although this norm is informal – as contrasted with formal legal restrictions against the use of chemical or biological weapons – it has served the purpose of reinforcing the practice of non-use. But since some nuclear weapon states, such as the United States, have retained the option of nuclear first use against non-nuclear states, the norm is not a full-blown taboo. Paul concludes that 'there is an informal normative prohibition against nuclear use and that different nuclear actors have behaved as if they have a responsibility not to use nuclear weapons vis-à-vis nonnuclear states' (p. 36).

Paul's argument is eclectic in its complex articulation of the logics of consequences and appropriateness in different decisional and temporal contexts. The former reflects rationalist arguments offered by realist scholars (concerning the strategic limitations of nuclear weapons and the character of deterrence reputation) as well as by neoliberal institutionalists (concerning how the shadow of the future strengthens the value of non-use). The latter incorporates theoretical

Box 3.4
T.V. Paul – Puzzles and eclecticism or foils and pigeonholing?

The key reason I adopted an eclectic approach in *The Tradition of Non-Use of Nuclear Weapons* (Paul 2009) is the puzzle- rather than paradigm-driven research agenda that I have adopted since I started my scholarly career. Many puzzles in international relations simply cannot be explained using a single paradigm. I favor instead analytical richness. International phenomena are much more complex than we understand, and often the historical contexts and specific situations in which states find themselves need to be explored to obtain a compelling explanation. While I see some value in paradigms, often they instill a dogmatic allegiance – and sometimes an ideological preference – that can affect social scientific investigations. By being intellectually open when conducting empirical research, one can develop original theories, whether or not these are grounded in any one paradigm.

To date, my book has received mostly positive reviews. But reviewers diverge in their readings. Some write that my book is normative, others that it is rationalist. Surprisingly, one even called it realist. In general, rarely have I seen a trenchant criticism of my work based on my preference for eclecticism. What is most noticeable is the tendency of scholars to place me in a paradigm category even when I clearly state that I am avoiding a single-paradigm approach. For instance, many of the citations of my *Power versus Prudence* (Paul 2007) treat it as a pure realist perspective even though I have provided a much more eclectic and situational analysis. This is so because many scholars, especially younger ones, often are looking for foils and pigeonholing authors to more easily prove their points of view. Sometimes I try to correct this misapprehension anonymously when reviewing book and article manuscripts on nuclear proliferation, often without much success. Open-mindedness and a willingness to work through the causal mechanisms and pathways rather than simply 'narrating variables' are essential to pursuing eclectic research fruitfully. We need to know how these different variables (often drawn from different paradigms) are connected, and how they affect or cause the outcome – alone or in conjunction with others – that we are trying to explain. Explanation, not description, should be the most important objective of social scientific theories. Eclectic approaches, if not carefully carried out, can end up in thick descriptions of a mish-mash variety, a danger that scholars should avoid. And sometimes a single paradigm can explain a phenomenon better than an eclectic approach can. In that case, scholars should opt for a paradigmatic explanation.

moves more typical of constructivists, emphasizing the role of iterated practice in turning individual calculations about non-use into an emergent tradition, strengthened by the actions of norm intermediaries who employ the logic of appropriateness to raise the reputational costs of nuclear weapons use. Finally, it is worth noting that Paul concludes his book by examining the implications of his argument for policy. The idea of self-deterrence, in particular, is a useful concept for capturing the practical and moral calculations that govern the choices of leaders in particular contexts when there are no mechanisms for punishment other than reputation costs (p. 203). Paul is wary that 'exaggerated notions about the restraining power of the tradition of non-use could result in military catastrophes' (p. 205). Nevertheless, from the perspective of the most powerful nuclear state in the international arena, Paul concludes that 'the tradition of non-use is one norm that Washington would be well advised to preserve, for once it is broken, it may not be easy to resurrect it even if future leaders wished to do so' (p. 212).

David Kang, *China Rising* (2007)

Kang's (2007) analysis of East Asian responses to China's rise begins with two surprising observations that contravene the expectations of established theories of international relations. First, China's rapid rise as an economic and military power has been accompanied by an unprecedented period of peace and stability in the region rather than intensified tensions or conflicts. And with the exception of Japan, most countries in the region see more advantages than disadvantages in China's rise, and thus seek to accommodate rather than balance against China's growing power. South Koreans, for example, are far from eager to be subservient to China. But they have responded to its rise by expanding and deepening cultural, economic, and diplomatic ties with China. And rather than pressing their claims to the disputed Spratly islands, Vietnam and the Philippines have joined China in pursuing joint exploration of oil reserves on the islands. Thus, most of the East Asian region appears to have accepted China's own pragmatic characterization of its 'peaceful rise.' They view China as 'more benign than conventional international relations theories might predict' (Kang 2007, pp. 5–6).

Realism offers the clearest theoretical foil for Kang because it has had the most consistently pessimistic view of China's economic rise.

A China that is growing rich will upset the balance of power in Asia and thus create a counter-coalition of Asian countries to oppose the United States in Asia. Power transition theories insist, similarly, that periods of rapid shifts are prone to produce deep conflicts, even wars. If balancing behavior cannot be observed, this must be due to the small size of East Asian states compared with China. Alternatively, the lack of balancing is due to the fact that 30 years is simply not enough time for such behavior to occur. Both arguments assume that fear of China is widespread, an assumption lacking much empirical support. The historical record suggests instead that among the world's main regions during the last 150 years, the balancing proposition holds only for Europe (Bennett and Stam, 2003, pp. 191–5). Equally problematic is the argument that 30 years is too short a time for balancing behavior to assert itself. Realist arguments are generally based on the assumption of widespread fear, and it is not plausible to assume that it would take fearful states many decades to develop balancing strategies. Contra realism, Kang argues that Asian governments and mass publics do not fear a strong China as much as the opposite. A weak China invites destabilizing regional rivalries. If its domestic difficulties or crises spill across national boundaries, this might be the source of dire political problems for many of China's neighbors.

Rejecting a framing of his question in the terms of realist theory, Kang challenges the simplifications accompanying the application of traditional realist concepts for dealing with external threats. Specifically, the conceptual distinction between balancing and bandwagoning strategies does not help to make sense of the relations among East Asian countries, past or present. Traditionally, external balancing has referred to the strategy of seeking allies to contain a threatening state. Bandwagoning has described a state's decision to align itself with the threatening power in order to minimize the threat and even benefit from the spoils of victory. Neither concept works well to capture the decision making of East Asian states. Defying realist expectation, no such military balancing has occurred since the end of the Cold War, even though China was the fastest rising power in East Asia. China's neighbors are not balancing against, bandwagoning with, or simply kowtowing to China. Conceptual innovations by balancing theorists, such as 'soft balancing' or 'under-balancing,' represent ingenious moves to reinterpret non-military tools and tactics through the lens of *Realpolitik*. But these moves have made balancing theory virtually unfalsifiable and have created problems of measurement. What is clear is that in the case of China and its neighbors, balancing of the traditional kind – that is, 'hard balancing' through military buildups and countervailing military alliances – is not occurring. Nor does bandwagoning – currying favor with a more powerful country through military alliances or various forms of cooperation – capture or subsume in a clear-cut way the range of strategies that is evident in East Asia (p. 52).

Kang argues that this conceptual dichotomy captures only two strategies at opposite ends of a much broader spectrum. In East Asia, the two terms accurately describe the behavior of only two states. North Korea is following a bandwagoning strategy, Taiwan a balancing one. In between, one finds a number of other strategies that do not reflect explicit strategic choices by actors responding to a potential external threat. Two in particular stand out: hedging and accommodation. The distinction is related to the fear instilled by a potential adversary. Hedging strategies are based on greater skepticism and anxiety about the adversary. In the absence of fear, it is possible to search for cooperation and the crafting of stable relations that fall short of slavish bandwagoning (p. 53). Not counting Taiwan, Japan is most skeptical of China's intentions; yet it chooses to hedge rather than to balance against China. Vietnam and Malaysia are least fearful of China and thus opt to accommodate China's rise, with Vietnam's engagement extending to military cooperation. Despite their strong ties to the United States, South Korea and the Philippines occupy an intermediary position between hedging and accommodation, as they pursue various forms of engagement on economic and security issues. In fact, most Southeast Asian states are neither opposing China's rise, nor abandoning their ties to the United States and other states (pp. 55–66).

Kang seeks to explain why these different strategies have emerged. Observable variations, Kang argues, are due to a mixture of causal factors: identities, interests, and relative capabilities. East Asia's response to China's rise constitutes an anomaly for how realist theory makes us think about a rapidly shifting distribution of power. Furthermore, Kang observes that while neoliberal theorists can point to growing economic interdependence as a basis for why China seeks peace, they admit to skepticism that interdependence alone could fully reassure China's neighbors or explain their reactions. Constructivists pay close attention to the effects of norms and identities on the foreign policies of East Asian countries, but they provide no explanation for which specific norms and identities matter most in explaining the region's surprisingly accommodating response to China's rise.

Since each of the conventional explanations has obvious weaknesses, Kang develops his own eclectic one for understanding how power, interests, and identities interact. In doing so, he gives primary emphasis to ideas; but he defines 'idea' in broad enough terms to incorporate strands of realist, neoliberal, and constructivist theorizing. Ideas are not treated solely through the lens of constructivism as a concomitant of identity, but are seen as the basis for building analytical bridges between different theoretical traditions, ranging from formal modeling to constructivist interpretations. Ideational explanations, for example, can coexist with the distinction that realists draw between status quo and revisionist powers. They accommodate the possibility that rising powers such as China can be socialized into supporting the existing international order rather than challenging or subverting it. Similarly, ideational arguments are not merely derivative of static understandings of national identity. China's nationalism is more variegated in its political and policy effects than is suggested by the narrative of its century of national humiliation. China's conceptions of sovereignty have changed in significant ways since the late 1970s, partly because Southeast Asia's regional identity has provided an opening toward lasting cooperation with China, and East Asia's emerging regional order has been adaptable enough to accommodate China.

For Kang, identity is more than the sum total of domestic politics: it is a set of unifying ideas that articulate how a nation perceives the world and its place in that world. These ideas result from two intertwined processes: interactions with other countries, and narratives about the past (p. 21). Recognizing these processes in no way relieves the analyst from contending with the formation of interests and the reality of power relations. As Kang puts this: 'To emphasize the importance of identities is only to recognize that interests and beliefs can vary widely. It does not preclude pragmatic interest-based foreign policy, but rather focuses research on determining which interests states judge as most important, and why' (p. 19).

While Kang includes interests in his analysis, he insists that they cannot be taken for granted. Rather, the crux of the matter is which interests states deem to be most important, and why. Understanding this requires attention to 'perceptions, beliefs, and intentions in the determination of threats' (p. 19). Moreover, a state's overall grand strategy is not likely to be affected merely by a myopic single-shot analysis of other actors' interests on specific issues. It requires a long period of interactions and relations among states that can give rise to deeper beliefs about other states' identities and beliefs. Power, too, shapes the way in which interests are defined and intentions are specified. Large, powerful, economically growing, status quo powers define their interests differently than do dynamic expansionist or revisionist powers. Calculations of interests are thus powerfully affected by the smaller countries' assessments of a larger country's self-image and its position in the world. The key to the definition of interest lies in the intersection between China's intentions and how these intentions are perceived by other East Asian states within the context of longstanding relationships (pp. 20–1).

In developing his argument, Kang thus acknowledges both interests and capabilities. Military and political capabilities set the constraints under which states operate. As defensive realists note, the constraints posed by nuclear weapons and geography give us grounds for optimistic views about East Asia's future. Furthermore, as Kang argues, pragmatic state interests come into play on a range of specific issues, particularly in the context of the opportunities that China's economic rise offers to its economic partners. In the end, both capabilities and interests have to be seen through the lens of an actor's intentions as perceived by various other actors; these perceptions are, in turn, the result of a geographically specific system that has been evolving for several centuries. That is, Kang's eclectic explanation stresses the interconnections among identity, power, and interest. Even if one is mostly concerned about contemporary developments, tracing these interconnections requires careful attention to history. As Kang puts it: 'History, and the manner in which it is interpreted in the present, are major elements in how states develop beliefs about themselves and the world' (p. 23).

However, there remains the question of whose history we should be taking into account. Most international relations theory has emerged from a Eurocentric tradition. Kang, however, sees no reason why developments in Europe should set the analytical, empirical, or normative baseline by which to judge current developments in East Asia. Over many centuries the Sinocentric system, as Kang argues (pp. 18–49), has been remarkably peaceful and stable. Importantly, this stability has coincided with patterns of relations between the Chinese empire and other East Asian countries that were hierarchical rather than anarchic in character. Also significant is the fact that this hierarchy did not involve much loss of political, economic, or cultural independence (pp. 43–5). Although the history of the East Asian system did not conform to the conventional expectations of realist, liberal, or constructivist theories, elements taken from each of the paradigms can be found in the complex relations that emerged in the region. Realist theories of hegemonic stability are consistent with the fact that China's neighbors accepted the preponderance of Chinese power instead of trying to balance it. The relations between East Asian countries, as liberal theories might suggest, were predicated on substantial trading links among the major states. And, consistent with constructivist theorizing, it is evident that a complex set of norms about appropriate behavior was shared and observed by the main actors in East Asia. Although this regional order eventually broke down, these intertwined processes left in their wake a set of baseline expectations that differed from European expectations concerning the possibility of a relatively peaceful, prosperous international system predicated on the logic of hierarchy (p. 49).

As with other eclectic treatments of security issues, Kang concludes with a clear discussion of the practical implications that follow from his analysis (pp. 197–203). His complex argument cuts across, and partially integrates, insights typically generated by separate theoretical lenses in Western international relations scholarship. While the argument does not lend itself to a general theory of regional power politics, it does give us a plausible and provocative account of why East Asia is not as perturbed by China's growing power as many Western analysts have been. With the possible exception of the very unusual case of Taiwan, no East Asian state is following a balancing strategy.

Informed by abstract balancing theory grounded in European rather than East Asian or world history, the expectation of instability and conflict in response to China's rise appears to be misplaced. The most likely destabilizing factor will not be China or its neighbors but a reorientation of American foreign policy, should American decision makers decide that they cannot tolerate the emergence of a regional power that would dilute US influence in East Asia. This at least is John Mearsheimer's (2001, pp. 375–7, 401–2) view of the most likely, even preordained, outcome should East Asian states fail to balance against an increasingly powerful

Box 3.5
David Kang – Explaining actual East Asian relations, not abstract balance of power

My approach grew out of the question I was trying to answer. Moving between theories and the empirical evidence led me in directions I would not have predicted when I began the research. My research is problem- rather than theory-driven. I wrote *China Rising* (Kang 2007) because of a straightforward observation around the turn of the century: East Asian states were moving closer to, rather than farther away from, China. Balancing behavior predicted by realists at the end of the Cold War was not really occurring. My goal was not to attack realism, but to provide a more accurate description and a more useful explanation of the relations among East Asian states. Realist and liberal variables such as balance of power and economic interdependence, I found, are relatively minor factors in the calculations of states. Regional states and peoples are instead more concerned with what China wants and how China defines itself in the region than they are about any abstract notions of the balance of power. This is true of most of the states in the region that are in the process of negotiating their own national identities. How these states sort out their relative statuses, and how they resolve their beliefs about each other's intentions and identities, are central to current and future regional relations.

The most interesting reaction to my book has focused on the measurement of the book's dependent variable. That is, a common response to my book has been for someone to say, 'Sure, but isn't X an example of balancing against China?' My response is always the same: 'Tell me what non-balancing looks like, and I'll tell you whether or not X is balancing behavior.' Theoretical rigor is important no matter what scholarly approach is used. In this book I thus spent a fair amount of time constructing a falsifiable measure of state behavior and paying close attention to distinguishing balancing from other strategies. 'Balance of power' is a central yet amorphous concept about which there exists little agreement.

I have learned that scholars choose between theory-driven and problem-driven research. And both styles of work have their strengths and weaknesses. Hypothesis testing and model building are important elements of our discipline. Yet scholarship that is theoretically motivated and arises out of real-world questions is just as interesting and important. The academy is large enough to accommodate both types of research.

China. Kang observes that East Asian states are hesitant to choose between stark alternatives; but if a choice is forced upon them by an American shift towards outright balancing against China, they may well choose China. Alternatively, US power may recede significantly in East Asia. In this case, there is no reason to rush to the conclusion that the stability of the region will be undermined by new conflicts and rivalries. In fact, the outcome is likely to be influenced by whether China remains a strong regional power, since historically, it has been Chinese weakness that has been associated with regional instability.

Another scenario is just as plausible: American accommodation, as in Europe, to a form of regional governance that differs from outright Chinese domination in strict power politics terms. Indeed, the extreme reluctance to engage in balancing behavior that Kang's book uncovers provides strong empirical evidence countering abstract arguments that favor a dramatic turn-about in American foreign policy. Whether or not one concurs with Kang's conclusions, his eclectic argument creates challenges for policy positions derived from more simplified models based on contending research traditions. Kang's analysis thus has implications for the United States that policymakers will need to consider seriously when fashioning strategies for coping with China's rise, the responses of its neighbors, and shifts in regional dynamics in East Asia.

Conclusion

Although they have dominated the field of security studies for most of the last century, arguments based solely on the logic of realism do not hold up when exploring questions that are not formulated in strict accordance with the boundary conditions of typical realist theories. For a wide range of important issues related to peace and security, we regularly encounter significant and persistent anomalies that realism cannot explain fully when questions are framed in an open-ended manner. Reformulating these questions within neoliberal and constructivist paradigms enables one to recognize other relevant mechanisms, such as those related to the rational interests of states and domestic actors, or to emergent national identities and international norms. Yet arguments developed within these latter paradigms, too, are often insufficient without taking account of factors normally privileged by realist accounts.

The books discussed in this chapter consciously adopt a more eclectic approach for addressing a variety of issues related to international security in different parts of the world. Jervis is concerned with the implications of an emergent security community of great powers for American foreign policy. Finnemore takes a long-term perspective as she explains global shifts in the ways in which the international community has defined and justified intervention. Solingen and Paul deal with nuclear security but with quite different questions in mind: Solingen is concerned with regional distinctions between states in East Asia and the Middle East as they pursue or eschew nuclear weapons, while Paul focuses on nuclear-weapons states and how their decisions not to employ those weapons have given rise to a de facto tradition of non-use. Finally, Kang addresses the implications of China's rise for other states that are located in, or have a stake in, the East Asian region.

All five books also exhibit the three attributes we employed to operationalize eclecticism at the end of Chapter 1. First, in their problem definition, they resist the temptation to oversimplify the phenomena they explain or to rely excessively on untestable assumptions. The authors focus directly on issues of conflict and security, in one form or another. However, their concern is not with filling gaps in the theoretical literature or with debating the limits of realism, which historically has held sway over security issues. Instead, all five are motivated by the desire to better understand particular real-world phenomena, ranging from emergent security communities and military interventions to nuclear use and proliferation. In each case, outcomes of interest are treated as puzzling phenomena that require a more comprehensive understanding, regardless of how such phenomena might normally be problematized within a given paradigm.

Second, all five books aspire to develop middle-range causal analyses. They resist both the temptation to pursue universal laws of political behavior, and the tendency to offer idiosyncratic narratives that are bound within highly specific contexts. In some instances, the authors find reason to add new historical interpretations, as in the case of Finnemore's survey of the shifting character of intervention over centuries, or in Kang's treatment of Chinese and East Asian history. In other instances, as in the case of Solingen's models of domestic political survival, new causal factors are identified that require us to rebalance particular realist, neoliberal or constructivist logics in a more complex story. But in all cases, the authors aim to generate complex causal stories that are portable to another universe of cases, and that incorporate a multiplicity of processes, neither insisting on any specific level of analysis nor rejecting out of hand either material or ideational mechanisms.

Third, all five books are, more or less directly, interested in engaging issues of political practice and policy. Although the authors are deeply steeped in the theories, concepts, and methods in the field, they offer arguments that are, in principle, of importance to both academics and policymakers. Jervis, for example, offers some clear prescriptions for American foreign policy that take into account the sensibilities and reactions of other members of the security community. Finnemore is less direct in engaging any particular foreign policy establishment, but her analysis has obvious implications for foreign policy debates over intervention as well as for epistemic communities engaged in international law and institutions. Solingen and Paul offer interpretations and arguments that are particularly salient for those in a position to update or refine policies dealing with nuclear policy and proliferation. And Kang's argument is clearly suggestive for contemporary debates in foreign policy establishments about the opportunities and threats presented by China's rise.

Beyond meeting our own three-point criteria for identifying eclectic scholarship, the shared eclectic orientation of the five scholars is also evident in their own assessments of their approaches and experiences (see Boxes 3.1 to 3.5). One recurrent theme that immediately emerges is a common insistence on problem-driven rather than approach-driven work. For Jervis, the general problem of tracking the sources and implications of a novel type of security community emerged out of the process of producing a series of separate articles probing the various implications of 9/11 for American foreign policy and for subsequent regional and international dynamics. For Finnemore, the absence of plausible hypotheses in the existing literature forced her to take more seriously the perspectives and motivations of the actors directly involved in making decisions about intervention. In contrast, there is no dearth of hypotheses in the area of nuclear policy. Yet both Paul and Solingen emphasize that they sought out alternative formulations of their respective problems to avoid what Solingen refers to as the 'straitjacket' of paradigmatic thinking. Paul insists that puzzle-oriented work has defined his scholarship throughout his academic career – even if his work has at times been pigeonholed inaccurately, especially by younger scholars seeking foils to differentiate their work from existing scholarship. Finally, Kang notes that his approach was driven not by either acceptance or rejection of realism, but by his desire to better understand why persistent behaviors and trends did not conform to the expectations of balance-of-power theories.

Another recurrent theme evident in several of the authors' statements relates to the relatively low status accorded to parsimony as a criterion of good scholarship. As Jervis argues, parsimony is of less value than getting the right answer to a given problem. For example, the lead chapter of Jervis's book, which expands on the presidential address to the American Political Science Association in 2001, makes clear that parsimonious arguments relying on paradigmatic 'isms' simply miss large parts of the story. This does not mean ignoring paradigm-bound theories entirely since, as Jervis notes, these can be used to discipline one's thinking, for example by supplying counterfactual arguments and prodding one to consider what evidence existing theories would require. At the same time, a more comprehensive understanding of interesting phenomena requires us to embrace complexity. Thus, Finnemore's desire to pursue a deeper and fuller understanding of intervention led her to consider different historical epochs and to incorporate – rather than bracket out – the complexities, anomalies, and surprises she encountered along the way. Solingen makes essentially the same point when choosing the plural for the title of her book, *Nuclear Logics*. Her multifaceted analysis is set up to accommodate, condition, or subsume the core constructs of the three main paradigms in international relations.

A third theme concerns the authors' conception of eclectic scholarship as analytically rigorous. That is, resisting parsimony and being open to complexity does not necessarily mean resorting to what Paul calls 'thick descriptions of a mish-mash variety.' What makes an eclectic approach rigorous is not the incorporation of each and every imaginable factor, but judicious attention to how a set of clearly defined causal mechanisms normally posited in different paradigms interact with each other and combine to generate interesting outcomes. Paul insists that the goal of good scholarship should be compelling explanations rather than comprehensive narratives, but he emphasizes that when paradigm-bound accounts cannot fully explain phenomena, there is a need to explore a wider range of causal mechanisms taken from different paradigms. Only in making this move, as Solingen argues, can we hope to generate theoretically rich, policy-relevant knowledge. This is also the central point of Kang, whose book is analytically rigorous in systematically differentiating between empirical phenomena rather than lumping them for the sake of convenience under an all-embracing and thus unfalsifiable category such as the balance of power. For him, theoretical rigor requires developing falsifiable measures of state behavior, and distinguishing among a variety of state behaviors, postures, and strategies in a systematic manner. Rather than finding quintessential examples or stylized facts that illustrate a specific paradigm-bound theory or hypothesis, these authors all contend that a central task of eclectic research is to find a workable balance between empirical richness and analytical rigor. That balance is a matter of intuition and judgment that is difficult to teach and impossible to describe.

In sum, while not all of the authors are equally explicit about their commitments to causal explanation and policy prescription, they do for the most part illustrate the character and utility of analytic eclecticism as we have defined it. Each has identified an interesting question that either represents an anomaly from prevailing theoretical perspectives or cuts across the boundary conditions of competing paradigms. Each has developed novel causal narratives offering portable middle-range accounts that identify and connect alternative mechanisms and logics. And each has found clear ways to articulate the implications of their theoretical arguments for both international relations theory and contemporary policy debates. Chapter 4 explores similarly eclectic approaches to aspects of the international and global political economy.

Chapter 4

Global political economy

The multiple causes of the deep crisis of the global economy, which exploded for all to see with the bankruptcy of Lehman Brothers in September 2008, will be debated for years. Consumers in the United States had convinced themselves, and been convinced by financial institutions and the media, that the price of real estate could only go up and not down. Like their credit cards, their homes became a functional substitute for the welfare state. Under both Republican and Democratic administrations, as a matter of social policy, the federal government sought to make home ownership available to a steadily growing number of Americans – even for those who lacked sufficient assets to make their monthly mortgage payments. Financial institutions fed the growing real estate bubble with new products that artificially reduced rather than accurately reflected the risks they incurred. After the bursting of the dot-com technology bubble and the Enron accounting scandal had receded from public consciousness, the administration of President George W. Bush decided to push hard for further deregulation. Subsequently economic incentives in the financial service and banking industries increasingly rewarded short-term investment strategies that turned out to be reckless in the extreme.

These factors also had enormous repercussions throughout the global economy, feeding the dramatically growing imbalances in trade and investment flows between the United States and China as well as other countries that depended on American consumer spending to fuel their export-oriented economies. In a matter of a few years, China became the largest creditor of the United States. With the world's most productive economies contracting, the demand for oil slumped, dragging down a Russian economy that had only just begun to experience economic growth after the turmoil of the 1990s. Whatever the causes of the deepest slump of the global economy since the 1930s, the financial losses of the Western banking system alone are estimated at a shocking US$1.5 to 3.0 trillion. In fact, a consensual valuation of losses turns out to be impossible. And losses in the financial sector are only part of the story. The losses incurred by individuals and institutions, in addition to government bailouts, guarantees, and stimulus packages, are much larger. The collateral damage of a near-collapse of the financial system has been enormous for the real economy in the United States and around the world.

These serious economic and policy failures also brought about an intellectual crisis for the fundamental ideas that guided the practices of business and government – in particular for rational expectations theory, which centers on the idea that individuals make choices based on past experience and available information. Current expectations, this theory holds, render an accurate picture of the future state of the economy, allowing economists to develop ever more sophisticated models to predict the future ever more accurately. In these models past outcomes and current expectations are closely linked; and in recurrent situations, such as daily trading on the stock market, the connection between past and future, outcomes and expectations, tends to be smooth and stable. Economic actors adjust their expectations in line with a consistent and predictable pattern in which unavoidable forecasting errors will be weeded out gradually. Expectations of the future thus are reflected quite accurately in current values, improving market efficiency and increasing profits for those mastering improved forecasting techniques. Financial economists had developed rational expectations theory so far that portfolio managers and CEOs were able to convince themselves – and policymakers in Washington – that new methods of combining risks in novel products had eliminated all risk from their asset sheets. But they overlooked the potential appearance of new systemic dangers, as all banks and financial institutions hedged their individual risks in similar ways across various asset classes and markets. As markets went up, this growing interdependence fed a boom in profits. But when they unexpectedly started to fall, it triggered a rapidly mounting cascade of losses.

For the followers of rational expectations theory, as in the natural sciences, there exists an objective reality independent of the observer which could be used as the basis of common knowledge shared by all market actors (Cassidy 2008). In this theory, the law of demand and supply functions like the law of gravity: a universally agreed upon generalization whose existence and effects were beyond question. Based on this assumption, banks became convinced that they needed to invest virtually none of their own capital to back ever more risky investments promising ever greater financial returns. When some large banks got into trouble, everyone looked for liquid assets, and markets tumbled, one after the other, as financial positions unwound. The end result was an unstoppable cascade that produced a gigantic financial collapse. Among the most prominent early victims was Goldman Sachs, one of the largest hedge fund managers until August 2007, when its most vaunted fund lost 30 percent of its value in just one week. David Viniar, Goldman's chief financial officer, famously declared at the time: 'We were seeing things that were 25-standard deviation moves, several days in a row.' The same week, Lehman Brothers also noted with surprise: 'Models (ours including) are behaving in the opposite way we would predict and have seen and tested for over very long time periods.'[1] For those thinking of economics as the physics of the social sciences, these were indeed startling admissions.

Since the crisis erupted, within the academe, proponents of rational expectations models have kept a relatively low profile in public discourse. When they do speak up, they too insist that this crisis is an anomaly, a freak exception to their robust models, something that might occur once in three generations. For many, however, the financial crisis has given us much to ponder about our standard practices and about the fundamental assumptions behind the models we employ. In a provocative new book titled *Lecturing Birds on Flying*, Pablo Triana (2009, p. 3) has launched a scathing attack on the conventional wisdom in economics, which he sees as predicated on a misplaced physics-envy:

> Economics, of course, is not physics. For one very simple, yet inevitably powerful reason: In one case the laws are immutably God-made and thus permanently exact (all one has to do is go find them and, with luck, express their structure down on paper); in the other, the rules are dictated not by God, but by His creatures, us humble humans. And if there is something that we know about ourselves it is that, when it comes to economic activity (which of course

includes the financial markets), we tend to be reliably unreliable. Our behavior is not set in stone, preprogrammed, preordained.

This is not merely an abstract metaphysical point. In fact, one of the most successful hedge fund managers and one of the leading philanthropists of the last generation would agree wholeheartedly with this assessment. George Soros (2008, 1998, 1987) argued that markets were confronting not only calculated risk but also genuine uncertainty. That distinction is for Soros the hallmark between the natural and the social sciences, between the analysis of unthinking objects and that of self-reflective agents. To be sure, markets often function on risk-and-reward behavior based on rational expectation. But they also contain a great dose of uncertainty, which Soros had experienced first-hand for decades. His intuition was grounded in practical rather than theoretical knowledge, and ran in a very different direction from the abstract models of mathematical economists, which he frankly acknowledged he could not understand – a fact that earned him polite contempt mixed with concealed envy over the billions of dollars he had earned in markets.

Soros's concept of reflexivity contradicts the assumptions of rational expectations theory. Reflexivity captures the notion that markets feature two kinds of functions, each of which essentially alters the independent variable in the other. In the cognitive function, participants in a market come to views based on their perception of the actual state of affairs; but in the manipulative function, these views become the independent variable and influence the status quo. The problem is that both functions not only operate simultaneously in markets, but are interconnected in ways that defy the assumptions and expectations of classical economic theory. Neither function can be treated in isolation, as economists are wont to do. In contrast to rational expectations theory, Soros argues that market actors act on the perceptions of their best interests rather than on some objectively determined set of best interests – a vitally important difference. Soros uses the concept of reflexivity to capture the lack of correspondence between the views of market participants and the actual state of affairs.[2]

Soros conveys the crucial insight that misjudgments and misconceptions have a noticeable effect on market prices, and that these prices, in turn, have a strong effect on the underlying fundamentals of markets. In direct contradiction to rational expectations theory, prices simultaneously reflect and shape economic fundamentals. Booms and busts thus become self-reinforcing and self-defeating. In a boom and bust cycle in financial markets, and under conditions of uncertainty, Soros argued, traders did not calculate risks rationally. Instead, they followed shared understandings, copied others, and speculated, thus generating herd behaviors that had little to do with economic fundamentals. What then Federal Reserve chief Alan Greenspan had in 1996 called an 'irrational exuberance' in markets was the central ingredient of both the high-tech and the real estate bubbles of the last decade. In the fall and winter of 2008–09, it became an 'irrational flight' from markets. In Soros's view, beyond a given zone of stability, markets are not self-correcting but tend to spiral out of control in either upward or downward directions, exacerbating economic imbalances. Conditions of uncertainty are thus beyond the reigning theories of risk and rational expectations that form the foundation for most of the work in the field of finance economics. Under such circumstances, when markets get out of balance, very large doses of government intervention are required to restore that balance.

The difference between rational expectation and reflexivity theory has a parallel in persistently differing paradigmatic orientations in the field of international political economy (IPE). Benjamin Cohen (2008a, 2008b, 2007) recently analyzed the characteristic differences between an economic-rationalist-quantitative American paradigm and a sociological-non-rationalist-qualitative British one. Seeing merits and limitations in both approaches, Cohen's analysis did not please everybody. Although he flatly contradicted the ex cathreda announcements of 'one right way' by some proponents of the American paradigm (Frieden and Martin 2002), British scholars took him to task both for accepting the American paradigm as a baseline against which to judge other approaches (Higgott and Watson 2008) and for overlooking American-inflected work within the British tradition (Ravenhill 2008). Cohen's characterization of the evolution of the field of IPE generated a set of spirited exchanges in a special issue of the highly regarded *Review of International Political Economy* (2009) debating the possible existence and consequences of this paradigmatic trans-Atlantic division. Issues of ontology (the basic units that make up the international political economy), epistemology (the foundations on which we make knowledge claims), and methodology (such as the choice between 'counters of beans' and 'tellers of stories') all become relevant to the debate over the extent and implications of a divide between an intellectually narrower and (allegedly) more precise American paradigmatic orientation on the one hand, and an intellectually more capacious and (allegedly) less precise British tradition.

To the extent there is an 'American school' of IPE, it is essentially an extension of the (neo)liberal paradigm, with realism, constructivism, and a once-influential Marxist approach all relegated to the margins (Maliniak and Tierney 2009, p. 14–16). At the center of this paradigm lies a model grounded in rational expectations theory – open economy politics (OEP), as outlined by David Lake (2009). OEP resonates with sweet common sense, at least on the American side of Atlantic. On economic issues, actors who are price takers with clearly ordered preferences will rank policies and outcomes based on how they affect their expected future incomes. OEP analysis seeks to make special adjustments for situations in which one or several of these assumptions are not met. OEP scholars start with sets of individuals 'that can be reasonably assumed to share (nearly) identical interests. ... Deducing interests from economic theory was the essential innovation of OEP' (Lake 2009, p. 50). In this formulation, individual (not social) interests are stipulated to exist (not inquired into). The great innovation of OEP was thus to derive parsimonious theories of politics entirely based on economic theory, a cause of worry to many students of politics.

The theories on which OEP relies are presumed to be falsifiable and empirically robust for explaining economic outcomes. Whether they offer any new insights into significant political outcomes, however, is a matter of considerable dispute. OEP generally brackets interests and preferences by taking them as given. Interests may be 'aggregated' institutionally and 'translated' via institutions into policy outputs and outcomes, but the interests themselves are not problematized. Moreover, OEP subscribes to a truncated view of what institutions are and do, focusing exclusively on their regulative power. In doing so, it neglects altogether the possibility that institutions, in conjunction with identities, may shape actors' preferences and interests as well as their capacities for acting on them. As Keohane (2009b, p. 38) notes, although it has contributed to the integration of comparative and international political economy, OEP has turned out to be 'too materialistic and much of it is too inclined to identify rationalism with egoism – an analytical mistake.' In effect, OEP essentially replicates the fundamental problem that Soros attributes to the rational expectation assumptions driving economic models.

The rationalist underpinnings of OEP are directly challenged by an emergent sociological perspective on international political economy. Stability and instability in the economy, in this view, are inherently social phenomena, open to individual and collective irrationalities that are not shaped by or subordinate to market dynamics but deeply intertwined with them (Beckert 2002). Of course, this is not a completely novel proposition. In fact, as Rawi Abdelal, Mark Blyth, and Craig Parsons (2010) point out, it is one of the deep insights of John Maynard Keynes. Keynes was not a mechanic who simply instructed the government to spend money during economic downturns to cover the shortfall of private purchasing power. He was a student of the complex social interactions that offer crucial insights into the functioning of markets. Materialist and individualist theories are not tailored to capturing social and ideational changes. Over short time periods – measured in terms of months, years and a few decades – the material infrastructure of the global economy, measured in terms of resources and individual motivation, does not tend to change much; the social infrastructure of conventions, norms, ideas, and identities, however, tends to vary considerably. This was reflected, for example, in very different definitions of what constituted the latest financial crisis in the first place: liquidity (United States), capitalization (United Kingdom), or Anglo-Saxon capitalism (Germany). Furthermore, in times of enormous uncertainty, expectations are not stable. Growing uncertainty can lead to a redefinition of identities and interests among a whole array of economic actors, from investors to more (rather than less) risk-averse individuals. A crisis is not only an event 'out there in reality,' but also a set of interpretive acts 'in here,' which can have different effects over time. For example, Japan was not in crisis in December 2008, two months after the collapse of Lehman Brothers; but it was very much in crisis by February 2009. The collapse in Japanese export markets, which was readily recognizable before Christmas, was not viewed as an enormous catastrophe until two months later.

This fundamental difference between the OEP paradigm and the sociological perspective is a development of the last two decades. Between the early 1970s rebirth of the field of international political economy in the United States and the mid-1990s, the paradigmatic fault lines were drawn differently. During the Cold War, Robert Gilpin's (1975, 1981, 1987) seminal writings both reflected and shaped a generation of scholarship organized around three paradigmatic approaches: realist-mercantilist, liberal, and Marxist, each with domestic and international variants. Realist-mercantilist theories put the state at the center of economic life, viewing state calculations and interests as derivative of the international balance of power. Liberal theories focused on the significance of individual and corporate interests in the domestic arena, and on the evolution of these interests in response to the growth of trade and interdependence in the international economy. And Marxist theories operated more freely across the domestic–international divide, linking the dynamics of class conflict in capitalist societies to the perpetuation of inequalities in the international capitalist system. The end of the Cold War, the economic rise of East Asia, and the spread of market reforms throughout the developing world have all combined to reduce sharply the political and intellectual relevance and attraction of Marxism, although it certainly retains a foothold in European, Latin American, and even Asian debates on political economy. Realist theories of political economy were either relegated to the margins or subsumed by variants of liberal theories. What emerged in the course of the 1990s, then, is a rationalist mainstream whose core tenets are identified with OEP. This mainstream extends the liberal paradigm but also incorporates insights from economics, viewed as the model social science which is admired and often copied by political scientists. In response, a distinct alternative has begun to crystallize, combining constructivist epistemology with insights from economic and historical sociology (Abdelal et al. 2010).

To the extent that there is a trans-Atlantic divide between American and British IPE (Cohen 2007, 2008b), surely both perspectives provide intellectual resources that can help us to make better sense of the world (Katzenstein 2009). But we are more generally concerned about the intellectual divides between paradigms, wherever they are constructed, that prompt scholars to frequently speak past one another even when they are interested in the same issues in global political economy. Cautioning against a monoculture in the study of political economy, Keohane (2009b, p. 40) calls for a 'synthetic interpretation of change' in which ideas, structural power, and diffusion processes all play crucial roles. He acknowledges that scholars now confront a larger volume of work and a greater degree of complexity, but he insists that 'those of us who are not in the field of IPE – scholars, policy-makers, or citizens – need to know what the best research says about the big questions.' This does not point to an alternative unifying paradigm to subsume rationalist and constructivist elements. Indeed, both camps have produced work of exceptionally high caliber, and it would be an intellectual loss to trade diversity in perspective for a new unified framework that informs any and all studies of political economy. Instead, as we argue in this book, scholarship benefits from accommodating work that is analytically eclectic in the study of specific problems by drawing on constituent elements of theories typically embedded in competing paradigms.

By making connections between paradigms that are typically disengaged from one another, analytic eclecticism holds promise for enhancing our understanding of different facets of the global political economy. As noted above, eclectic approaches conceive of questions whose scope extends beyond conventional field boundaries, develop complex arguments at the level of middle-range theory that incorporate mechanisms drawn from competing paradigms, and explicitly or implicitly engage 'messy' issues of policy or practice. Obviously, this conception of analytic eclecticism is an ideal-typical one; not all eclectic scholarship will score high on each of these three criteria. But on balance, studies that are reasonable approximations of analytic eclecticism will rank high on at least two of these dimensions and will make a concerted effort to incorporate concepts and mechanisms of at least two distinct paradigms.

This chapter reviews an illustrative sample of eclectic scholarship addressing different aspects of global political economy. These include works on finance (Seabrooke 2006), credit and bond rating (Sinclair 2005), trade liberalization (Woll 2008), European integration (Jabko 2006), and national and regional experiences with economic growth (Stubbs 2005).[3]

Leonard Seabrooke, *The Social Sources of Financial Power* (2006)

Seabrooke's (2006) book is a prime example of an eclectic perspective. Its inquiry into the social sources of state financial power weaves together concepts and mechanisms drawn from different research traditions in international political economy, comparative politics, the new institutionalism, and economic sociology. One of the book's most noteworthy and imaginative aspects is a radical expansion in the scope of the problem that Seabrooke defines. While he, like many other IPE scholars, is concerned with the basic question of how states enhance their financial capacity, Seabrooke does not limit his focus to the interests and interactions of the most visible actors at the 'big end of town.' Rather, he considers the possibility that less prosperous groups at the 'small end of town,' whose members are individually powerless, can collectively affect a state's ability to generate financial capacity. The question, then, is whether and how states recognize and tap into the latent power of these groups as they seek to enhance their financial power base and shape the international financial order. While scholars and policymakers have wined and dined with representatives of high finance, they have overlooked the potential effects of norms and practices of those at the 'small end of town' on a state's financial capacity in the international arena. Seabrooke thus defines his problem in a distinctive manner which deviates sharply from, but still engages, typical approaches to comparative or international political economy.

For his purpose, Seabrooke finds existing paradigm-centered scholarship to be quite unhelpful. Theories emphasizing either factor endowments or institutional logics are too static. They recognize the opportunities generated when the circulation of credit is increased, but fail to consider political and social responses to the manner in which this credit is allocated among different groups. Theories focusing on the constraints posed by financial globalization and various state structures offer partial explanations for variation in financial systems and policies. Some even recognize that 'factor endowments are not natural but born from political struggles among rational economic actors' (p. 5). But they do not and cannot explain why similar states may have quite different capabilities in projecting their financial power to shape the international financial order. Furthermore, neither theories focusing on opportunity nor those focusing on constraint take into account 'the role of economic social norms that inform struggle over how the economy should work' (p. 6). Constructivists do emphasize the significance of norms, but only a few studies link those norms to the stability and power of financial institutions; and even these tend to confine their attention to moments of radical uncertainty and to adopt a top-down view focused primarily on the role of 'ideational entrepreneurs' (p. 9).

Seabrooke is not interested in promoting or debunking paradigms. He simply notes that, while each of the prevailing approaches has important insights to contribute, none can by itself shed light on the processes that link lower-income groups to international finance in the way that Seabrooke seeks to do. For this purpose, a more expansive analytic framework is needed, one that simultaneously cuts across and utilizes comparative political economy, international political economy, the new institutionalism, and economic sociology (p. 7). Put another way, Seabrooke seeks to bring Max Weber back in (p. 11):

> For Weber, everyday economic struggle is more important than moments of crisis and uncertainty. While charismatic leaders can lead us down the garden path, it is the relationship between state and society on everyday matters that has the real capacity to transform environments.

Specifically, Seabrooke employs the Weberian concept of *legitimacy* to build an analytic framework that incorporates mechanisms from different traditions in diverse fields of scholarship. Weber's notion of legitimacy incorporates both 'top-down' and 'bottom-up' processes. As Seabrooke (p. 12) puts it: 'legitimacy is a process by which those with power claim that their actions are morally just and legally right, but where the conferral of legitimacy upon such actions can only come from the expressed consent of those subordinate within the power relationship' (see also Bendix 1977; Beetham 1991). One of Seabrooke's central insights is that legitimacy among lower-income groups provides the indispensable social foundation for sustainable financial power. He argues that when lower-income groups view access to credit, property ownership, and tax burdens as fundamentally fair, this has a strong effect on state influence in international finance in ways that conventional treatments of political economy simply fail to recognize and thus cannot explain. But states can undertake policies that shape or respond to the views of lower-income groups. Seabrooke (p. xii) distinguishes between two ideal types. Positive state intervention for lower-income groups on questions of taxation, credit, and access to property deepens and broadens the domestic pool of capital, and encourages financial practices that increase the flow of capital back to the state. Negative state intervention has the opposite effect, giving more scope to rentier interests that restrict the flow of capital into state coffers. Positive or negative state intervention exerts strong effects on the strength of domestic financial systems and the ability of the state to shape the international financial order.

Seabrooke develops an institutional analysis that is organized around the core concept of legitimacy. In this effort he is quite specific in distinguishing his Weberian approach from two alternative forms of institutional analysis, rational and historical, which he finds wanting (Chapter 2). He also distinguishes his approach in important ways from economic constructivism, to which he shows some affinities. Rational institutionalist arguments borrow from microeconomic theories of market failures: institutional structures maintain a social equilibrium disturbed by exogenous shocks that produce uncertainties and information asymmetries, requiring self-interested actors intent on maximizing their utilities to work out a new equilibrium. Well suited to the task of explaining institutional endurance, this approach is often criticized for failing to explain the creation of institutions, the chosen task of historical institutionalism. It focuses also on problems of change rather than how to minimize transaction costs. In this approach, rationality is not assumed to be an unproblematic given, as in rationalist institutionalism, but the product of political constructions that are based on variable mixes of instrumental rationality and social norms. The focus is on specifying why institutions differ, and how these differences inform the process of change. The emphasis of rationalist institutionalism on punctuated equilibrium and path dependence is replaced by evolution and path dependence. Rather than adapting in a functional way to change, actors learn in a self-reflexive manner.

Economic constructivism merges central insights of these two institutional arguments. Rejecting the notion of external shock, economic constructivists explain change by focusing on actors who are motivated by ideas and norms that are endogenous to institutions. But like the institutionalist approaches on which it draws, economic constructivism tends to focus on moments of uncertainty as the crucial periods in which ideational entrepreneurs assert their autonomy and create legitimacy 'from the top down' by proclamation. Seabrooke's Weberian approach builds on a more robust conception of legitimacy, insisting instead that legitimacy is fought out 'from the bottom up.' Through normal, daily contestations, people fight for their life-chances and live out their normal life experiences. In doing so they are informed by their perceptions of how the world works and how they should act, adhering to instrumental and value-oriented beliefs. Compared with rational institutionalism with its emphasis on 'thin' instrumental norms, in Seabrooke's analysis rationality is deeply penetrated by 'thick' substantive norms. And compared with historical institutionalism, this analysis of change highlights processes of political conflict and contestation rather than institutional logics.

Seabrooke (p. 12) is explicit in characterizing his approach as a middle-range rather than a general theory. He is also explicit in using the language of mechanisms to capture the complex processes that link types of state interventions to the legitimation of finance reform, and its consequences for the breadth and depth of the pool of capital that can then be deployed internationally. Standard labels for characterizing economies, for example as 'liberal' or 'coordinated' as in the tradition of varieties of capitalism, are useful for understanding the forms of different political economies in the aggregate; but such labels should not blind us to different mechanisms and patterns of behavior that operate within such aggregates (p. 13). Coordinated political economies, for example, centralize power in pilot agencies to better cope with external shocks in the international economy and to save time in domestic politics. Greater fragmentation in uncoordinated economies undercuts timely response and may undermine the ability to soften the blow of externally induced crises. But beneath the difference in institutional form lies the political purpose informing positive or negative intervention. A state that is kept in check by its public is likely to enjoy more legitimacy and thus greater amounts of socially backed financial power than a state that is not kept in check. Rather than seeking the correlation among key abstract variables (such as forms of state intervention, extent of legitimation of financial reform, and extent of a state's international financial capacity), Seabrooke is interested in specifying and observing the linking mechanisms within this broad constellation of variables.

In articulating his theoretical approach, Seabrooke employs a broad understanding of mechanisms: 'mechanisms seek to tie down not only structures and institutions that provide constraints upon action, but also outline how actors can work toward their life-chances' (p. 50). His analysis (pp. 14–15, 50–2) identifies three sequentially linked mechanisms. Contestation, redistribution, and propagation, he argues, form a complex causal chain. The initial driver of change is political contestation between lower income groups, rentiers, and the state over the legitimacy of financial reforms in a given social and institutional environment. This contestation drives lower-income groups and rentiers to draw upon ideational and normative resources to influence the state's chosen form of intervention. That change can be either positive or negative for lower income groups, as it entails *redistribution* of benefits and costs among social groups. Redistribution encompasses the direct reallocation of assets and opportunities as well as broader reforms in how public and private institutions interact with society. The cumulative effect of contestation and redistribution is to trigger a third mechanism, propagation, whereby the state promotes ideas about how the economy should work for the purpose of legitimizing its policies and either encouraging or discouraging the use of financial innovations among lower-income groups. These norms feed back onto lower income groups which will react, depending on their beliefs of how the economy should work, and thus start a fresh cycle of contestation. Seabrooke tracks these mechanisms' effects on the three policy domains of credit access, property ownership, and taxation, with the help of a variety of sources, including archival and documentary data for the historical cases and interviews for the contemporary ones.

Comparisons of England and Germany (at the end of the nineteenth century) and the United States and Japan (at the end of the twentieth) provide empirical support for Seabrooke's argument (p. 15–17, 194–9). Broadly speaking, the late nineteenth century was an era of an international rentier economy, which reflected England's domestic legitimacy dynamics. The English state proved too weak to prevent the turn to a rentier economy in an era in which state regulatory regimes more generally were gradually built up. The late twentieth century was an international credit economy, propelled by changes in the domestic legitimation of US financial reforms which dismantled most regulatory regimes. Whereas England's strong position was eventually weakened by the political protest of lower-income groups opposing negative state policies, similar opposition in the United States produced very different results, giving rise to positive state policies after the mid-1980s that increased the legitimacy of national financial policies and enabled the United States to extend its hegemony in the international financial order, at least until the financial crash of 2008. In sharp contrast, Germany (at the beginning of the twentieth century) and Japan (in the 1970s and 1980s) lacked the political institutions and policies to build a sustainable social foundation for financial power. In the area of finance, this absence of power doomed their bids to move from a position of rival to the position of principal.

Seabrooke (p. 173) concludes that 'if a state intervenes positively to legitimate its financial reform nexus for lower-income groupings, it can provide a sustainable basis from which to increase its international financial capacity.' While this may not be the norm, particularly in rentier states, his case studies and comparisons suggest compellingly that the legitimacy and financial capacity of states in the international arena are directly and significantly affected by the fundamentally domestic choices of state elites with regard to lower-income groups. Greater access to credit, property ownership, and lower tax burdens enhance the social foundations of a state's financial capacity, often coupled with the use of financial innovations. They not only serve technical or regulatory functions but become essential tools for propagating new economic and social norms relevant for financial practices.

The policy implications of this analytical strategy are clear. There is little to be gained from mimicking the institutional forms of those states or political economies enshrined (often erroneously) as 'winners' or 'models' at a particular historical juncture. What may have worked in one case may not work in another, given the different baselines and expectations of lower-income groups and the varying will and ability of state elites to consider these in designing their policies. It is thus necessary to look more carefully at the particular mechanisms affecting a state's legitimacy and the extent of its financial capacity in the international arena. This analysis also has implications for scholars and policymakers concerned with the relationship between democracy and economic policies, since democracy creates regular institutionalized opportunities for lower-income groups to punish state elites (although the long-term viability of policies adopted by semi-authoritarian and authoritarian regimes also depends on some degree of social support). In sum, between domestic social policy and international financial policy, Seabrooke's eclectic analysis builds an intellectually and practically useful bridge – one not previously recognized by either students of international political economy or policymakers.

Box 4.1
Leonard Seabrooke – Exploring the full cocktail menu

The analytic eclecticism in *The Social Sources of Financial Power* (Seabrooke 2005) comes from a combination of annoyance and awareness. I was annoyed with the Gramscian and Foucauldian scholarship in international relations that dominated my undergraduate studies in Australia. A common approach was to make a normative commitment, apply concepts like 'social forces,' and then run already-formed conclusions through case material. Such a 'plug-and-play' approach was not good enough, or even true to anti-foundationalist ideas. But reading Foucault led me to Max Weber, where discontinuity, interests as ideas, and analytic pragmatism were present. Weber's clarity on sociological concepts matched with his thick descriptions in other work. The main lesson I took from Weber was that political economy, the new institutionalisms, anthropology, and economic and organizational sociology provide a range of analytical tools and concepts that were not 'plug-and-play' but could be fit for purpose. This is particularly important in understanding concepts like legitimacy and everyday politics, since imposing my own judgment on what is 'best' for a population would distort the findings. Through Weberian sociology, my approach in social sources was deliberately eclectic.

I know that my analytic eclecticism has generated mixed responses. Prominent rational choice scholars have tutted at how the causal relationships in social sources can be partially explained by interest group analysis, suggesting that norms simply add noise. Constructivists have furrowed their brows at my endorsement of methodological individualism. Marxists have told me publicly that the lack of ideological commitment within my analysis has the consequence of 'making poor people poorer'. Hardly. I do think that people should enhance their life-chances in ways they see fit, and that seeing how they think the economy should work requires analytic eclecticism.

I see no reason why intellectual ground should be conceded to scholars who provide the 'default' model in various social science communities. This is especially the case when we know that it is the less-monist and more 'quirky' scholars – Abbott, Bendix, Elias, Weber, Zelizer, and many others – who transform how we understand social and economic change. Finally, my advice to authors considering an eclectic approach is that the academic market – both publishing and jobs – does not punish eclecticism because it produces interesting, often counterintuitive work. And why drink lager or Pinot Grigio when the full cocktail menu is there to be explored?

Timothy Sinclair, *The New Masters of Capital* (2005)

Since the beginning of the 1990s, Sinclair argues, the liberalization of financial markets has increased exposure to risk and the value of information, investigation, and analysis. As a result, knowledge provided by intermediary institutions such as rating agencies has become extremely important in a more global economy. American bond rating agencies in particular have become especially influential. These agencies are tiny in terms of their employment and are largely unregulated, but the effects of their activities are huge. Sinclair's book studies the two major bond-rating agencies – Moody's and Standard & Poor's (S&P) – which maintain ratings on roughly US$30 trillion worth of debt issued in American and global markets. Many in business and politics are interested in the obvious question of whether the ratings provided by these agencies are technically correct or incorrect. Instead, Sinclair insists that the more interesting underlying question is the source of the authoritative knowledge that gives these tiny organizations a virtual chokehold on access to global capital markets. Although they are American, rating agencies enjoy high esteem in national and international politics, and the information they provide is relied upon by banks, firms, and governments around the world.

Rating in a world of financial globalization certainly has a technical side that needs to be respected and taken seriously. Cheaper securities markets have caused traditional bank lending to diminish sharply in importance. The assessment of creditworthiness that banks used to offer before lending their capital is now being performed by the grading of securities by bond-rating agencies. Largely unregulated by governments, this facilitates transactions between buyers and sellers operating on a global scale. But focusing exclusively on this technical side conceals the broader political significance of the rating agencies – the esteem in which they are held, and the authority they enjoy. Like Seabrooke, Sinclair focuses on the factors that make rating agencies reliable in the eyes of those who depend upon them. Although he does not use the term legitimacy, by focusing on the authority imparted upon rating agencies, Sinclair is able to expand the scope of the question so that it encompasses a range of non-technical aspects that are frequently unrecognized and certainly undertheorized. Sinclair puts forward a new question: what factors affect the high level of social esteem, trust, and authority that rating firms enjoy?

This move is somewhat reminiscent of Robert Gilpin's (1981, p. 31) treatment of reputation as 'everyday currency' in international affairs. But whereas Gilpin remains committed to the primacy of realist logics and material capabilities, Sinclair sees the independent significance of the esteem enjoyed by ratings agencies, and is focused on exploring the complementarities among processes emphasized by competing paradigms. Sinclair's analysis treats the theoretical orientations of different paradigms as heuristics, and seeks to identify complementarities between rationalist (that is, realist and liberal) approaches and those based on economic and organizational sociology (that is, constructivist). Rationalists argue that in an environment of high uncertainty and risk, rating agencies give economic agents the transparent and impartial assessments of conditions they need for a rational assessment of conditions and efficient allocation of scarce resources. By downgrading the quality of bonds, rating agencies can coerce debt-issuing institutions to change their ways. But what is the source of this coercive power? And what processes generate the unquestioned assumptions that influence the generation and consumption of the knowledge offered by ratings agencies? These are important questions in IPE that rationalist approaches neither raise nor answer.

Sinclair seeks to enrich the study of rating agencies with a deeper and more complex understanding of the political and social processes through which their knowledge is created and monitored. This requires incorporating the heuristics developed by constructivist-economic sociology, without claiming that this research tradition is inherently superior (p. 17). Sinclair is quite permissive in his stance toward the substantive usefulness of realism and liberalism, which he sees as offering a helpful rationalist baseline. Actors with fixed preferences compete for scarce resources and act on the basis of material interests. The beauty of this heuristic is that it can be used to inquire into the likely motivations of actions in any number of different social institutions and settings. The alternative approach drawn from sociology focuses less on instrumental rationality and more on processes through which identities and preferences of actors are built up and down, thus affecting conceptions of interest that inform action. Broadly speaking, in this sociological perspective knowledge and culture comprise intersubjective structures that define who the economic actors are and what they want. These are aspects of markets that rationalist approaches typically hold constant or bypass altogether. Sinclair insists that for his question both approaches – rationalist and constructivist – are relevant. He argues also that the field of international political economy has neglected the latter unduly, but he does not then insist on treating the latter as a preferred alternative that should replace or subsume rationalist analyses.

Rating agencies certainly take on the technical task of providing to their clients and the general public a condensation of massive amounts of data about market developments. But what makes them effective in this role is the fact that they also constitute 'embedded knowledge networks.' Building on, but going beyond, the concept of 'epistemic communities' (Haas 1992), Sinclair sees knowledge networks as embedded in the very processes that constitute financial globalization: they share certain normative beliefs but also enjoy legitimacy based on their conformity to public expectations in certain environments (pp. 14–15). The power of ratings agencies lies not only in the information they provide, but in the beliefs and worldviews they foster in diverse societies concerning how their data is to be interpreted by different actors. A striking illustration is the fact that the major international rating agencies are all located in the United States, a defining aspect of the knowledge networks they embody. Their legitimacy worldwide, however, is a function of these agencies' self-portrayal to market participants everywhere as networks that are endogenous, not exogenous, to financial globalization. Hence they are normally accepted by market participants as legitimate. Rather than constraining markets, rating agencies contribute to their internal constitution, thus affecting the social context in which corporations and governments map their strategies. Thus, beyond brute coercive power impelling behavioral change, rating agencies offer interpretive frameworks that specify what constitutes proper economic conduct and thus should be rewarded by the flow of additional private investments.

Sinclair's analysis is self-consciously modest (p. 11), offering a plausibility probe for subsequent hypothesis testing. He is not interested in developing a universal model of rating-agency behavior, nor does he offer a general theory about the effects of this behavior on aspects of global political economy. Instead, he seeks to develop, and provide an empirical basis for, mid-range arguments about rating, investment, knowledge, and governance (p. 50). Sinclair proceeds inductively, tracking processes that reflect back on a number of different theoretical orientations in the field of international political economy. For Sinclair, these orientations are heuristics that point to possibly relevant variables and causal logics that combine to influence the outcome in question: the role and authority of rating agencies in global finance.

Sinclair's relational perspective sees actors as embedded in larger social contexts such as networks. It differs from the rationalist emphasis on self-regarding actors mingling in decentralized or anarchic structures. Markets are not freestanding structures but integral parts of social life, connected by history and culture. Instead of invariant behavioral properties that we can model to uncover universal, lawlike patterns of behavior, Sinclair points to variability over time and space. This is not to deny the existence and analysis of general patterns of cultural homogenization on a global scale – pervasive myths and mental frameworks that enhance or reduce the legitimacy of specific organizational forms. Rating agencies have morphed from national and American institutions to become an intrinsic, unquestioned part of global finance writ large. Collective attribution of meaning and conferral of trust, esteem, and authority, either in national societies or on a global scale, are political phenomena with very considerable consequences for the functioning of modern capitalism.

What is true of society at large is also true of the internal life of an organization such as Moody's. It too follows its own scripted rules, develops its own organizational routines and practices, cultivates and perpetuates its own myths, and validates its existence and conduct through publicly told stories. Professional judgment and analysis are a central part of the mental framework motivating people who work for rating agencies, and of the public story that these agencies stand for and represent. Professionally recognized competence and expertise bestow the power of issuing authoritative claims, constituting a dimension of power that corporations and governments neglect only at considerable risk.

Sinclair's central claim (p. 17) is that rating is not neutral, technical, detached, and objective. Instead, the gathering and processing of vast amounts of information is informed by judgment that helps to coordinate market activities. In normal times, the judgments of rating agencies acquire the social status of accepted facts in the eyes of market participants even when, occasionally, ex post analysis shows that the assessment was faulty. Typically, the authority that market participants ascribe to agencies outweighs their technical proficiency. Agency judgments have risen to the status of orthodoxies which, between the mid-1980s and 2008, pushed organizational and strategic logics toward the prevailing American institutional pattern. Or, as Sinclair puts it: 'In this emerging order, norms are increasingly shared, and policy converges around characteristically American "best practice"' (p. 17).

Sinclair supports this central view through three, more specific, mid-range arguments that collectively account for the 'unconscious power' (p. 50–71) that rating agencies acquire and project in global finance. First, with the growing importance of capital markets and the declining importance of banks, investment decisions are increasingly shaped by rating agencies rather than banks. Orthodox understandings of investment best practice are now shaped by conforming to standards set by rating agencies rather than assessed by financial institutes that consider lending money. The result is a 'centralization of investment judgment' (p. 18), as rating agencies take on more and more of the 'gatekeeper power' once held by banks. The relationship between corporate ratings, the cost of debt municipal ratings, the rating of the automobile companies, and the spread of US rating agencies abroad, as well as the emergence of local agencies in emerging markets, all provide strong evidence for this argument.

A second supporting argument concerns knowledge, which is normally thought to transcend particular situations and times. Instead, Sinclair seeks to identify the tipping point when the idiosyncratic view of a small group of individuals acquires the status of being widely accepted as common sense. Rating judgments are in this sense not objective, but intersubjective and collectively consequential. Furthermore, the sort of knowledge that rating agencies privilege – and claim to excel in – is analytical and technical, highlighting specific cause–effect relations (p. 19). This kind of knowledge excludes from inquiry broader questions of how institutions originated and how they might transform themselves. Instead, the underlying assumption holds that the world is fundamentally unchanging – reflected, for example, in the assumption that across time and space, markets have always and will always perform the same function as they do today. This knowledge is plainly inadequate to anticipate big and unforeseen events such as the Mexican debt crisis of 1982, the Asian financial crisis of 1997, 9/11, or the financial crisis of 2008. Supportive evidence comes from the growth of the rating industry, municipal ratings, and the creation of Japanese rating agencies.

Finally, a third supporting argument tracks the emergence of new forms of governance based on the static worldview of rating agencies. Governance, for Sinclair, is about how institutions are hierarchically organized and how they shape our daily lives as citizens and consumers (p. 20). Without full awareness of historically derived norms and practices in various locales, rating agencies end up promoting specific constitutional arrangements and corporate governance approaches that emerged within the United States but are regarded as universal standards to be emulated everywhere. Although rating agencies did not invent these governance structures, they act as interpreters, advocates, and enforcers of these arrangements, which may or may not be suitable to particular local circumstances. The experience of Japanese banks, New York's financial problems, and political controversies in Japan, Australia, Canada, and several developing economies all illustrate this third supportive argument.

Sinclair's analysis captures the ways in which typical rationalist understandings of investment, knowledge, and governance can be challenged and complemented by a more historically oriented constructivist treatment of these three aspects of international political economy. These twin competing images of the three aspects of international political economy have specific implications for the extent and manner in which American political influence spreads globally. Rating is now applied not only to corporations but also to sovereign states. Hence the rating activities of US firms have serious implications for national autonomy. Furthermore, Moody's and S&P have opened branches in many parts of the world and have served as a model for the establishment of local rating agencies. Sinclair argues that rating is an American innovation that spreads American norms and practices. Yet, he also notes that these agencies view themselves as transnational entities offering standardized, objective knowledge. Rationalist and synthetic views are thus complementary and interactive, combining to influence the way in which rating operates in contemporary settings. Even though rating has become a transnational activity in the global economy, its origin remains clearly rooted in American institutional conditions and practices.

The policy implications of this dual image of rating agencies are most profound for actors in the world economy who use, or are

Box 4.2
Timothy J. Sinclair – Not being deterred by the ultimate taboo

I attribute my analytic eclecticism – and I happily accept the label – to growing up in a society slowly becoming unhinged by economic decline. My initial response was to embrace Marx as so many have before me, and I know that some readers see this influence clearly in *The New Masters of Capital* (Sinclair 2005). This interest in unpeeling the mechanisms of capitalism is important because something has to explain the resistance to criticism characteristic of the credit-rating agencies. Their resistance is structural – the agencies are in a 'useful' position. They seem to 'fit.' But there was a detached quality to the Marxist analysis I encountered. Serving as a junior analyst in the New Zealand Treasury forced me – it was not something I sought – to acquire the outlook of a beat cop or private investigator, trying to understand where money was being made and spent, and how an activity could be done more efficiently (or not at all). This is how I got my feet wet in research. Arriving subsequently in Toronto, I met Robert W. Cox and Stephen Gill, and started to develop an approach that combined empirical investigation, specification of mechanisms, and the political management of institutions.

Rating agencies were a concern of Robert Muldoon, New Zealand's prime minister between the late 1970s and mid-1980s, who was an inspiration to me. I thought them important too, but I came to think that the rationalism of Marx or Samuelson did not capture the way in which their outputs helped to constitute the securities markets, when traders spoke of 'AAA' or 'BBB' bonds, without thinking. Few had read Keynes recently, so not many scholars were interested in these insights at first. Instead, panel audiences wanted to know how the agencies 'wielded power.' But the more I investigated, the more I concluded that their role in making markets was crucial. Rationalism identified a resilient 'function' for the agencies but not the real consequences. Answers to this question had to come from elsewhere.

I never set out to be eclectic – it was the ultimate taboo in graduate school, after all – but I could not find a solution to my puzzle using just one paradigm. The important thing I learned from this journey is that once I am interested in a puzzle, I should not worry much what others think. Instead, I should pursue my interest until I have a cogent solution, even if it challenges established paradigms.

judged by, the knowledge provided by these agencies. If such actors decide to question the processes through which information is gathered and circulated, then the role and influence of ratings agencies may not remain what they have been during the past decade. In the aftermath of the financial crisis of 2008–09, the main focus of attention has been on executive compensation and the improvement of regulatory frameworks' capitalization requirements for the financial sector. It remains to be seen whether the rating agencies, which are alleged to have failed so dramatically, will also be subjected to reform. Assuming that the pressure will be concentrated on state institutions, this would validate Sinclair's intuition of the centrality of private power in the political economy.

Cornelia Woll, *Firm Interests* (2008)

The central question informing Woll's book reflects her own personal experience. As a high school student in the United States, she spoke to her family, then living in Europe, only once a week for 15 minutes. This was a period when flying across the Atlantic was very expensive. A decade later she would often talk several times a day; and flights, especially in Europe, had become dirt cheap. This shift in her own personal experience is intertwined with Woll's scholarly interest in the liberalization of telecommunications and the partial liberalization of air transport. Woll's initial intuition was that she surely was far more enthusiastic about the drop in prices than were old European network monopolies, which probably were forced to accept liberalization by user demands and pressure from international institutions. The winners surely would be American firms and new market entrants. Established European firms most likely would see their market shares and profits drop as a result of policies they would presumably want to resist (p. xii).

Woll's exploratory interviews suggested a different reality. European firms expressed happiness with new agreements liberalizing services in telecommunications and international aviation. But why would this be the case, given that firms with large protected home markets normally seek and benefit from protection? Woll initially suspected that her interview subjects were simply trying to cover up a past policy defeat. Over time, however, it became increasingly clear that a genuine shift in perspective had taken place: her interview subjects acknowledged that they had not liked the liberalization at first, but that they and the world had changed (p. xiii). This transformation became the basis for the problem explored in her book: 'Why had preferences evolved so decisively over such a short period of time? What did it take to move a business actor from protectionism to support for liberalization?' (pp. xiii–xiv).

This question had been asked before, but only one major study of American trade policy yielded outcomes that did not neatly fit the expectations of conventional trade theory (Bauer, Pool, and Dexter 1963). The ten-year study had found (to the consternation of economists who simply disregarded its findings) that not only large and competitive firms but also medium-sized and small ones, which were much more vulnerable to foreign competition, favored tariff reductions. Economists typically assume – instead of seeking to demonstrate – that a firm's product and position in the economy tell us everything we need to know about its trade policy preferences. At the dawn of liberalization, this turned out to be an inaccurate shortcut for the analysis of American trade policy. Based on over 900 interviews, the authors of the study concluded that communication and new norms of free trade had a profound effect, undercutting and deflecting the influence of firms' material conditions and incentives (Bauer, Pool, and Dexter 1963, pp. xi–xii).

Several decades later, Woll finds very much the same kind of shift occurring in Europe. That businesses lobby government on issues of trade policy in services is as much about the definition of preferences as about influencing trade policy. When economic stakes are clearly defined, material interests are often unambiguous. But, typically, the world of trade negotiations and manufacturing is more complex, and incentives are often unclear. Firms, for example, have multiple operations in different sectors of the economy and different parts of the world. This makes it virtually impossible to impute economic interests from products or position, as a given trade policy may help one part of operations and hurt another.

In her specific case, large multinational corporations, such as Citigroup and American Express, were key players and early and strong supporters of trade in services liberalization, as conventional trade models would predict. Their support of US trade policy helped to build a coalition and generate momentum for liberalization of trade in services in the Uruguay Round. At first glance, this account appeared to support the conventional story of large, powerful businesses recognizing the benefits they could reap from trade liberalization, and then using their power and resources to influence trade policy (p. 2). But there were also a range of other actors, such as NYNEX and regional telecommunications operators in the United States and Europe, who were more ambivalent activists; they did not necessarily stand to benefit from trade liberalization in clear-cut ways but eventually were major promoters of international liberalization. There were also late starters, such as public service companies in Europe, which had little enthusiasm for liberalization before the mid-1990s.

What does the difference between first movers, ambivalent activists, and late starters tell us about the true interests of firms and how they are activated? Woll argues that 'preference formation of economic actors is socially embedded' (p. 3). Beyond the thin rationality that talks about the efficiencies of means and distributional consequences of liberalization, which economic assumptions handle well, the regulatory and political arrangements among firms, governments, and competitors are decisive in defining the content and evolution of firms' interests. Without close attention to the changing political and social context of firms, the attempt to define preferences is doomed to failure. Thus, it is essential to track how political stances emerge in interaction with competitors and government representatives, with crucial shifts often hanging on ideational and strategic conditions. Woll readily acknowledges that firms act rationally in seeking to maximize their goals, once these goals are clear. But the process through which such goals become defined and altered requires problematizing the microfoundations of political economy that economic explanations simply take for granted (pp. 4–5).

Woll's most significant finding is that firm behavior and the goals economic actors pursue are embedded: because identities, beliefs, and political opportunities depend on the political and regulatory contexts, 'business lobbying varies between cases, even when material conditions would indicate that behavior should be similar' (p. 5). Economists, she writes, were not pleased by her commitment to take seriously the answers of businesspeople. If trade theories were inadequate to render a plausible and more fine-grained answer, they told her, then other economic theories (such as network economics or the economics of foreign investment) would surely be adequate, and certainly preferable to deploying wooly concepts such as norms and identities. For one simple reason, Woll decided against the route of ever greater disaggregation of firms' incentive systems: Since it was increasingly difficult for her to discern incentives by following this research strategy, how could such an approach guide firms in choosing their lobbying strategies?

Sociologists criticized her for the opposite reason. Rather than merging insights from the international political economy and sociological perspectives, they encouraged a straightforward sociological analysis of the micro-foundations of economic action. In their view, studying economic decision making at the macro-theoretical level through the prism of international relations theory would be a waste of time. Confronted by two strong disciplinary critiques that appeared to speak entirely different languages, Woll chose to write a more self-consciously eclectic book that would seek to build bridges between dueling analytical traditions. In doing so, she found inspiration in Max Weber's understanding of economic action as a type of social action, setting her sights on understanding how economic action under conditions of uncertainty can defy expectations based on the standard rational actor model (p. 7).

Firms do not behave in ways that contradict their economic interests. Rather, they make sense of their interests in a complex political environment that includes their historically embedded relations with governments and competitors (p. 8). The issue is not how to defend but how to define interests, particularly under conditions of uncertainty. Although neoclassical economists certainly pay close attention to uncertainty, Woll finds that they tend to employ a very narrow understanding, focusing on costs or benefits given the likelihood that an anticipated event will occur. Economists working in fields such as transaction costs or signaling attempt to model firms' confusion about their interests by predicting a time lag for informational updating. Building on these models, uncertainty is often reduced to a world of computable probabilities and risk assessments in the literature of international political economy. Actors have subjective probabilities and are assumed to rationally anticipate the choices of other actors based on information that is grounded in past behavior. Assuming that actors share the same information and the same subjective probabilities, this statistical form of computational rationality permits the calculation of risk in an uncertain environment.

In contrast, economic sociologists treat uncertainty as a more fundamental 'lack of knowledge about relationships between means and ends' (p. 9). Following the work of Jens Beckert (2002) and Mark Blyth (2006), Woll notes that gathering information is not only costly; its marginal utility cannot be determined. Economists may make sense of risk, which refers to a situation in which probabilities can be assigned. Coping with situations of uncertainty (as characterized by the economist Frank Knight), however, requires a different approach. Uncertainty refers to a situation where there is no information on which to base calculations of probabilities. In complex environments, actors do not calculate in isolation but make sense of their self-interests through their interactions with others. These interactions define, preserve, and transfer ideas about the proper relations between means and ends; shape which means to pursue; and predict the most likely courses of behavior. Such a socially and historically embedded conception of individual behavior argues that self-interested maximizing behavior lacks purposeful content and thus is radically indeterminate in what it can tell us about the world.

To analyze this form of behavior in institutional settings, Woll draws upon the notion of 'intentional action' as developed by Renate Mayntz and Fritz Scharpf (1995; Scharpf 1997) as well as the analysis of embedded economic action as developed by Mark Granovetter (1985). These approaches recognize the utility of combining a rational actor model with a sociological understanding of how routinized behavior and shared cognitive orientations enable individual action under conditions of uncertainty. This approach appeals to Woll because it refrains from universal generalization and instead seeks a 'middle ground' (p. 11) between predicting and understanding individual behavior. More importantly, it recognizes that regularities orient the behavior of economic actors, particularly in times of stability. At the same time, Woll emphasizes that divergence from this behavior under conditions of uncertainty can be better understood through the embeddedness perspective. Thus, for Woll, if firms can overcome uncertainty by updating economic information and then verifying whether assigned probabilities match up with facts, then one would expect merely a short time lag between change and actor adaptation. In situations of uncertainty, however, firms seek to reduce that uncertainty through reliance on any number of social or political devices such as networks, institutions, and alliances. Such devices are crucial features of any causal story that claims to specify which particular pathway will maximize self-interest in a given environment.

Woll's approach mirrors efforts to introduce complexity to the field of IPE, which she sees as dominated by an implicit material determinism that makes the evolution of the field at least partly a function of changes in material conditions (pp. 24–5). In contrast to materialist approaches, which treat preferences as exogenously given, constructivist approaches and historical institutionalism open the door to problematizing individual interests against the backdrop of the ideas, identities, and social relations that operate in a given environment. At the same time, there exists a crucial difference between emphasizing the causal priority of ideas as independent variables and making sense of the mutual constitution of ideas and interests in a given context. The latter, favored by Woll, requires the integration, but not the privileging, of constructivist insights into the complex process of preference formation. More importantly, Woll recognizes the centrality of analyzing specific contexts – including those in which materialist assumptions are unproblematic – rather than relying on programmatic statements or assumptions: 'recognizing that interests are intrinsically bound up with ideas is of little analytical value if scholars cannot specify when and how these mechanisms operate and what this implies for an understanding of policy change' (p. 17).

Woll's study focuses specifically on trade in services in the United States and Europe. The question driving her research has to do with the factors that shape the evolution of firms' objectives and behaviors in new contexts characterized by uncertainty. In contexts where new trade issues have arisen, the logic of international exchange is not yet clear, and firms may be operating in regulatory contexts in which they are not necessarily in direct competition. Under such conditions, traditional trade models, while helpful for predicting tariff negotiations in the trade of goods, come up short. Arguments emphasizing the pressure exerted by firms on the basis of a preexisting goal simply do not work. Instead, it is necessary to develop 'a nuanced conceptualization of business interest in international trade that takes into account ideational and strategic changes induced by firms' political and regulatory interactions' (p. 25). This process is shaped by contests over not whether, but how, to liberalize in a given sector. It is likely to vary across countries depending on their regulatory context.

Woll's empirical study, based primarily on interviews, focuses on negotiations related to the Basic Telecommunications Agreement of the World Trade Organization (WTO) and the liberalization of international aviation (particularly, the negotiation of a Transatlantic Common Aviation Area). Woll's studies confirm her intuition that traditional theory does not predict which actors ended up supporting liberalization, and they point to two more specific conclusions. First, the political institutional arrangements in Europe and the United States differ significantly, making it difficult to simply extend to Europe analyses of business–government relations as they have evolved in the United States. Europe's multi-level polity gives trade negotiators more liberty to ignore interest group pressure and to work selectively with those supporting their own objectives. For business lobbyists, this means that some demands are difficult to voice or simply unfeasible. This creates strategic constraints that shape outcomes in important ways, causing European firms to embrace policy positions that one would not expect in the American context. Varieties of political systems and regulatory regimes thus have an impact on preferences. Those variations need to be taken into account in comparative policy research and cannot simply be assumed away in order to facilitate simplified models predicated on fixed material incentives. In the case of trade in services in the United States and Europe, such models are demonstrably wrong.

Second, since political context is so important to preference formation, an atomistic and demand-side-driven model of interest formation is misleading. Governments are not merely arbitrators of competing demands, and government strategies do not merely conform to pressures from firms and other social actors. Rather, in the case of service trade liberalization, large service companies frequently shifted their positions, often in response to strategies and ideas coming from the government. The case studies and comparisons suggest that business demands do not merely determine, but are formed in response to, government policy. In the process, ideas and strategies interact to produce a more complex evolution of preferences on both sides: 'ideas explain how firms reorient their policy demands, while strategic changes trigger often profound transformations of firm preferences' (p. 19).

The final chapter of Woll's book takes up, as a pragmatically oriented eclectic study should, the implications of the study for normative and policy questions. Specifically, Woll is concerned about the nature of the power business wields and the importance of democratic decision making and accountability in international trade negotiations. Among other observations, she notes that the fluid nature of business interests in negotiations over new issue areas potentially enables greater participation in a more pluralist approach to global public policy. Although multinational firms still retain advantages over smaller firms, non-government organizations (NGOs), and social movements, trade negotiations increasingly take place in a more public sphere, enabling a more diverse set of actors to participate in the debates (p. 158). Moreover,

Box 4.3
Cornelia Woll – Getting it right

My education was not organized along the lines of American political science. After initial training in international relations at the University of Chicago, I moved back to Europe to work on a PhD in comparative politics and sociology. None of my colleagues was particularly interested in international relations theory. The theoretical value of my work was grounded in empirical findings. When I had to explain the stakes in international relations theory to colleagues outside that field, I treated the dominant strands as ordering devices that regrouped elements and methods present also in other disciplines. Because I did not consider the theoretical currents in international relations as paradigms, I was not particularly conscious of being eclectic when I began work on *Firm Interests* (Woll 2008).

Nonetheless, I wanted to address the literature in international political economy directly. The first real contact with colleagues in the field came when I began to try to publish my work. I quickly learned how paradigmatic the struggle in international political economy had become. Publishing is always difficult. The reactions to articles I submitted in comparative politics generally commented on whether or not the argument was empirically supported. In the field of international relations, reviewers were more concerned with paradigmatic and methodological issues. Picking a paradigm might have made my work more readily accessible to those working on similar issues. But I simply did not see how I could answer the most relevant questions from my research within one of the dominant approaches in international relations.

Eclectic reasoning is not an easy task. Academic work is always a compromise between the substance of our research and the constraints of our profession. Scientific innovation comes from crossing disciplinary boundaries and moving beyond paradigms. Yet education and evaluation need to be structured in recognizable fields in order to be transferable. For young scholars, it is very difficult to begin a career if they sit between all stools. I would therefore recommend an analytically eclectic approach only if the main theoretical argument speaks to an identifiable academic community elsewhere, even if it is outside of the field of international relations. Finally, to hedge against critics, scholars should not confuse 'getting it right' with 'making lots of interesting points.' The rule of thumb, 'one article – one message' seems particularly relevant for analytically eclectic scholarship to avoid falling into the trap of analytically informed real-world description.

in the case of the European Union, while European negotiators seek to expand their capacity to bargain with US counterparts, they also risk attenuating the already limited level of democratic accountability evident in EU trade policy decisions. Thus, Woll's analysis not only sheds light on the limits of trade theory, but also links her own analysis of negotiations over service liberalization to the need for formal and transparent rules for the participation of all economic and social actors in trade and other policy areas (p. 160).

Nicolas Jabko, *Playing the Market* (2006)

Europe's quiet revolution during the 1980s and 1990s gave renewed impetus to the idea of a united Europe, and produced a 'distinctive European model of political economy' (p. 2). This revolution, Jabko argues, is the result of a political strategy by initially weak and opportunistic political actors. This was true, specifically, of the European Commission, which smartly deployed ideas about market liberalization to build a broad-based coalition in favor of deep institutionalized integration. While the idea of Europe certainly had its committed advocates, they were probably in the minority until the 1980s. The plasticity of the market concept proved to be politically crucial in attracting other actors to a broadened coalition that favored the strengthening of European institutions. In developing his argument, Jabko questions standard characterizations of European integration as an opaque, elitist, ineffective, and technocratic project that has resulted in a growing democratic deficit. Instead, he sees the evolution of a 'Janus-faced European Union' (p. 179) that served as an ardent advocate of market liberalization and also managed to engineer the concentration of decision-making power at the supranational level.

In developing this argument, Jabko challenges three conventional arguments of European integration in the 1980s and 1990s, finding each to offer, at best, a partial account of the phenomenon. The most prevalent view treats European integration as fundamentally embedded in an inexorable process of market globalization. According to this utilitarian view, globalization shifted interests and power relations, enabling European multinational corporations and financial actors to gain influence and to promote market-friendly policies through the European Union. A second view is institutionalist. It emphasizes the path-dependent processes of change through which the European Union has expanded and become more deeply institutionalized, sometimes quickly and at other times more slowly. A third view is constructivist. It emphasizes the centrality of key ideas that become decisive in moments of uncertainty. In this view, the apparent failure of Keynesian policies in the 1970s paved the way for a more market-driven program for relaunching Europe in the 1980s. Each of these views, Jabko argues, 'sheds light on particular aspects of the broad structural and ideational context of late twentieth-century Europe.' However, none manages to adequately capture the politics that account for 'the pathbreaking nature of change in European economic governance in the 1980s and 1990s' (p. 3).

Jabko's own argument proceeds eclectically, drawing upon constructivist theories as well as insights of rationalist ones, to develop a complex analysis that emphasizes the creation of a political strategy in a time of uncertainty. Contra simplified utilitarian or institutionalist perspectives, Jabko sees ideas as playing a pivotal role in marking key shifts in both the evolution of the material interests of key actors and the development of institutional characteristics. At the same time, he veers away from typical constructivist treatments of ideas by emphasizing that 'ideas are important not so much as pure beliefs but because, in any given policy area, the parties involved must resort to ideas to articulate and advance their interests' (p. 8). These two reformulations combine to form the basis of what Jabko calls 'strategic constructivism.'

Jabko argues that the big push toward a distinctive European political economy in the 1980s and 1990s was a fundamentally important political project. It is best explained by the complex interaction between ideas and institutions that are activated by and acted upon by diverse coalitions of self-interested actors. Market reforms were promoted strategically in a manner that enabled actors with limited power resources to bring together new converts to the cause of European integration, while at the same time strengthening the social and economic structures of Europe. In the 1980s, European decision making thus moved to the center of the political stage. At the same time, success was not preordained, even for actors who thought and behaved strategically. Institutional inertia put up difficult roadblocks; but it also created political spaces, as Jabko highlights. Institutional contradictions and incongruities are both impediments and opportunities for creative political action.

The simultaneity of dynamic market liberalization and deep regional integration was possible because Europe's quiet revolution was not supported only by federalists or by ardent champions of other institutional solutions. Instead, it was aided also by a broad coalition of political actors with divergent political objectives. The new converts to Europe included supporters and opponents of free markets, adherents of the political Left and Right, bureaucrats and business leaders, and highly placed government officials in all countries. The coming together of so heterogeneous a political coalition was not a chance event but the result of a political strategy led by the European Commission, which fully understood the need to rally a broad constituency in support of its ambitious plans. Specifically, it engaged in a creative crafting of new institutional rules that were broadly acceptable to a heterogeneous coalition of actors under the rubric of a market-based Europe. The market provided a 'conveniently broad repertoire of justifications' for a diverse set of actors who 'were given a stake in the European Union's quiet revolution and thus encouraged to reframe their interests around the achievement of Europe's market and monetary integration agenda' (p. 6).

Standard institutionalist and constructivist arguments typically downplay tensions or incoherence in order to highlight the causal power of, respectively, institutions and ideas. In contrast, the originality of Jabko's argument is grounded in the possibility for the political exploitation of such tensions and incoherence. Since the Commission was more interested in the issue of power at the European level than in any specific approach to market reform, the programmatic coherence of the EU reforms was not a crucial imperative. Moreover, the European Commission varied its characterization of the market, playing up different and potentially competing ideas depending on its audience. It advocated Europe, both as a method of economic adaptation to novel market conditions and as a political approach to managing globalization.

For some, the market was a constraint that undermined existing institutions, but it was accepted on pragmatic grounds in the form of a single European entity. For others, it was understood as the most sensible and legitimate norm for organizing economic life, even in sectors such as energy that had been shielded from market competition for decades. For many, the market conveyed the idea of an energetic pursuit of economic prosperity; but since a market does not guarantee fair outcomes, it made sense to embrace the European Union's developmental efforts as a natural complement for advancing prosperity. Finally, the market represented what Jabko calls a 'talisman of political discourse' (p. 7), a political metaphor that served to bridge the chasm between those who ardently supported markets and those who were less committed but were willing to accept it as a pragmatic necessity in the pursuit of higher, normative goals. The idea and program of market reform were thus left ambiguous, an ambiguity that was never resolved precisely because 'the polyvalence of market ideas served to cement an otherwise heterogeneous coalition to a far-reaching reform agenda' (p. 7). This is what made the simultaneous extension of market reforms and buildup of political competence at the European level politically possible.

Jabko examines four cases to illustrate his argument. These cases capture variation in the pace, scope, focus, and profile of the most significant EU efforts to cope with market globalization. First, in sectors such as finance and telecommunication reform, market pressures were already in evidence, but market liberalization accelerated dramatically. In the case of the single financial area, a rapid succession of market-oriented reforms swept through banking, securities, and insurance. Financial regulations and administrative controls, in place since the Second World War, were quickly dismantled. This was followed immediately by the establishment of new regulatory frameworks wedded to market-based governance mechanisms. A second case examines the broad scope of market reforms that spread to sectors, such as energy, where market pressures were much less pressing than in finance or telecommunications. For example, although public utilities in the energy sector were subject to low market and technological pressures, early on the European Union imposed reforms on energy, and later in the electricity sector, as part of the single market initiative. The pace was gradual but the scope was broad, as reform steadily moved in the direction of full liberalization, and extended into areas that were at best tangential to the European Union's reform agenda. In some instances liberalization even led to the privatization of public sector corporations that had been in place for decades. The third case features reforms with divergent focus, as reflected in structural policies of regional development designed to enhance European competitiveness. These policies combined centralized control with decentralized implementation. Eventually structural policy became the second largest of the European Union's budget allocations, with significant amounts of financial resources redistributed among regions. Finally, the economic and monetary union (EMU) stands out as a case of a high-profile response to the process of market globalization. The creation of a central currency, the euro, managed by an independent European Central Bank (ECB), was a politically dramatic act with enormous, elusive long-term consequences. Economic and political gains and losses were difficult to estimate. But the symbolic significance of the reform escaped nobody. This reform involved a shift to more market-friendly policies while at the same time concentrating a great amount of power at the European level.

In the context of such varied cases, two features of the integration process stand out as puzzles that are better explained by Jabko's argument than by prevailing explanations. First, Europe's shift toward market-based governance does not correspond neatly with the strength of market pressures in various sectors, as a market-based utilitarian argument might suggest. In the fast-changing sectors of finance and telecommunications, for example, the move towards a single market merely accelerated existing domestic regulatory reform programs. The effects of a single market were discernibly stronger in sectors that provide collective services such as energy. Second, the shift of policymaking from national capitals toward Brussels went hand in hand with a reassertion, not dilution, of public power. For example, the EMU created a powerful ECB rather than transferring authority to markets. Indeed, inasmuch as EMU protected the European economy against currency fluctuations, it dampened rather than reinforced the operation of free markets. Europe's shift to market-based governance thus represents a conundrum (pp. 24–5). These two puzzles point to a story that goes beyond Europe's responses to market globalization and the ascent of neoliberal ideology. Both are important factors, but they need to be considered as part of the more complex argument that Jabko offers.

Jabko's analytic framework captures the complex interplay of ideas, institutions, and interests within the context of the emergence of a deliberately ambiguous political strategy that could support market reforms across quite diverse sectors with quite distinct characteristics. Rather than treating this framework as a general model of the process of supranational integration, Jabko restricts himself to the level of middle-range theory. He focuses on the European context in order to 'disaggregate the various elements of that process and evaluate theoretically derived hypotheses at a more concrete level' (p. 20). At the same time, he notes that the European Union's quiet revolution, while it could not be considered a

---

Box 4.4
Nicolas Jabko – Know thyself: Constructivism and strategy

When I started out my research as a graduate student at Berkeley, I identified, ontologically speaking, as a constructivist. (I still do.) But I already knew that I was not dogmatic about the power of ideas. When I began work on *Playing the Market* (Jabko 2006), my initial hypothesis was that actors pursued late-twentieth-century European integration under the banner of a coherent neoliberal doctrine. I thought that neoliberal ideas mattered a great deal because they were necessary to mobilize interests; but then, I also thought that actors had utilized these ideas for political purposes. In the course of my research, I was surprised to observe that EU actors were rarely very doctrinaire when they justified their actions in terms of 'the market.' So I ended up quite far from a pure version of constructivism that would identify ideas as straightforward causes. I now see myself as a constructivist who studies strategy, i.e., an object that many constructivists dismiss for dogmatic reasons. And I am thus more self-consciously anti-dogmatic – which, I guess, means eclectic – than when I started.

I have often noticed that many colleagues do not know how to make sense of me theoretically. Some mistake my work for a 'synthesis' between constructivism and rational choice. Others think (even worse!) that I am a closet rational choice scholar. So I find myself having to reassure constructivists that I am not the enemy. And I have to resist the pull of rational choice scholars who try to claim that what I say is not new and has already been said (but better) by them. In sum, I have learned that it's challenging to not be a well-behaved follower of one of the main political science churches.

My most important advice to would-be eclectic scholars is – however pompous it may sound – to 'know thyself.' To reject dogmatism should not be an excuse for adopting a lame mix of every existing approach in the literature. There is certainly something to learn from all the different approaches, but we also have to make clear ontological and epistemological choices. The most difficult part is not to make these choices, but to say something truly new and original. Frankly, I am not sure I have achieved that. But if I have, then I owe it as much to my firm commitments at the outset as to my desire to go beyond conventional approaches to Europe's integration.

commonplace occurrence, is not idiosyncratic. It represents an instance of contemporary institutional change, and as such, offers analytical observations that are potentially transferable to other situations – particularly the insight of the strategic opportunities opened up by institutional tensions and incongruities (p. 9).

Jabko's eclectic approach has important practical implications for the European Union. As he emphasizes, because of the historical specificity of the political processes that gave momentum to European integration, there is no guarantee that this momentum will continue given that the institutional context has changed since the turn of the century. It is even possible that 'the remarkable success of the integrationist strategy of the 1980s and 1990s could become a liability for future political integration' (p. 186). Jabko notes that while the European Union may have strengthened its capacity for supranational governance, this has not been at the expense of the member states' capacities, even in the area of monetary policy. Thus, the European Union, while more powerful than was anticipated in the 1970s, 'remains less than a federal state with a unified government' (p. 184). As such, it remains vulnerable when it comes to the legitimacy of its decision-making processes in the eyes of Europeans. Jabko notes: 'In the absence of a unified EU government elected by a united European people, there is still no fully legitimate selection procedure among competing actors and their visions at the EU level' (p. 9). This explains why the European Union's key actors tend to approach conflict resolution through deferment, approaching their separate agendas in roundabout ways to avoid the risks of popular backlash against the decision-making process. Even so, Jabko notes that the 'progressive decomposition' (p. 186) of the European Union is not unthinkable among some of its initial backers so long as Europe's internal market remains functional.

Richard Stubbs, *Rethinking Asia's Economic Miracle* (2005)

Stubbs starts his inquiry with the startling contrast of East Asia as the site of capitalism's most stunning economic miracle during the last two generations, and of some of the most devastating and horrendous wars during the second half of the twentieth century – from the Second World War to the wars in Korea and Vietnam. Scholars tend to view these two sets of phenomena as entirely separate, and their explanations for each tend to be embedded within mutually exclusive domains. Not so Stubbs. The central question that drives his book – and the answers he offers – emerge by juxtaposing what others have tended to compartmentalize. What are the causal connections between these two dramatic sets of phenomena in the same region?

Specifically, Stubbs seeks to challenge typical explanations of East Asia's economic miracle by expanding the scope of the problem to include the effects of a string of violent wars. Citing a World Bank study, Stubbs notes that, assuming a random distribution of economic growth, the chances of so high a concentration of growth in so condensed an area as East and Southeast Asia normally would be just 1 in 10,000 (p. 2). Could the recurrence of violent wars have something to do with the highly concentrated economic growth in seven highly successful East Asian countries – Japan, South Korea, Taiwan, Hong Kong, Singapore, Malaysia, and Thailand – over roughly the same period? The very formulation of the problem opens the door to a range of causal forces previously excluded by fiat in analyses of East Asia's economic growth.

Stubbs goes further by spinning out several more specific auxiliary questions that derive from this general conundrum. How exactly did the various 'hot wars' of the area as well as the more drawn-out Cold War impact capital formation and growth? And how did they influence the variation in levels of growth, since not all countries experienced the East Asian economic miracle? Furthermore, if the Cold War was so important for East Asian growth, what was the significance of the role played by the United States, and how did this role change with the attenuation and end of the Cold War? Did the patterns of economic growth and the political and economic legacies of the Cold War era have something to do with the dynamics of the Asian financial crisis and the subsequent revival of the region's economies? To what extent are these processes responsible for the growing sense of regionalism that appears to have emerged since the late 1990s?

Stubbs aligns five alternative explanations, some of which overlap, and all of which rival his own preferred account: neoclassical economic, statist, cultural, regionally hegemonic and Japan-centered, and globally hegemonic and American-centered. Each of these five explanations has a natural disciplinary home: economics, comparative politics, sociology and anthropology, and international relations. As a result, each is subject to blinders that preclude a more comprehensive understanding of the various political, economic, and social dynamics that have characterized patterns of economic change in East Asia.

For economists working in the neoclassical tradition, East Asia's miracle is due to 'getting prices right' and letting unfettered market competition, not governments, drive economic growth and take advantage of the opportunities the world market offers. Government should have a minimal role of protecting property rights (through the rule of law) and providing some public goods (such as national defense). Dismantling trade barriers; permitting markets to set foreign exchange and interest rates, the price of labor and inputs for industry; encouraging high savings, high rates of capital formation (both human and physical) and high investments in research and development; keeping exchange rates stable and effective; attracting foreign investment; and promoting the export of manufactured products – all of these will increase the chance of economic success. In brief, 'getting prices right' in competitive markets is the secret to success. This is precisely the East Asian story that neoclassical economists have researched in depth. But the story they have offered is, at best, only partial and leaves unexplored a number of important prior causes. Two in particular stand out. First, because neoclassical economists were ahistorical in their approach, they could not account for the resources – capital, technology, and a skilled labor force – that proved critical for the development of export-oriented strategies and an expansive economic infrastructure. Second, because the economic explanation failed to take seriously the role of government, it completely missed the causal significance of state intervention in the most successful cases of economic growth, in areas ranging from coordinating the development of particular industries to the shift to export-oriented industrialization and the overall orchestration of the economy.

The statist explanation focuses on the guiding hand of the state rather than the invisible hand of the market. It sees the state as driving East Asian economies to their unrivalled success. States not only plan the general strategy of economic development but often intervene in specific sectors to micromanage choices at the sectoral or firm level. Industrial policy becomes the hallmark of state intervention. Advantage is not comparative by the logic of markets, but competitive by the logic of politics. East Asia's miracle is derivative of the innovation of a 'developmental state.' As Alice Amsden (1989) famously argued, the secret to success was to have 'gotten prices wrong' deliberately – by directing industrial capital into particular high-growth sectors. But statists also confronted troubling questions to which they did not have good answers. What kind of state intervention is most effective in causing high growth? Should it be market conforming or market distorting? Furthermore, statist explanations do not consider the changing global economic environment. With the growing interconnectedness of the global economy, governments are increasingly at a disadvantage to intervene effectively, lacking both relevant information and political capacity. And given the difficulties encountered by weak states seeking to engineer growth in the developing world, what is it about the state in the East Asian region that enabled such effective forms of intervention in each of the seven most successful economies?

The quarrel between the two perspectives was not resolved either by the World Bank's 1993 special report on East Asia, or by the Asian financial crisis. The World Bank report leaned toward the economist explanation while offering plenty of data that supported the statist case. And the Asian financial crisis of 1997 turned out to be the result of the meddling of increasingly corrupt Asian governments in the setting of interest and exchange rates, as well as the increasingly rapid movement of hot, speculative, global capital that national governments were no longer seeking or able to regulate.

The other three explanations, though less prominent than the first two in debates over East Asian economic growth, also have their own distinctive contributions and limitations. The culturalist argument focuses on the specific cultural traits of Japan and East Asia. As a value system that is shared across many parts of the region, Confucianism (sometimes in combination with Buddhism) and its core elements – such as family loyalty, obedience to legitimate authority, and the value placed on education and duty – are thought to have given rise to distinctive patterns of industrial relations and economic development. The cultural argument, however, cannot account for either change over time (considering the long period of economic stagnation before China's economic growth) or the emergence of high-growth economies in Southeast Asian countries without strong Confucian legacies (Malaysia, for example). Japan-centered explanations draw attention to the unintended beneficial effects of Japan's colonial occupation as well as its role as an engine and a model for East Asia's postwar economic take-off. However, this explanation also falls short, since it leaves out the story of economic growth in places not colonized by Japan (for example, Hong Kong, Singapore, Malaysia, all former British colonies, as well as Thailand, which maintained its independence), and ignores the fact that many economies that supposedly benefited from Japanese aid and investment in the 1970s were already heading towards sustained economic growth. Finally, explanations centered on American hegemony or primacy, while useful in pointing out the significance of the continuing and multidimensional interests of the United States in the region, fail to account for either the manner in which American hegemony might impact economic growth or the emergence of regional variations across East and Southeast Asia.

In this thicket of theories, no one theory is truly compelling by itself. Yet for Stubbs, the contributions and limitations of the five explanations suggest some conclusions. First, history and geography matter. It is only through their lenses that we can appreciate fully all the different factors that have shaped Asia's economic miracle. Second, the explanations operate at different levels of analysis – global, regional, and national; all three levels, Stubbs argues, need to be integrated into a comprehensive analysis. Finally, any useful analysis must specify correctly the decision-making processes and economic and administrative policies in East Asian countries. It is not enough to simply assert the relevance of multiple factors. Stubbs' own explanation is developed against the background of these partly complementary and partly rivaling explanations. He offers an original account, centered on the effects of recurrent major wars, that provides an overarching explanation for the emergence or impact of factors posited in existing explanations.

Put simply, the key to economic success in East and Southeast Asia was fighting wars and the preparation for wars, as well as the geopolitics of the region and the anti-Communist containment policy of the United States. Apart from its direct effects on economic variables such as investments and consumption, the historical sequencing of these factors had a profound impact on institutional arrangements and policies. That said, wars should be conceived of broadly, encompassing devastating conflicts such as the Second World War as well as localized insurgencies or terrorist campaigns. In addition, specific circumstances matter. For example, the Korean and Vietnam wars occurred in different parts of the region, had different effects on different countries, and drew the United States into regional affairs in different ways. Yet, despite these differences in context, war and the threat of war had remarkably similar effects in each of the seven countries where economic success followed. Wide political and policy differences narrowed over time. And these similarities carried forward into the 1990s, shaping the economic rise of China and the growing importance of regionalism as a political force.

War is a horrible political institution. But it is one that can have profound effects, as it did in the case of East Asia, on individuals, institutions, society, and economy. In classifying the consequences of wars, or preparation for wars, Stubbs builds on the work of Bruce Porter (1994). First, war's effects are *destructive* and *disintegrative*, featuring loss of life, social and political dislocation, and the weakening or destruction of the state. But war preparations and war fighting are also *formative* and *developmental*, with long-term consequences for society and economy. Not only do territorial gains provide new resources, but external threats provide a basis for unifying society, justifying expanded state bureaucracies, and boosting employment related to the development of new war-fighting technologies. Finally, wars can be *reformative* and *redistributive*. Mobilization of society in the context of an ongoing or imminent war provides a basis for socializing and educating larger portions of the population, while government intervention in the economy as well as increased government spending can become established as legitimate.

The magnitude of each of these effects certainly differs across space, depending on where wars break out and how they are fought. States in whose territories wars are fought will experience the destructive and disintegrative effects more than others. States that are peripheral to but allied with the actual fighting will experience the formative, reformative, and redistributive effects most strongly. And the manner in which civil and guerilla wars are fought will determine the relative strengths of disintegrative and formative effects. Duration and timing also matter. In the presence of the threat of war or during the early stages of war, formative effects will predominate. As wars drag on, however, disintegrative effects tend to become more pronounced.

Stubbs is not interested, however, in employing the similarities and variations to build a universal theory of how war affects economic growth. Different settings and experiences lead to different outcomes. The seven most successful economies (including Japan, South Korea, Taiwan, and Singapore) are readily distinguished from the Philippines and Indonesia, which have not grown nearly as rapidly. Stubbs' concern is with articulating a more modest argument revealing the similarities in the complex processes through which the various 'hot' wars and the all-encompassing Cold War influence the prospects for economic growth. His argument is 'that economic success was the product of the virtuous interplay of a number of social, political and economic institutions and that these institutions were shaped in good part by the regional and international geopolitical environment' (p. 25).

The economic success of the seven most advanced economies in East and Southeast Asia, Stubbs argues, was the result of the beneficial interactions of a variety of social, economic, and political institutions, each of them affected by the repeated onset or threat of war in the region. These institutions regularized procedures, practices, and norms that structure the relations between individuals and groups, ranging from formal institutions (such as parliaments and government bureaucracies) to informal ones (such as government–business links and networks of politicians). Economic activity results from these institutions. Indeed, markets are the most central institution of any economy, accompanied, complemented, or rivaled by state institutions. Yet, the efficacy of markets has depended crucially on the emergence of a strong developmental state capable of managing the public–private divide and enlisting a well-trained elite bureaucracy to promote economic growth as part of a national project to ensure survival in a hostile environment (p. 29). Crucial for Stubbs' argument is an extension of Peter Evans's (1995b) concept of 'embedded autonomy': both state and markets are embedded to different degrees in society, with social ties and institutional channels providing the basis for balancing autonomy and embeddedness (p. 27). Also significant are cultural factors – particularly ideas, values, beliefs, and norms. They influence how a society perceives threats, how its range of options is constrained, and how certain policy proposals are legitimized (p. 33).

Stubbs' argument also takes advantage of important concepts developed by historical institutionalism. Path dependency is relevant to Stubbs' causal story in the durability of institutions and institutional arrangements established at some initial point: although circumstances change and create pressures for institutional change, initial policy choices and institutional interactions can certainly delay or prevent the emergence of new institutions and policies. Critical junctures also feature prominently in Stubbs' account. Relatedly, feedback processes can strengthen or weaken the viability of an original institutional arrangement; although the longer an arrangement is in place, the more likely it is that

Box 4.5
Richard Stubbs – Experience leading to eclecticism

My approach to undertaking the research for *Rethinking Asia's Economic Miracle* (Stubbs 2005) was heavily influenced by an eclectic set of academic experiences. As a student in Britain I delved into aspects of twentieth-century history, strategic studies, and 'English school' realism. In Canada, I spent an intriguing year in a Department of Political Science, Sociology and Anthropology, and later, my doctoral years in a relatively conventional Political Science Department. In 1972 I went to Malaysia to carry out research for my doctoral thesis on the Malayan Emergency. While there, I discovered how significant the Korean War-induced commodity boom had been for the government's counterinsurgency campaign, and how crucial the combination of the two had been for the subsequent economic, political, and administrative development of the country. At the same time, as I traveled around the region I experienced first-hand the economic, social, and political impact that America's prosecution of the Vietnam War had on Singapore, Thailand, and Malaysia.

Out of these experiences, I began to explore the links between security and regional and international political economy issues. However, my tentative eclecticism was challenged at a series of informal Toronto-based workshops on the emerging East Asian regionalism, by thoughtful and knowledgeable colleagues from a variety of disciplines and different international relations and comparative politics paradigms. I was forced to take their points into consideration and to think through my ideas in a more systematic way, a process that was reinforced by teaching graduate courses on the regional political economy and comparative politics of East Asia.

The key to research, then, was finding a compelling empirically, rather than theoretically, driven puzzle. My puzzle was the relationship between East and Southeast Asia's conflict-ridden recent history and its dynamic economic development. Frustratingly, I discovered that many analyses of the region's prosperity were more attempts to use the East and Southeast Asian experience as a way of confirming the supremacy of one paradigm over another than they were explorations of the complex interplay of the multiple factors that led to the region's economic success. However, it is clearly important to stay open to empirical findings derived from theoretically driven enquiries as well as to see value in theoretical approaches from various sub-disciplines in political science as well as cognate disciplines. Certainly, the amalgam that was provided by fusing paradigms and empirical findings from political science with those from history, economics, sociology, and geography proved extremely productive.

self-reinforcing positive feedback will outweigh negative feedback, making it difficult to choose alternative pathways. In addition, timing and sequence affect the manner in which the effects of crises can be magnified or diffused in a given context; in Stubbs' argument, the sequence in which the destructive, formative, or reformative effects of war are felt is particularly significant (p. 32).

In the end, Stubbs' argument stands out for its effort to provide a comprehensive explanation. While aspects of his analysis have been developed in isolation by various other scholars, Stubbs seeks to establish the linkages between these aspects within specific regional and international geopolitical contexts. This process requires cutting across levels of analysis to connect international and domestic factors in ways that neither international relations scholars nor students of comparative politics are inclined to do. The result is an eclectic analysis that not only provides an original explanation for high economic growth in East Asia, but also provides insights into how regional and international geopolitics – particularly war and the threat of war – influences many of the factors that are posited by proponents of competing explanations. This points to a more comprehensive understanding of security which incorporates and has implications for both scholars and policymakers who tend to underestimate the 'security dimension' (p. 238) in discussions of economic policy and economic growth. Stubbs' analysis also provides a balanced view of institutional change, recognizing the changes that have resulted from crises or from subsequent global pressures, as well as the slowness of the change owing to the political and social embeddedness of institutions (p. 239). At the same time, Stubbs is fully aware that his analysis does not offer obvious lessons for developing countries that have not experienced wars or a sustained threat of war. For such countries, more creative efforts are needed to provide the capital necessary for boosting state capacity and promoting economic development and social stability (p. 240).

Conclusion

All five scholars whose work we have discussed in this chapter are deeply committed to rigorous scholarship that is driven not by dogmatic commitments to paradigms, but by interesting substantive problems. The books reviewed above are not the only ones adhering to an eclectic stance in the study of international political economy. Nor is analytic eclecticism a necessary condition for excellent scholarship on political economy. In our search for books that exemplify an eclectic approach, we have run across many studies that, while not meeting our specific criteria, are truly impressive in their originality, sophistication, and methodological rigor. We have also been constrained by space and time from discussing other works that are more obviously eclectic. Having said that, we believe that the books discussed above illustrate well the benefits of problem-driven eclecticism in framing and analyzing questions of interest to diverse communities within and beyond the academe.

The five studies collectively make a strong case for the promise of eclecticism in analyzing different facets of the global political economy. Seabrooke offers a novel analysis that connects domestic politics to states' relative positions in global finance. Sinclair examines the various mechanisms and processes through which rating agencies have acquired power in the global financial system. Woll inquires into the changes in politics and perceptions accompanying the liberalization of telecommunications and air transport. Jabko studies the evolution of a distinctive political strategy that enabled key actors to promote market liberalization while engineering support for supranational governance structures. And Stubbs explores the connections between war-fighting and preparations for war, on the one hand, and the dynamic growth experienced by seven East Asian economies, on the other. All five certainly fall outside of the 'American IPE monoculture' (Weaver 2009, p. 1), at least insofar as this is currently identified with the sort of open-economy politics embraced by David Lake (2009) and others. To varying degrees, each exhibits the three features that we employ to identify and distinguish eclectic scholarship in international relations (see Table 1.1 in Chapter 1).

First, each of the books has identified and articulated problems that extend beyond the theoretical scope of competing paradigms in international political economy. Stubbs, for example, articulates a problem that connects issues – the patterns of war-fighting and the dynamics of economic growth – normally explored in very different literatures. Seabrooke similarly explores a research question that requires connecting the distribution of states' financial power in the international economy to patterns of domestic politics related to social policy. These and the other works examined above are all creative in their effort to identify a puzzle that is substantively interesting, rather than useful for refining existing paradigm-bound theories or advancing intra-paradigm progress.

Second, in their theoretical aspirations, all five studies operate at or near the level of middle-range theory, taking spatial and temporal contexts seriously but seeking out mechanisms and processes that are, at least in principle, portable to comparable cases. The majority of the authors do not, like Seabrooke and Woll, explicitly use the language of causal mechanisms in formulating their arguments. They do, however, forgo the search for parsimony and instead offer complex causal stories that draw together a wide range of factors and logics drawn from diverse paradigm-bound theories.

Third, the five works generate findings that are explicitly or implicitly related to the practical challenges that policymakers and ordinary actors encounter. Jabko, for example, cautions against treating European integration as an irreversible evolutionary process. Sinclair's analysis, especially in light of the recent American and global financial crises, raises important questions about the authority universally bestowed upon ratings agencies originally set up in the United States. The authors do not necessarily start off with the intention of offering policy prescriptions; but they are self-conscious about how the problems they investigate and the analytic frameworks they offer bear on important issues of policy and practice.

In reading the assessments the five authors themselves give of their road to eclectic scholarship (see Boxes 4.1 to 4.5), one cannot help but be struck by the relationship between biography and scholarship. All of the authors mention, of course, that empirical puzzles require answers that normally transcend the explanatory power and causal stories of any one paradigm. But beyond that, they reveal how their own intellectual and personal journeys proved to be very important in shaping their eclectic scholarship. Whereas the scholars featured in Chapter 3 were mostly raised and trained in the United States, our search for eclectic scholarship on questions of political economy has led us, unexpectedly, to scholars who have been trained elsewhere or spent significant time studying or working outside the United States. For whatever reasons, the American academy may have had a particularly strong effect on shaping the field of international political economy.

Seabrooke, for example, received his training in Australia, where his intellectual journey led him to reject predetermined conclusions derived from normatively committed scholarship. Instead, he embarked on a search for alternatives to this kind of 'plug'n'play' mode of argumentation to find eventually an eclectic approach to political economy that harkened back to Max Weber's sociological concepts and to 'quirky' scholars who offered more interesting insights than did the 'default' model of scholarship. Woll began her training in the United States but soon thereafter moved to Europe; in the process, she also moved from international relations to comparative political economy and politics. Living between different worlds, she was in a position conducive to picking and choosing different analytic elements from different intellectual traditions to solve puzzles that interested her. Like Seabrooke, she has made peace with the paradigm-driven criticisms that she has encountered along the way; she views them not as an obstacle that impedes her research but rather as a spur that serves to validate her eclectic strategy.

Sinclair was born in New Zealand, received his undergraduate degree in England, and did his doctoral training in Canada. This path coincided with his road to eclectic scholarship, which began when he found both Marxism and modern economics to be inadequate for understanding the world he encountered as a junior analyst working for New Zealand's Department of the Treasury. Sinclair did not set out to be eclectic, which was the 'ultimate taboo' in graduate school; but his search for answers to the functioning and consequences of markets led him to recognize the role of various actors, institutions, and knowledge structures in the making of markets. Stubbs's training in the United Kingdom and Canada grounded him broadly in intellectual terms, and his dissertation field research experience in Southeast Asia showed him at first hand the important linkages that connect war and the economy. As a result of both his training and his experience he was able to develop his causal story, informed by rigorous disciplinary criticisms he received along the way.

Jabko was born in France and went to Berkeley for his graduate training before returning to France to begin his academic career at Sciences-Po. But it is his internal journey that is more relevant to his scholarship. Anchored in constructivist ontology but without a rigid analytic dogmatism, he advises us to know ourselves as individuals and to be clear about our ontological and epistemological choices. Of the five authors, Jabko is perhaps the most clear in emphasizing that eclecticism cannot be treated as a new dogmatic commitment or an excuse to unthinkingly combine every possible argument. Original analyses and novel insights follow from balancing our initial commitments as individual scholars with a willingness to go beyond conventional arguments.

It is impossible to synthesize these varied intellectual and personal journeys into a guide on how to conduct eclectic research on global political economy. Although it is conceivable that further evolution of international relations scholarship away from paradigm-centered to eclectic work might generate greater demands for such a guide, we remain skeptical about the utility of such a venture. Analytic eclecticism as we define it is incompatible with the idea of rigid injunctions or formulas for how to define and analyze political economy. What we can do fruitfully is to take seriously the insights of scholars who self-consciously resist identification with any particular paradigm; to ask whether the motivations and principles guiding their work match the three criteria we have been employing to identify eclectic scholarship in international relations; and to consider the contribution of each work to scholarly dialogue as well as to normative and policy debates beyond the academe. This is what we seek to do in the concluding chapter in relation to all of the substantive topics in this book. For now, we turn to eclectic approaches to problems related to regional and global governance.

Chapter 5

Order and governance, regional and global

The contemporary study of world politics consists of more than the analysis of security and political economy and the focus on states and markets in world politics. States are both too big for some tasks and too small for others. Markets are both spontaneous and constructed. And the international system shows both great continuity and dramatic, often unexpected change. Some of the most interesting processes in current world politics evolve beyond, around, and in between states, markets, and the international system.

Recent developments in security and economic affairs make the analysis of world politics a vibrant field of scholarship and reveal the need for more encompassing analytic schemes. The broadening of notions of security as attached to individuals and human communities and not just to states and nations, for example, indicates that governments confront a greatly altered and more complex security agenda than that of a few decades ago. Public health and global warming have direct and indirect security implications for state and citizen that do not come into clear focus if we analyze only traditional interstate relations. Similarly, the 2008 financial crisis that led to a freezing of capital markets and a freefall of international trade originated in the United States. Its ramifications, however, were global. European banks in particular were as badly affected as American banks. And the future of American fiscal policy and the weakness of the American dollar will put not only American but also Chinese savings at risk. These observations point to the need for problematiques and analytic frameworks that identify emergent forms of regional and global governance that go beyond international rivalries or the balance of power and beyond the interplay of global and national markets.

During the last several decades, scholars have attempted to develop a conceptual vocabulary that stretched conventional boundaries of analysis and anticipated later eclectic approaches to transnational forms of governance. Within the context of realism, for example, balance-of-power theory was adapted to support a new theory of hegemonic stability that sought to account for the political changes that followed with the end of the fixed exchange rate system, the oil price increase of 1973, and the US defeat in Vietnam. Spurred by anxieties that international politics could again drift towards 1930s-style protectionism, hegemonic stability theory invited international relations students to rethink the fundamentals of international politics with the aid of a concept that had its origin in Antonio Gramsci's writings on Italian politics during the interwar period. The distribution of material capabilities thus became a basis not only for the balance of power but also for the possibility of powerful hegemons deploying their resources to support enduring institutions of governance. Complementing that effort and taking their cue from the field of international organization and law, scholars articulated the concept of international regime. The elaboration of regime theory was an attempt to understand the continuation of order, absent a hegemon, in various issue areas of world politics. Constructivism of course arrived later, taking the place of Marxism among the three prevalent paradigms. As a newcomer to the study of transnational order and governance, it had to contend with well-developed arguments and analytic frameworks that realists and liberals had been developing for some time. It is not surprising, then, that contemporary treatments of regional and global governance frequently build on versions of the three dominant paradigms which were being stretched unduly, opening the door to greater analytic eclecticism.

Anticipating today's canonical distinction between realism, liberalism, and constructivism, European integration theory during the 1950s and 1960s had three main strands. In their analysis of European affairs, realists were skeptics who insisted that states would not relinquish their sovereign prerogatives on questions that mattered most (Hoffmann 1966). In contrast, functionalists like Ernst Haas (1958, 1964) argued instead that the logic of integration was dynamic and would convince states to surrender more of their sovereignty claims as the efficiency costs of not doing so became clearer. Finally, communication theorists like Karl Deutsch (1957) remained skeptical that any progress in European integration was actually occurring, as underlying rates of national communication, trade, and integration outpaced observable international ones, suggesting that collective identity formation at the European level was going to be a very slow affair at best. As was true of the 1980s and 1990s, the paradigmatic debates of the 1960s were spirited and strong. At the same time, these debates were mitigated by the fact that all the major protagonists shared a strong substantive interest in Europe, to which each had strong personal ties. Hoffmann, Haas, and Deutsch were all brilliant, first-generation immigrant scholars who had made it to the United States between the 1930s and 1950s. Their debates reflected distinct analytic prisms that would shape later debates on the possibilities for governance, in Europe and elsewhere.

Half a century later each of the three perspectives, refurbished in the language of contemporary realism, liberalism, and constructivism, finds its central claim supported by some aspects of the empirical record. Although EU member states are coordinating their foreign policies more effectively now than in the 1960s, realists are correct in pointing to the lack of any substantive evidence indicating that any state is willing to relinquish sovereign control over the many issues it considers to be vital to its national security. The emergence of a multi-level European governance system in the European Union, liberals correctly insist, is pooling sovereignty across numerous policy domains that once had been under sole national control. In addition, constructivists can point to the growing density of Europe's social interactions and cultural shifts, which have facilitated the emergence of a collective European identity, especially at the level of elites, alongside (but not in place of) existing national identities.

In response to dramatic changes in the international economy in the 1970s, however, Europe receded as the prime focus of international relations theory. The move to flexible exchange rates, the revolution in oil markets that followed in the wake of OPEC's dramatic price increases in 1973, and the US defeat in Vietnam signaled to many that an era had come to an end. Against this backdrop, the central question became what would hold the world together in an era of US decline. Without US leadership, would the world slip back into protectionism, depression, and war, as during the 1930s? Or would it find new ways of defending the advances of the past without the presence of a central power? Realists and liberals offered different answers to that question.

Looking at the 1930s, pessimistic realists expected international politics to turn dramatically worse with the receding of American influence. In their analysis, order and peaceful change rested on the balance of material capabilities. Irresponsible behavior and political instabilities were preordained as the Organization of Petroleum Exporting Countries (OPEC), other raw material cartels, and the Group of 77 (Third World states) demanded a New International Economic Order while lacking the capabilities to either impose or defend new rules. Optimistic realists argued instead that US capabilities were not declining as dramatically as pessimists were assuming, and that any change in world affairs would be gradual. The difference between pessimists and optimists was rooted in different conceptualizations of power. Pessimists focused primarily on material capabilities, and paid little attention to the ideational dimensions of power that the optimists were also taking into account. In the latter view, what continued to make the United States a powerful actor was in part its ability to persuade, inspire, and serve as a model for others. This view was influenced by the Marxist tradition, specifically the strand closely associated with the work of Antonio Gramsci. Most realists related more easily to the behavioral than the structural aspects of Gramsci's arguments about power and hegemony, and thus failed to ponder whether the observed behavioral changes pointed to a mere modification or to a fundamental transformation in the structure of world politics.

Liberals offered a very different answer, although they too felt Gramsci's influence. They agreed that American hegemony had ended and that the recalibration of power had created a world 'after hegemony,' as captured by the title of Robert Keohane's (1984) book. Keohane's analysis went beyond his earlier study of complex interdependence (Keohane and Nye 1977) to combine elements of liberal and realist theory while departing from 'the crude theory of hegemonic stability' (1984, p. 39). For Keohane, a refined, more loosely structured version of hegemonic stability theory could serve as an interpretive framework that, while not a full-blown explanatory theory, could help to reconceptualize the meaning and significance of hegemony in another way. Such an approach would not simply explain outcomes in terms of power, but lay out the features of an international system in which leadership is exercised by a single state. Significantly, Keohane (1984, pp. 43–5) explicitly noted that his analysis is substantively, if not terminologically, similar to that of Karl Kautsky, and that his approach is deeply indebted to Gramsci's conceptualization of hegemony. In short, in Keohane's analysis of the problem of international hegemony, the boundaries of liberalism were being stretched to incorporate insights from competing traditions, including the soon-to-be-marginalized tradition of Marxism.

A different liberal perspective stressed the rise of more 'complex interdependence' (Keohane and Nye 1977) and increasingly robust international regimes as taking the place of American hegemony in providing a degree of governance (Krasner 1983). These regimes were traceable, if not in full-blown organizations, then in the growing coordination of state policies across discrete policy domains such as trade, money, finance, and energy. Spurring on this process were the convergent expectations and interests of states that had been shaped by and benefited from the US-centered international order after 1945. To be sure, the relative importance of principles, rules, norms, and decision-making procedures varied across issues and periods. But overall, regimes were more durable than pessimistic realists were willing to recognize, and less dependent on American power than optimistic realists were arguing. At the same time, the theoretical horizon of liberals remained limited by its continuing view of the world from the perspective of state interests, treating international organizations as handmaidens of the state with virtually no agency of their own. International regimes were simply sites for the strategic interaction among states.

With the end of the Cold War, scholarship on world politics changed once more. The disintegration of the Soviet Union, the preponderance of US political and economic power in the 1990s, and the growing prominence of globalization heralded a further stage of theorizing about processes that rivaled or complemented the world of national states and markets. The 1990s became the decade of globalization. This concept was embraced enthusiastically by those focusing on new changes and seeking new opportunities – Wall Street bankers as much as Chinese entrepreneurs, media moguls as much as savvy consumers. Globalization optimists talked about the compression of time and space, and the creation of new communities and possibilities. New sets of positive and negative externalities and the attendant policy interdependencies would diffuse throughout an increasingly borderless globe. In its strong version, globalization theory replicated core features of the technological determinism seen in 1960s theories positing the transformation of societies driven by evolving technologies. In its weaker version, it refined liberal theories of the 1970s emphasizing the effects of complex interdependence and transnational processes (Keohane and Nye 1977). Globalization skeptics insisted that the phenomena picked up by the new theory were in fact manifestations of age-old processes of internationalization that had existed for many decades, even centuries. The World Wide Web was simply a global version of the Internet, an invention funded by the US Department of Defense. Flows of capital and information may have sped up, but they were not qualitatively different from the increase in flows of capital and information made possible by earlier shifts in technology. Internationalization describes processes of increasing dynamic density that do not fundamentally transform the character of actors, such as states, corporations, groups, or movements. Instead, these actors fundamentally remain who they were, continuing to drive and to a substantial degree control the extent, pace, and direction of the various dimensions of globalization.

Finally, 9/11 refocused scholarly attention on the concepts of empire and world region, building on themes that had been theorized differently in different contexts in the 1960s and 1970s. After the attacks of 9/11, the quick victory of US troops over the Taliban government initially seemed to offer a striking contrast to the inability of the Soviet army to win a decisive victory over Afghanistan in the 1980s. In addition, it expedited the Bush administration's adoption of a national security doctrine of preemptive attack and a foreign policy of unilateralism. Both were implemented over widespread opposition in the United States and throughout the world, as was evident in reactions to the US decision to attack Iraq based on, at best, flimsy evidence of Iraq's concealed weapons of mass destruction (WMD) program. A new body of literature began to re-evaluate international and global governance through the concept of empire, in light of this dramatic change in US foreign policy. Supportive of the foreign policy agenda of neoconservatives in the administration, such as Paul Wolfowitz, and enamored by their partial reading of the benefits and costs of the British Empire, some observers openly advocated a return to imperial policies (Ferguson 2004a, 2004b). Others were more dispassionate, pointing to the structural transformations in world politics that made empire an impossible form of international order (Brzezinski 2004). Still others analyzed the American empire in historical perspective (Maier 2006) or acknowledged that, as had been true of past empires, the United States occupied a position that was qualitatively different from that of all other states today (Münkler 2007).

Beyond the study of empires, the aftermath of 9/11 has also spurred investigations into the characteristics of world regions. This literature builds on elements in the European integration literature, albeit in less Eurocentric fashion. Going beyond studies of national security and international political economy that happen to focus on particular areas of the world, the scholarship on regions is evolving towards a multi-disciplinary understanding of how geography, history, political economy, security, and identity concerns combine to produce distinctive regional responses to typical issues in international relations (Buzan and Waever 2003; Katzenstein 2005; Lewis and Wigen 1997; Mansfield and Solingen 2010; Solingen 1998). Here, too, we see distinct strands of analysis emerging from quite different theoretical and disciplinary perspectives, along with efforts to cut across theoretical and disciplinary boundaries in eclectic fashion. Classical theories of geopolitics stress the material base of regions. One argument, for example, traces the dynamics of regional politics to the nature of the terrain or the imperatives of land or sea power. Ideational theories of geography insist that regions are not given but politically and culturally made. Regions are not only shaped by processes that separate economic cores from peripheries. Regional symbols act also as instruments or labels designating the domination of specific places in the world by particular groups of people. Space, in ideational theories, is a social invention and practice. And from the perspective of behavioral theories of geography, the variable of spatial distance in different regions was thought to have a direct and statistically robust effect on the behavior of actors in those regions. Each of these approaches offers important partial insights, but none independently provides a satisfactory account of how actors define and understand regions or their place in them. Here is where analytic eclecticism, supported by the inherent interdisciplinarity of geographical science, can open the door to more comprehensive frameworks that reveal connections between the mechanisms and processes privileged by each of the three approaches.

During the last 40 years, international relations research thus has given us ample conceptual material to deploy eclectic styles of analysis. These broad shifts in theoretical concepts and frameworks have their roots in past theoretical debates. They also reflect the limits of the major international relations paradigms in capturing the complex processes through which state and non-state actors have sought to establish order and governance in regional and global contexts. The possibilities for integration and institutionalized cooperation across borders, the reconstruction of hegemony as a possible foundation for order in a system with a single dominant state, the reformulation of the concept of empire to characterize the far-reaching power and foreign policies of one state, and efforts rooted in geography to analyze the shape and structure of regional orders – all point to the need to extend our analyses of contemporary forms of governance beyond existing theoretical frameworks constructed solely around familiar problems of security and political economy. The studies considered in this chapter take important steps in this direction, employing eclecticism to analyze the internal dynamics of international organizations (Barnett and Finnemore 2004); the character and accomplishments of the International Criminal Court (ICC) (Schiff 2008); the importance of legitimacy in the deliberations and decisions of the UN Security Council (Hurd 2007); the eastward expansion of European regional organizations such as the European Union and the North Atlantic Treaty Organization (NATO) (Schimmelfennig 2003); and the negotiation and evolution of regional order in Southeast Asia (Ba 2009).[1]

Michael Barnett and Martha Finnemore, *Rules for the World* (2004)

Barnett, who had the opportunity to work at the United Nations, and Finnemore, who had previously done research on the World Bank, note at the beginning of their book (2004) that their training and academic engagements had not prepared them for 'what international organizations were *really* like' (p. vii). Through the 1980s, the field of international relations took little notice of international organizations, focusing instead on relations among states. Even those who were concerned with international governance framed their arguments around interdependence and convergent interests among states. When the field did eventually begin to think about international organizations, it was through the lens of microeconomic theories of organization. This generated a positive normative bias by defining international organizations as instruments that help states to cooperate and diffuse good norms. For Barnett and Finnemore, international organizations (IOs) are neither passive instruments that states manipulate to achieve their objectives, nor intrinsically positive facilitators of cooperation.

Instead, IOs are characterized by 'the logic of bureaucracy' (p. viii), and as such exercise power through the impersonal rules they construct. In the process, however, they can produce both positive change and 'undesirable and self-defeating outcomes' (p. ix).

This is the starting premise of Barnett and Finnemore's inquiry into the dynamics of international organizations in world politics. The premise is anchored in substantial research in the field of organization theory, documenting that many IOs behave in ways that are not sanctioned by their members and that are clearly unanticipated by their founders. Sometimes they generate negative outcomes that subvert their own goals, and at other times they take on new missions and responsibilities that have little to do with their original mandates. All bureaucratic organizations have a life of their own, which is often surprisingly independent from, even resistant to, external influence. They evolve over time, adapting to new environments and 'drawing from experience that has become encoded in rules and embedded in the organizational culture' (p. 3). In the context of world politics, there are now 238 IOs dealing with a wide range of issues, from humanitarian crises and environmental concerns to the management of violent conflict. Barnett and Finnemore's objective is to understand the behavior of such diverse IOs through a focus on internal bureaucratic features.

Much of the conduct of IOs is explained best by paying attention to the internal dynamics of IOs, specifically to their bureaucratic nature. Thus, Barnett and Finnemore devote an entire chapter to analyzing the different ways in which different aspects of bureaucracy shape the behavior of IOs. As bureaucratic organizations, IOs are defined by hierarchy, continuity, impersonality, and expertise. Impersonal rules are central to how bureaucracies behave. Rules prescribe actions both inside and outside of bureaucratic structures. They frame the way in which bureaucrats conceive of problems and perceive the world. They help to create or constitute the world in which bureaucrats act. They make that world amenable to legitimate bureaucratic action. And they help shape the identity of the organization itself. In all these ways, rules create a culture of bureaucracy. By the term 'culture,' Barnett and Finnemore (2004, p. 19), citing Diane Vaughan (1996, p. 64), mean 'the solutions that are produced by groups of people to meet the specific problems they face in common. These solutions become institutionalized, remembered, and passed on as rules, rituals, and values of the group.' Bureaucratic cultures are important to a full understanding of how, in interaction with external legitimacy and professional norms, the actions of IOs help various actors to interpret and shape world politics. They do so by guiding action that is aimed at realizing a rationally specified, independent objective. In this view rationality is not a context-free, neutral way of maximizing efficiency in the accomplishment of a specified task. Instead, the very means and ends that bureaucratic actors value are shaped by the culture in which they operate. Finally, the relation between bureaucratic rules and actions is mutually constitutive and dynamically evolving over time: 'Bureaucracies create rules that shape future action, but action, in turn, shapes the evolution and content of rules' (p. 20).

Four aspects of the behavior of IOs are of particular interest to Barnett and Finnemore. First, there is the question of their *autonomy* vis-à-vis other actors. Here, international relations theory has generally relied on some version of principal–agent analysis, which emphasizes the correspondence between state interests and IO behavior. This view tends to neglect factors internal to the IO bureaucracy that can contribute to an independent set of IO preferences and generate an autonomous basis for authoritative knowledge and practices. Second, there is the question of *power*, which in the case of IOs is linked to their material capabilities, their ability to deploy information strategically, and their role in both regulating and constituting the social world. As Barnett and Finnemore note, 'IOs are often the actors to whom we defer when it comes to defining meanings, norms of good behavior, the nature of social actors, and categories of legitimate social action in the world' (p. 7). Third, there is the *dysfunctionality* of organizations, which has not received significant attention even among students of IOs – since conventional international relations perspectives simply assume that IOs are worth analyzing only to the extent that they are responsive to state interests. In reality, an IO may frequently 'act in a manner that subverts its self-professed goals' (p. 8), even when these goals are defined autonomously. Sometimes this dysfunctionality is related to staffing and resource issues. More often it exists because the very factors that make bureaucracies efficient – division of labor, standardization of rules, and rational compartmentalization of relevant knowledge – become liabilities by creating tunnel vision and inflexibility in dealing with complex challenges. Finally, Barnett and Finnemore seek to understand sources and pathways of organizational *change*. Mainstream treatments of IOs tend to view organizational change as indicative of changes in the demands of states. Yet, frequently, IOs are slow to evolve even when their most influential stakeholders are pushing for change; at other times, they can surprise states by embarking on new tasks and routines that states neither want nor expect. Understanding this difference requires us to understand the internal bureaucratic structure and culture of IOs, which can account for resistance to change as well as significant transformations, including mission creep. In all four dimensions of variation among IOs, 'we can better understand what IOs do if we better understand what IOs are' (p. 9).

In analyzing the cases of the International Monetary Fund (IMF), the Office of the United Nations High Commissioner for Refugees (UNHCR), and the UN Secretariat, Barnett and Finnemore evaluate their bureaucratic-centered perspective against conventional state-centered accounts. Their book is a salutary correction for the disproportionate attention paid to statist arguments in international relations theories. That said, Barnett and Finnemore concede all along that state demands are extremely important, and that rarely if ever do IOs have the ability to compel powerful states to act against their expressed interest. However, it would be a mistake to make this the only test of the autonomous power of IOs. In many situations, IOs act independently from but not necessarily in direct opposition to states. Often, these actions turn out to have significant effects on world politics which are neither anticipated nor desired by states. In the interest of a more encompassing explanation, Barnett and Finnemore thus develop an eclectic style of analysis that focuses on IOs as bureaucratic actors in their own rights without seeking to overturn the central and valid insight of a statist perspective. Their analysis establishes that IOs have sometimes pursued important policies in accordance with the wishes of strong states, but that often they 'might fail to carry out state interests, oppose state interests, or change state interests' (p. 11). Of particular interest is the ability of IOs to shape state preferences by setting the agenda on issues that most states have not initially had an opportunity to examine closely. Furthermore, even in situations when the interests informing an IO's actions paralleled those of states, they often acted for different reasons. Their perspective thus stresses the dynamic interactions between IOs and states, rather than viewing IOs as simply playing the role of agents of states.

In their investigation of the relation between knowledge and power, Barnett and Finnemore make a second eclectic move, integrating the regulatory and constitutive styles of analysis favored by neoliberal institutionalists and constructivists respectively. In doing so, they follow Max Weber in emphasizing that bureaucratic power is essentially 'control based on knowledge' (p. 29) – a point that neoliberal institutionalists readily appreciate when they equate knowledge with control over information. Information and other resources are certainly important in the bureaucratic manipulation of incentives to induce or compel actors to follow bureaucratic rules. In this sense, bureaucracies can use information to regulate behavior. IOs such as the IMF, for example, use their expertise in the form of economic advice to regulate government policies either directly or indirectly. However, bureaucratic power 'also includes the ability to transform information into knowledge, that is, to construct information in ways that give it meaning' (p. 29). Put differently, bureaucratic action not only reflects social reality, it also creates it. When IOs define a problem as a moral issue, identify what are considered legitimate means to pursue collectively agreed-upon ends, and articulate rules that limit the scope of human action in specific contexts, they are creating the political world in which IOs operate and in which states form their preferences. While rationalist theory focuses on the regulation of conduct in a given world, constructivist theory concerns itself with the production or constitution of that world. In using their authority, knowledge, and rules, Barnett and Finnemore argue, IOs both regulate and constitute a world which then needs further regulation.

Three mechanisms enable IOs to accomplish this task. First, IOs classify the world. They create categories of problems, actors, and practices. This classification process reflects both a template for interpreting the world and a means to exercise power. It enables IOs to frame and prioritize problems, and thus to shape the possibilities for action. 'Classification schemes shape not only how IOs see the world but also how they act on the world in ways that can directly affect the behavior of others' (p. 32). This is true, for example, in the manner in which the IMF categorizes economies and the UNHCR distinguishes among refugees, migrants, internally displaced peoples, and others. Second, IOs serve to fix meanings attached to the social types and categories they create, enabling them to orient action within established boundaries. Borrowing from symbolic interactionism (Blumer 1969; Goffman 1963), Barnett and Finnemore note that 'the ability to invest situations with a particular meaning constitutes an important source of power' (p. 32). Typically, IOs accomplish this task by using frames 'to situate events and to interpret problems, to fashion a shared understanding of the world, to galvanize sentiments as a way to mobilize and guide social action, and to suggest possible resolutions to current plights' (p. 33).

In addition, IOs regulate and constitute world politics by actively seeking to diffuse new norms and rules that inform political practice. This is in part a function of the fact that IO bureaucrats define their mission to include the spread of global values and norms. Because of their rational-legal character, IOs are in a position to define rational-legal solutions and designate rational-legal authorities to implement them. For example, IOs devoted to the seemingly basic mission of preserving civil peace end up promoting a more expansive set of norms and reforms, as peace requires policing. This, in turn, requires a legal system, a professional judiciary, and the creation of law schools (p. 34). These three mechanisms enable IOs to exercise power and influence in the world in ways that cannot be explained solely on the basis of the interests and power of states.

In their three empirical case studies, Barnett and Finnemore deploy this analytical apparatus to analyze the IMF, the UNHCR, and the UN Secretariat. The three cases cover substantively diverse issue areas covering security, finance and humanitarian affairs. Furthermore, these are all areas in which we have well-developed statist explanations, which makes them hard tests for Barnett and Finnemore's more eclectic approach. Finally, the three IOs involved also feature different types of authority claims, with the IMF relying more on expert authority, the UN Secretariat more on moral authority, and the UNHCR on a more evenly balanced mixture of both. Finding common patterns across such diverse cases – for example, the tendency exhibited by each to steadily expand – enables Barnett and Finnemore to develop some provisional arguments about how different kinds of authority affect the behavior of IOs.

The case study of the IMF showcases the authority and autonomy that flow from professional expertise. The IMF created intellectual technologies embodying specific economic models to advise policymakers on balance of payments issues. Rather than hoarding these models and seeking to keep them inside the organization, the IMF adopted a dissemination strategy, reducing the information and knowledge gap between itself and its member states. The models became persuasive and worth adhering to only once member states understood them. Because the economic conditions that were attached to the extension of loans to deficit-plagued states rarely produced the hoped-for results, the scope of IMF requirements expanded over time. Leaving behind its original narrow focus on balance of payments problems, IMF programs expanded to include more and more variables that were thought to influence deficits, eventually resulting in sweeping structural adjustment programs. In addition, the IMF established technical assistance programs to make recipient countries adopt new institutions and enable them to absorb and act on the technical advice the IMF proffered. Beyond regulating vitally important economic policies, the IMF thus sought to reorganize the basic make-up of recipient countries.

The UNHCR offers a second case that illustrates vividly how an IO can deploy its political and moral authority. Although the UNHCR was created in 1951 with only a three-year life span, a very limited mandate, and virtually no autonomy, the organization has since flourished, acting as a center for an entire culture of repatriation. Initially, in accordance with the core principle that refugees should not be returned against their will to a situation in which their lives might be threatened, the UNHCR sought to resettle refugees in other countries. However, starting in the 1980s, changing patterns of refugee flows and states' increasing reluctance to accept refugees precipitated a shift in the direction of repatriation. Voluntary repatriation had always been a possible solution; however, since states were not always ready to wait until the refugees were ready to return, there was growing pressure to exercise or threaten forced repatriation. In response to these external pressures and some internal rethinking, UNHCR moved towards a 'repatriation culture'; repatriation not only became the preferred solution, but the meaning of the term 'voluntary' was significantly relaxed, as were the protections for refugees. Specifically, UNHCR began examining how to 'encourage' refugee repatriation without exploring the possibilities of third-country resettlement and asylum. This approach was implemented, Barnett and Finnemore document, in the early 1990s, when UNHCR forcibly repatriated tens of thousands of Rohingyan refugees who had fled from Burma and attempted to settle in Bangladesh. Repatriation now continues to figure centrally in solutions to refugee problems. Its moral and delegated authority continues to give UNHCR considerable discretion over the timing of repatriation. What had started as a small European refugee organization has thus evolved into a global humanitarian organization.

The third and final case study focuses on the peacekeeping role of the UN Secretariat, specifically in the case of Rwanda through late April 1994. During the Cold War, the United Nations adhered to clear rules for peacekeeping involving consent of the affected parties, impartiality, and neutrality in the execution of the mission. However, an explosion in the number of missions involving humanitarian emergencies, civil wars, and exercises in nation-building raised questions about the utility of these rules, especially as the United Nations became both more ambitious and more assertive in its missions. Failure, especially in Somalia, made UN officials fearful that a departure from the classical rules of peacekeeping was putting at risk not only any individual operation but also the entire enterprise of peacekeeping. In the fall of 1993, the old rules were reestablished and strictly enforced as a way to preempt further failures on the part of the United Nations. It was these rules that guided UN officials when the killings in Rwanda exploded on April 6, 1994. They interpreted what turned out to be the first stages of genocide as the beginning of a civil war, and concluded that there was simply no basis for intervention to stop what in the end was the slaughter of 800,000 people. The United Nations' behavior in this case was not so much a matter of indecision or inaction, but rather a function of the classical rules of peacekeeping, which were intertwined with the imperative of organizational survival after earlier failures.

Barnett and Finnemore's eclectic approach is thus deployed on a wide-ranging and substantively important set of cases. In the end, the authors draw two main conclusions. First, following Max Weber, they note that IOs and bureaucratic rule tend to expand and evolve in ways that statist or rationalist explanations cannot easily account for. Over time, debate and discourse within large bureaucracies generate a constellation of understandings and interests that support this expansion. Theoretically, these observations draw attention to the broader moral principles or aspirations underlying the specific mandates of IOs; these principles and aspirations provide motivations for diverse actors to demand changes where they find organizational structures too confining. In the process, IOs not only evolve towards broader missions but also end up with greater power to reconfigure both international and domestic social spaces. Barnett and Finnemore caution that the result of this power for weaker actors can mean emancipation for some and domination for others.

Box 5.1
Michael Barnett – Pack lightly, but welcome nuance and complexity

Why did we reason eclectically in writing *Rules for the World* (Barnett and Finnemore 2004)? We were driven by empirical puzzles and substantive questions regarding the behavior of international organizations. Dominant statist and rationalist theories of international organizations, however, were unable to explain what relatively autonomous international organizations do after their creation; indeed, it was impressive how little existing theories had to say on the subject. We turned to organization theory for help for several reasons. Organization theory has always been attentive to organizations and their environment. Also, it represented a rigorous yet non-sectarian approach to all organizations, including international organizations, and thus matched our intellectual disposition. Our research design reflected this non-sectarian, eclectic approach.

One of the decisions we had to make early on was whether we would try to develop a competitive test by setting up our argument as a direct competitor to rationalist approaches. In many respects the 'discipline' expected a wrestling match. We refused to play along. Instead, we built a theoretical framework that could be competing at some moments, complementary at others, and most importantly, identify the pregnant silences of existing theoretical approaches. We knew that this ecumenical approach might lead mainstream, statist-oriented scholars to fault us for not offering a 'definitive' test to 'falsify' existing theories, but we also feared that the very process of establishing a competitive test on rationalist terms would severely hinder our desire to create a theoretical and empirical space for non-rationalist approaches. We never regretted our decision, and are heartened to see other scholars develop alternatives to rationalist and statist scholarship.

Our advice is to begin by packing lightly. Do not take more than you need. Following Occam's razor, ask 'what is the simplest explanation for the puzzle?' Then ask, 'what are the strengths and limits of this explanation?' Do not get trapped by a 'usual suspects' approach to alternative explanation. Taking 'off the shelf' explanations from hardened paradigms is seductively simple; however, it invites you to create a straw man of alternatives, and potentially leads to the failure to imagine nuanced and complex ways of blending existing theories. Moreover, do not underestimate the data demands of eclectic theorizing. And do not minimize the difficult process of interpreting the data in ways that might be consistent with alternative theories. Finally, be very clear about the strengths and weaknesses of your chosen alternative, particularly as causal complexity can potentially be mistaken for a 'garbage can' approach in which everything matters.

The second conclusion that Barnett and Finnemore draw has to do with the linkages between rationalism, liberalism, and democracy. 'Rationalization has given IOs their basic form (as bureaucracies) and liberalism has provided the social content that all IOs now pursue' (p. 166). However, rationalism and liberalism are not always easy to fuse. The procedural legitimation of action lies in the domain of the former. It can be used to undercut the substantive legitimacy attached to important values such as the extent of voluntarism and participation enjoyed by IO members. On the issue of accountability, too, while IOs set up procedures to ensure transparency, the mechanisms on which they rely frequently fail to keep up with their own growing reach and power. The result is significant variation in the extent to which various constituencies feel they can hold IOs accountable. These concerns prompt Barnett and Finnemore to point to the dangers of an 'undemocratic liberalism' whereby the pursuit of socially liberal goals through impersonal procedures is not matched by mechanisms to ensure democratic participation and accountability. The challenge facing both scholars and practitioners dealing with IOs are thus plain: 'the very source of their power to do good might also be the source of their power to do harm. ... Managing our global bureaucracy and learning to exploit its strengths while moderating its failings will be an essential task' (p. 173).

Benjamin Schiff, *Building the International Criminal Court* (2008)

The ICC is a novel and highly political institution marked by lofty ideals and ambitious goals. By prosecuting perpetrators of genocide, those committing acts against humanity and war crimes, Schiff notes, 'it seeks to deter depredations against citizens in violent conflicts and to contribute to justice, peace, political transition, and reconstruction' (p. 1). However, the nature of the international society of states makes it exceedingly difficult for the court to carry out these objectives. In domestic politics, legitimate political processes and legal institutions are designed to devise and enforce laws in a manner that is expected to be objective and dispassionate. In the international arena, by contrast, there is no legislative structure to legitimize the making of international law, no consolidated authority for its enforcement, and no mechanism to constrain sovereign states and preserve the autonomy of international organizations.

Despite these differences, advocates of law have tried to extend the logics and structures developed in the domestic context to the international sphere. Developments since the 1970s have led to a growing legalization of international politics. Arbitration and judicial decision making have come to complement diplomatic maneuvering and the use of power as ways to settle conflicts between sovereign states. Equally important, international legalization has given the concept of the individual and personal responsibility of leaders within and across state borders a direct political relevance that it did not have before. The ICC is the most visible manifestation of this development. Initially submitted for signature and ratification in July 1998, the ICC came into existence on July 1, 2002, after the minimum of 60 states had acceded fully to the treaty. It has since grown from a five-member transition team in 2002 to an institution employing 700 staff members in 2007. Its organization, rules, and operations build on ad hoc tribunals such as those used in Yugoslavia and Rwanda, but it also incorporates features of civil law and common-law systems in order to investigate cases, issue warrants, take custody of arrested suspects, conduct international criminal trials, and protect witnesses and victims of crimes.

Because the ICC is a relatively new institution, Schiff's is one of the first extensive studies of the Court. Unavoidably, it is thus more descriptive than the other books analyzed in this chapter. At the same time, Schiff does seek to relate his work to competing streams of international relations theory in the process of explaining the emergence of the Court as well as selected aspects of its functioning during the first years of its operation. We focus here on the self-consciously eclectic analytic framework Schiff develops to analyze this novel institution.

Schiff does not view the three canonical theories of international relations – realism, neoliberal institutionalism, and constructivism – as mutually exclusive rival theories as much as tools to explain and make intelligible different facets of a very complicated world. Realists are well positioned to explain why some states have sought to limit the Court's powers and defend their own sovereignty while others have decided to go along with it once it came into existence. They are not, however, able to offer a convincing account for why such an elaborate institution was created in the first place. Neoliberal institutionalists see the Court's autonomy and legitimacy as varying with its ability to serve the mutual interests of states, and this helps them to understand aspects of the Court's evolution and organizational form. They cannot explain, however, why international criminal law, and specifically the anti-impunity norm, became significant in international affairs in the first place. Social constructivists, for their part, do well when it comes to explaining why states collectively committed themselves to cooperate within the ICC without any clear material incentives. However, their weakness lies in anticipating which kinds of identity shifts and collective orientations are likely to define important transformations in the international system. Thus, none of the three perspectives is able to provide a compelling account of the lengthy process through which the ideals and norms underpinning the ICC emerged and became extensively institutionalized. At the same time, Schiff (p. 9) notes that all three approaches shed light on different segments of this process:

> The constructivists explain development of the consensus on which the Court is based; the realists explain states' compulsions to protect sovereignty and to seek relative advantage; the liberal institutionalists explore how the ICC embodies states' cooperative efforts to improve absolute welfare.

Rather than identify and analyze a specific puzzle, Schiff uses the combinatorial power of the three theoretical perspectives to explain some of the key conundrums that the Court faces. And there are many. There is, for example, a tension between the ICC's role as a judicial institution, which is theoretically autonomous, and the political ramifications of this role, as seen through the eyes of states and other actors. The ICC's organizational structure is also problematic as it seeks to reconcile a commitment to judicial insularity with its goal of administrative efficiency and coordination. There is also the dilemma created by the Court's broad mandate to combine traditional retributive justice, which focuses on punishing offenders, and new forms of restorative justice, which focuses on repairing the harm inflicted by the offender on the victims and the larger community. Clashes have also emerged between the Office of the Prosecutor, which is influenced mostly by common law, and the pre-trial chamber judges, whose roles are influenced more by civil law. And, finally, there are the often-competing objectives of bringing perpetrators to justice and establishing peace between warring parties.

In tracing the emergence of the 1998 Rome Statute that set up the ICC, Schiff employs the metaphor of a river to capture the evolution and expansion of the international justice movement. He describes how various 'normative tributaries, eddies, currents, and dams, as well as a cascade or two' (p. 15) have combined over time to produce a swelling of the river of international justice, culminating in the promulgation of the Statute and the establishment of the ICC. Any given moment in the construction of that arc is but a snapshot that should be located within broader streams of events. This is precisely why the Statute embodies potentially contradictory elements with which the Court must now contend in its daily operation.

Schiff analyzes various moments in the evolution of international humanitarian and criminal law. This evolution has its roots in the articulation of an international variant of natural law from the time of Hugo Grotius through the nineteenth-century efforts to establish international humanitarian law, most notably by the International Committee of the Red Cross. More recent developments were crucial for converting these initial conceptions of international law into a mandate to establish the ICC. They include the first acts recognized as 'crimes against humanity,' as well as the precursors of genocide during the First World War and the interwar period; the further development of international criminal law from the Second World War and the Nuremberg trials through the United Nations' adoption of the Genocide Convention, the Universal Declaration of Human Rights in 1948, and the Nuremberg Principles; the rise of the human rights and environmental movements spearheaded in the 1970s by non-government organizations (NGOs) rather than states, as well as the recognition of international law in the Helsinki Accords of 1975 as part of the effort to minimize the risk of war between East and West in Europe; and finally, since the 1980s, the establishment of Truth Commissions and the opening of police files in societies that had undergone processes of democratization (in Latin and Central America, Africa, and Eastern Europe) as well as, in the 1990s, criminal tribunals in Yugoslavia and Rwanda. All of these developments represent the 'swelling river' of international justice.

The metaphor of a river helps to describe the process through which a gathering stream of ideas about international criminal law ultimately resulted in the Rome Statute of the ICC. It does not, however, clarify 'how nonmaterial objectives without clear advantages for states as sovereign actors could motivate those states to create an international organization' (p. 39). Schiff's explanation begins with a constructivist account of the role played by the growth of collective justice norms, marshaled by norm entrepreneurs and channeled into norms cascades, in helping to reconfigure conceptions of state interest. By 1998, it was not the norms as much as the mechanisms for their implementation that remained controversial. Realists see power as constitutive of law rather than the other way around. This assumption conforms to some aspects of the Statute, such as the strong protection of state sovereignty, the limited form of Court jurisdiction, the checks on the Court's independent power, and the necessity of the states' cooperation for the Court's success. Liberal institutionalists, finally, see the Court as an instance of the process of international legalization by which states replace unpredictable power politics with more orderly legal processes. Once state interests have been reconfigured in relation to an emergent set of norms (as constructivists explain), and refined in the context of negotiating specific features of the Court (as explicated by realist theory), a neoliberal institutional framework becomes the most useful in analyzing the organization and operation of the ICC in its first years.

Schiff also explains specific facets of two ad hoc criminal tribunals that served as prototypes for the Rome Statute: the Yugoslav and Rwandan tribunals. Here, too, each of the three analytical perspectives provides important insights that need to be integrated. Realists point to states' extreme reluctance to become involved in either of these two conflicts, which involved no vital interests of major states. Russia, the United States, and the European states, trying to avoid a conflict among themselves, relied upon the UN Security Council's establishment of the two tribunals in order to claim that something useful had been done after all the blood that had been spilled. Thus, the tribunals represented legalistic post-hoc responses to disasters that major states, following the do-nothing dictates of *Realpolitik*, had chosen to disregard. Constructivists offer an equally plausible account of a different aspect of the story. The tribunals symbolized a convergence of the international community around the notion that crimes of the magnitude committed in Yugoslavia and Rwanda were unacceptable and could not be tolerated. The creation of the tribunals thus was a response to the perception of mounting domestic political pressure. In this manner, state interests were redefined in response to shifts in norms and identities among publics which forced the hands of their leaders. Finally, neoliberal theory tells us something useful about the responses to the atrocities, specifically the emergence of an epistemic community of legal experts and a consensual understanding of the institutional machinery required to administer international criminal law. In this regard, the work of the International Law Commission (ILC), specifically the fact-finding mission of legal experts (who also were advocates for setting up tribunals) to Yugoslavia and the subsequent establishment of an ad hoc tribunal, offered an enduring institutional solution to the pressure that was building from publics to governments and to the UN Security Council. The ILC draft, supported by the US State Department, created a rickety institution that eventually took on a life of its own, spurring the growth of the tribunals and providing crucial lessons that would shape the rules and structures of the ICC.

The three different analytical perspectives also offer complementary accounts of the signing of the1998 Statute, the institutional design of the ICC, the emergence of NGOs as powerful actors within the Court, and the evolution of the relations between the ICC and states. In all of these cases, as in the case of the Yugoslav and Rwandan tribunals, a comprehensive understanding of the choices and motivations of various actors requires a complex framework in which principles of sovereignty and self-help are systematically connected to divergent expectations and objectives of self-interested actors, and to broader currents in the international arena that elevate the significance of particular norms.

Thus, from the perspective of constructivism, the Court's creation, its administration of justice, and its subsequent expansion to incorporate NGO actors reflect a shift in the international society of states toward restorative justice and individual accountability. The inclusion of NGOs, in particular, speaks to the significance of 'norm entrepreneurs' and other civil society actors in consolidating specific norms and pressing state actors and international organizations to uphold them. At the same time, realists rightfully note that these normative shifts do not prevent states, especially the most powerful ones, from insisting on their sovereignty in an environment they still see as characterized mostly by self-help. For realists, states uphold the Court's various features and missions in a selective manner, when it suits their own interests, or at a minimum, when it does not contradict those interests. This is precisely why the ICC has fared better in prosecuting crimes against humanity than in taking measures against crimes of aggression, an issue on which there is much less agreement among states, particularly the most powerful members of the UN Security Council. Finally, liberal institutionalist analysis points to the role of a growing epistemic community in promoting the notion of a stable institution for systematically circumscribing the impunity it saw as impeding the defense of international peace and security. The subsequent expansion of the Court, in spite of the numerous obstacles and internal conflicts it has faced, also speaks to the neoliberals' optimism concerning the possibility of positive-sum outcomes through the efficient and exemplary implementation of institutional procedures.

Schiff's sophisticated eclectic treatment of constructivist, realist, and neoliberal perspectives is not just intended as a theoretical move in response to scholarly debates. Each of the approaches sheds light on a process that has significant practical implications, both for the Court and for the prospects of international organizations and law writ large. As Schiff (pp. 259–60) puts it:

> From a constructivist's standpoint, the creation of the ICC denotes a pivotal historical moment in the development of international society. From a realist's standpoint, further complexity has been added to the anarchic international system without fundamentally changing it. For neoliberal institutionalists, states added to the panoply of organizational mechanisms intended to mitigate anarchy and enable collective gains.

To be sure, state sovereignty, divergent state interests, and the logic of self-help remain important features of international politics. But they now coexist with a new, consolidated stream of commitments to international criminal law, which is here to stay and is becoming progressively more institutionalized as state and non-state actors feel pressures to frame impunity as fundamentally problematic for justice, stability, and the possibility of mutual benefits. Even though the ICC's future trajectory is uncertain, it is promising so long as the political forces emphasized in the three analytic perspectives are kept in balance. As Schiff (2008, p. 260) puts it:

Box 5.2
Ben Schiff – Without loyalty to any theoretical gods

Having written two prior books on international organizations, one self-consciously embedded in regime theory and another that dispensed with theory altogether, I approached *Building the International Criminal Court* (Schiff 2008) without loyalty to any particular theoretical gods, but willing to engage one or more if they seemed benevolent.

The more I thought about the ICC, the more I found my own ideas falling into the categories of the three frameworks I ultimately employed in the book. Realism, liberal institutionalism, and constructivism seemed useful heuristics, although I did not want to be responsible for all of their complex permutations. I was fascinated by the ICC's development as a milestone in international law generally, international criminal law in particular, and as a major case of contemporary norm institutionalization. Since my objective was explanation, not theory building, I saw no reason to limit the exposition to one theoretical tradition – my objective was to express as broad and complete an understanding of the Court as possible within the confines of a short and readable book.

Employing the three frameworks together seemed to me helpful to show undergraduates how theories aid understanding, and to assist more expert audiences in tracking the explanations. Moreover, since the three frameworks jointly enabled me to make assertions about the Court and its problems and future that would have been precluded in a single-theory approach, eclecticism seemed natural.

The rarity of published, explicitly eclectic approaches led me to worry that readers would not take seriously the book's theoretical aspect, although I hoped the descriptive material would nonetheless support their interests. The book's very positive reception among reviewers in both international relations and international law leads me to believe that the approach at least did not detract from its usefulness, and may even have helped.

My research has always been driven by questions and substance rather than theories. Now that I have imbibed international relations and international organization theories for about 35 years, however, the theories shape my thinking – not one at a time, but together. I recall vividly my mentor Ernie Haas's lecture about the virtues of mid-level and 'islands' of theory. Grateful to Ernie, I am content to be a mid-level islander. I have never understood why single-theory explanations are inherently better than eclectic ones. If the trade-off of parsimony for fuller understanding points in the direction of eclecticism, given a complex world with multiple explanatory possibilities, what is the harm? Try eclecticism. The gods will smile.

the future of the organization rests upon its ability to navigate political currents while being responsive to states' interests yet resisting their pressures, as humanity builds a court to try individual perpetrators of its worst crimes, to bring recognition to their victims, and to restore the rule of law and help heal societies.

Ian Hurd, *After Anarchy* (2007)

Drawing on diverse literatures in sociology, psychology, and management studies, Hurd's far-ranging analysis develops a general understanding of how legitimacy affects the power, behavior, and limits of international organizations. Focusing on the UN Security Council, Hurd makes two contributions. In theoretical terms, he constructs a bridge between rationalist and constructivist styles of analysis. In substantive terms, he improves our understanding of the relationship between states and international institutions. The questions guiding his study are crafted without reference to any a priori assumptions about the relative weights and overall significance of material and ideational factors. While it is commonly acknowledged that the loss of legitimacy is problematic for organizations, Hurd asks how and to what extent the presence of legitimacy enhances an international organization's power, and therefore its ability to attain its goals. He also raises the issue of the limits of legitimacy as a means to exercise power, especially in light of efforts to challenge the status quo.

The significance of the general question of legitimacy and the specific issue of its relevance to the UN Security Council is apparent in the importance attached, by both proponents and opponents of the Iraq war, to the 2003 Security Council deliberations over resolutions pertaining to the preemptive use of force against Iraq. Both groups sought to appropriate the legitimacy attached to the Security Council for their own purposes. Both sides expended enormous energy lobbying Security Council members to achieve their ends. And both were sorely disappointed with the outcome, believing that the Council had 'failed' a crucial test. 'One side believed it had failed in its responsibilities by refusing to authorize the US-led war, and the other believed it had failed by being unable to stop it' (p. vii).

This episode demonstrates for Hurd 'that legitimacy is central to the power of international organizations ... and also that we can use it to begin to explain some phenomena in world politics that were hitherto unaccounted for' (p. viii).

Legitimacy, defined as 'an actor's normative belief that a rule or institution ought to be obeyed' (p. 7), is a difficult concept to study. Due in part to an intersubjective quality that cannot be observed directly in the behavior of actors, legitimacy does not figure prominently in materialist approaches to international politics. But disregarding legitimacy is risky. It causes us to overlook important aspects of world politics such as saving face, offering justifications, using symbols, and exercising authority. The central argument that Hurd builds throughout his book holds that international organizations and some other organizations, like states, exercise sovereign authority, understood as 'the right to exercise final authority.' This finding is at odds with realist understandings that only states are endowed with sovereign authority, and that the relations among them are always and only characterized by international anarchy. In contrast, Hurd argues, the international system consists of different fields in which states as well as other organizations with legitimate power exercise sovereign authority. At the same time, constructivists' attempts to capture empirically the 'logic of appropriateness' in world politics, although taking for granted the significance of legitimacy, have not been grounded in a systematic exploration of the concept and its operation. In the context of the Security Council, much of the complexity surrounding even the most basic questions about its behavior and role is the result of 'an underappreciation of the role of legitimacy and legitimation in the routine business of the Council' (p. 3).

Drawing upon Hardt and Negri's (2000) discussion of the Security Council, Hurd acknowledges frankly that the sovereign authority of the Council is built on an apparent paradox. If we regard sovereign states as legally free to make their own decisions following their own interests, and if we see the regulatory and supervisory activities of international organizations as constraints on state freedom, then the result is a fundamental 'contradiction between international commitment and state sovereignty' (p. 5). This contradiction lies at the heart of the tension between the UN Security Council's Charter, which makes it the world's most powerful international organization, and its attempts to use its power in addressing issues of international peace and security. A conventional way around this contradiction is to note that states choose to obey the Council, either by joining or by complying with or disregarding specific decisions. That is, the power of the Security Council is presumed ultimately to rest on the consent of states. The central thrust of Hurd's book is to show how problematic this presumption is, and how much more can be explained by taking into account a different understanding of power as linked to legitimacy.

The limits of the 'consent' approach become evident when one considers that state leaders often take some of their international obligations seriously even when they might prefer to disregard them. Even when states violate their obligations, Hurd notes, that violation is normally accompanied by the effort to make it appear consistent with the state's obligation. Consent thus is not free, but constrained by the presence of a legitimate international organization. At the same time, the legitimacy of an organization does not guarantee compliance with its edicts. The reality lies somewhere in between: 'States generally try to manage their relations with international organizations such as the UN and to influence their development rather than ignore them or pretend they do not exist' (p. 6).

Hurd goes on to demonstrate that the power that an international institution derives from legitimacy has little to do with the consent or choice of state actors. Instead, it stems from socialization processes and symbols that are internal to the actor. Legitimacy for Hurd is not only intersubjective as a shared or collective property of an institution or rule. It also rests on an actor's subjective belief that the institution or rule ought to be obeyed. Thus, legitimate institutions do not operate as external constraints on actors; rather, they constitute actors and their interests, and those interests are conceptualized in a way that accounts for existing, legitimate institutional rules. In the case of the Council, as a matter of institutional design and political practice, legitimate power was deliberately circumscribed to minimize conflicts of interests between the Council as a whole and its largest and most powerful states.

How do we know that legitimacy based on internalization has occurred? There are two clear indications. First, there are cases in which states are acting instrumentally to achieve their purpose, but within the context of rules and institutions that they take for granted. In such cases, it is reasonable to suspect that 'states have internalized the content of the rule or the authority of the institution into their schedule of private interests' (p. 32). This was the case in the deliberations over the UN Charter in 1945, when the substantive outcome had already been negotiated in accordance with the preferences of the Great Powers. It is also evident in the fact that small states seek symbolic affiliation with the Council even absent any obvious material gains. Second, there are cases in which states manipulate others by drawing on resources derived from legitimate institutions – for example, when states use appeals to international norms or make cynical comments about the Council in an attempt to get other players to respond in terms that suggest the Council's rules and decisions do have legitimacy. This latter move, suggestive of the 'rhetorical action' highlighted by Schimmelfennig's (2003) analysis of EU and NATO enlargement (discussed below), depends on an 'audience' acknowledging that adherence to certain international norms is at least of some value. Even states that have not fully internalized the Council's authority can find their behavior affected by others that accept its legitimacy. Hurd's perspective thus differs from the consent theory of realists and liberals, who see legitimacy as useful for states as they defend their interests against possible opponents. It differs also from the approach of constructivists, who take for granted the emergence of stable intersubjective understandings but neglect the importance of subjective perceptions and the possibilities of manipulation linked to actors' interests.

Legitimacy exercises social control in three distinct ways: through affecting the internal make-up of actors, through affecting the payoffs of actors, and through the construction of resources made available to all actors in the system. First, at the unit level, the significance of legitimacy depends on its internalization by the actor, as the proscriptions and procedures of an institution are integrated into the state actor's sense of identity, interests, and strategies. Besides its intrinsic qualities and needs, such as survival, which is essential for continued existence in the state system, this is how a state learns from its environment what it wants. Learning here is more than the simple improvement of a means–ends calculus; it refers to a deeper social reconsideration of beliefs and goals. At the unit level, the significance of legitimacy is different from that of compliance. Legitimacy might lead to enhanced compliance, and it often does; but compliance does not inhere in the very concept of legitimacy. What matters critically is the internalization of an external norm, not the behavioral result. Finally, at the level of the international system, both the structures of payoffs and constraints and the distribution of symbolic resources among actors are affected by 'the embeddedness of the individual in an environment of legitimated power' (p. 41). To the extent that the system generates states that take it to be a legitimate order, it possesses a social validity based on general expectations and the probability of coercive enforcement. These general expectations make even the strong and those opposed to the system's legitimacy take account of legitimacy in their political calculations. Moreover, legitimate institutions dispense and give access to valuable symbolic resources. Symbols are tools of power that both serve the instrumental purposes of actors and enhance the power of international organizations that control access to symbolic resources.

It is perhaps easier to define legitimacy by what it is not rather than what it is. Legitimacy is neither coercion nor self-interest. Legitimacy, coercion, and self-interest represent distinct ideal-typical modes of social control, each depending on a distinct mechanism. Although all three are often present in observed practices, the operation of legitimacy needs to be distinguished analytically from the other two concepts. Coercion is based on a relationship of asymmetrical physical power deployed to alter the behavior of the weaker actor. Coercion acts directly, and is costly in that it generates resentment and opposition which in the future will require the application of more coercion, possibly at greater cost, to elicit the same amount of compliance. It is an expenditure of precious social capital, and difficult to sustain in the long term. The belief of serving one's self-interest is a second motivation for compliance with rules. Self-interest is similar to coercion in that both are forms of utilitarianism in practice; but self-interested actors continuously assess all institutional rules and social relationships, and thus contemplate more far-ranging change in terms of a wide range of psychic, social, and physical incentives and disincentives. What is significant of self-interest is its role in maintaining or limiting long-term relationships depending on whether these relationships continue to produce the expected stream of positive benefits. Neither coercion nor self-interest captures the distinctive feature of legitimacy, which is its ability to influence other actors through the internalization of particular norms and the subjective perception that these norms are worthy of obedience for their own sake. There are certainly complex relationships among coercion, self-interest, and legitimacy, but one must take care to analytically distinguish the operation of each rather than succumb to the temptation of reducing one to the other.

Hurd's eclectic approach brings together elements of realist, liberal, and constructivist perspectives on the sources of power among international organizations. For realists, the power of international organizations rests fully and solely on the underlying distribution of states' material power. Specifically, strong states shape the range of international options that are open to small states, and the kinds of international organization that come into being in the first place, as Lloyd Gruber (2000) shows for the European Monetary Union. For liberals, the power of international organizations lies in offering efficient solutions to coordination problems. The formality of an organization and the public character of membership in the organization are important tools for creating credible commitments. The power of institutions is thus measured in the reduction of transaction costs among states. In highlighting the fact that international politics is social rather than strictly material, constructivists focus on how institutions constitute state actors and the interests they hold. Hurd's conceptual apparatus takes on these controversies directly, and his treatment of how legitimacy relates to coercion and self-interest makes it possible to proceed eclectically. Legitimate international institutions both empower and constrain states. And when states view them as legitimate, these institutions become endowed with sovereignty and power in ways that no single paradigm can capture by itself.

Hurd's book has several implications for both scholarship and policy, particularly in relation to assessments of the United Nations' performance and its future prospects. First and foremost, Hurd demonstrates compellingly that 'sovereignty exists in multiple locations in the international system, and is exercised by institutions beyond the state' (p. 196). In this process, it is worth noting that the UN Security Council's original legitimacy was not acquired because it was perceived as inherently fair, or because it allowed explicitly for the over-representation of powerful states. It derived instead from being procedurally fair: that is, by being correct in giving all voices the opportunity to be heard. Ever since its establishment, the Council has experienced ups and downs in terms of the extent of its legitimacy. It has enraged those in powerful states who saw it as sometimes failing to uphold their interests; and it has sorely disappointed those who wanted to constrain the powerful in their willful exercise of power on issues of overriding state interest. Although

Box 5.3
Ian Hurd – Practical politics and conceptual implications

In writing *After Anarchy* (Hurd 2007), I pursued what I thought was an interesting and puzzling phenomenon in world politics, namely the deference states seemed to give to the UN Security Council and the fights they engaged in over the resources of the Council. The Security Council seemed to be at once a place where power politics was being played by states, an independent actor in those struggles, and a prize. I was interested in both the practical politics of the Security Council's life and the conceptual implications of the politics surrounding it for international relations (IR) theory. To get there, I looked for conceptual tools and approaches to help make sense of these politics, and this took me to sociology and organization theory for the ideas of legitimacy and authority, and to constructivism in IR theory.

The book is motivated by my curiosity rather than by the urge to validate a research program, and as a result it incorporates aspects of the world that the stridently paradigmatic scholar might prefer to keep separate, such as strategic actors, the social construction of power politics, and the concerns of international security. It takes the attitude that the paradigms in IR are like a drawer full of left-handed mittens: each is useful to a point, but it will only take you so far. The book shows that international rules and norms are inseparable from states' ideas about their interests. Focusing exclusively on either, one misses what is interesting about the situation. Paradigmatic boundaries should not force us to choose between them. Similarly, the processes of legitimation that interested me do not fit well into the language of dependent and independent variables, and trying to squeeze the project into that model would be counterproductive. As I see it, the freedom that comes from 'eclecticism' leads to an obligation. Sil and Katzenstein rightly emphasize in this book that eclecticism neither solves the problems of epistemology and philosophy nor reconciles the differences that separate the approaches. Instead, it represents the pragmatist's bet that we can set aside some of these questions long enough to present interesting research on a problem. But as a result, it carries the obligation to eventually return to these questions and reflect on what the research says about them. Eclecticism is both a strategy for getting on with research in the face of difficult philosophical questions and an instrument for gaining insight on these questions.

both reactions are understandable, it is worth reminding critics of the Council of its carefully calibrated mandate. The Council has the power to resist the unilateral decisions of the powerful but not the power to oppose them on matters of vital interest. Furthermore, Hurd's careful examination of the Council's various decisions suggests that our expectations of how international institutions exercise power should be framed not generally, but in specific issue domains within which these institutions and other actors exercise sovereign power. Hurd's analysis also suggests the possibility of increasing or decreasing legitimacy as weaker powers cloak their arguments in language and symbols of the powerful – with varying degrees of success – to get the latter to support their interests. Looking to the future, Hurd suggests that full blown delegitimation of the United Nations is highly unlikely: 'The 'collective legitimation' that the Council can provide is extremely valuable to states, and the political contestation that takes place around the Council tends to reinforce ... the belief among states in its legitimacy' (p. 193).

Frank Schimmelfennig, *The EU, NATO and the Integration of Europe* (2003)

Schimmelfennig explores what he considers 'the most consequential political project' (p. 2) for European organizations in the last decade: the post-Cold War eastward enlargement process of Europe's two most important regional organizations, the European Union and NATO. He finds that the actual increased salience of the topic of EU and NATO enlargement has given rise to a good deal of scholarship on the subject. However, he establishes also that most of this scholarship is either descriptive or focused on single enlargement rounds, or on single member or accession countries. A theoretically oriented approach should start by articulating a central research question that focuses not only on the requests of the many countries seeking to join an organization, but also on the expansion decisions of different European organizations and the positions of their member states.

Why Central and East European Countries (CEECs) would want to join these organizations in the wake of the Cold War is not particularly puzzling for Schimmelfennig. Rationalist arguments suffice to explain this development. What is more interesting is why Western member states in these organizations should bother to embark on the complicated and risky course of steady enlargement when there is no clear indication of the gains from doing so. Specifically, why did the European Union and NATO decide to acquiesce to the CEECs' desires for membership? How did the members arrive at their decisions to support eastward expansion? And how did they decide on the criteria for accession? These questions are relevant not only for understanding post-Cold War European politics, but also for 'exploring novel ways of conceptualizing institutional effects and actor behavior in international politics' (p. 3).

Schimmelfennig's approach is premised on the observation that, in the emerging architecture of the New Europe, organizations such as the European Union and NATO have signified a Western community of states that is constituted by shared liberal values. These values have a significant impact on questions of membership as well as the appropriate rules governing its behavior. Rather than insisting that in the process of enlargement, state behavior is governed by the interests of Western states, as would be consistent with a rationalist framework of analysis, or by rules of appropriateness, as would be consistent with sociological institutional theory, Schimmelfennig develops a novel theoretical framework that rests on two main arguments. The first stresses the significance of 'the constitutive liberal rules of the Western international community' in explaining expansion; the second, the significance of 'rhetorical action' in explaining how these liberal rules have affected the enlargement process (p. 3). Below, we briefly consider the first, straightforward constructivist argument and the empirical evidence provided to support it. It is the second argument, however, that we find to be more novel and self-consciously eclectic in offering mechanisms that cut across and connect competing rationalist and sociological-institutionalist perspectives.

The first argument stipulates that EU and NATO enlargement are best conceived as exercises in community building. Both regional organizations are representatives of broader international communities, and define their collective identities in terms of the shared values of those communities. The European Union represents a European community, NATO a wider Euro-Atlantic one. The overlap between these two communities is reflected in a shared set of Western liberal norms and values, among which is that 'belief in and adherence to liberal human rights are the fundamental ideas and practices' (p. 4). In the domestic affairs of the member states, these common liberal principles are reflected in social pluralism, the rule of law, democratic participation and representation, private property, and a market-based economy. In the international arena, a liberal conception of order is premised on multilateralism and non-violent conflict management among the members of the community. These values find their institutional expression in the constitutive organizational rules that govern the policies of both the European Union and NATO toward non-members and potential future members. Both organizations disseminate liberal values and attempt to socialize non-members and potential members to adhere to liberal values. Enlargement results if these states are willing to be appropriately socialized – that is, if they are prepared to adopt a liberal identity, norms, values, and conduct. This perspective explains why Eastern enlargement worked for those former Communist states that were successful in adopting democratic values and practices, and the constitutive rules of the European Union and NATO. States that remained undemocratic or were less committed to liberal values and practices were more likely to be denied membership.

The empirical evidence in support of the community approach to enlargement gives a generally satisfying explanation for the Eastern enlargement of NATO and the European Union. Identification with the Western community of states and their liberal practices has been a sufficient but not a necessary condition of the CEECs' interests in joining NATO and the European Union. While all of the CEECs with a sustained effort at democratization and liberal reforms have applied for membership, several have fallen short on that score. Western organizations considered expansion into Central and Eastern Europe because they were intent on aiding ongoing democratic transformations in the region. By agreeing to formal accession, these organizations recognized reform processes that had succeeded so far as to make states legitimate community members. The community approach receives further support from the fact that no CEEC that has systematically violated liberal norms has been invited to accession negotiations. Where this approach falls short, however, is in its ability to differentiate between the motives of applicants and non-applicants and its ability to project the exact number, timing, and sequence of invitations to accession negotiations. Lithuania and Slovenia, for example, should have been part of the first-tier accession countries. Similarly, considering their domestic track record, Bulgaria and Romania were invited too early to enter into accession negotiations. In both instances, geostrategic considerations involving the relations between Western organizations and Russia probably played a significant role. Furthermore, the European Union and NATO were not fully congruent in their timing of when to invite CEECs to enter membership negotiations, due most likely to the different function of the organizations and the US presence in one (NATO) and absence in the other (the European Union). These limitations notwithstanding, Schimmelfennig's statistical analysis of other episodes of enlargement tends to support his basic finding that demonstration of democratic, liberal norms is the most robust and significant factor in explaining the enlargement processes of Western organizations in Eurasia. Certainly, it is more robust than other prevailing explanations emphasizing the organizational imperatives of the European Union and NATO, or the material incentives of member states.

The eclectic core of Schimmelfennig's analysis is most clearly evident in the book's second main argument. This argument highlights the importance of *rhetorical action*, 'the strategic use and exchange of arguments to persuade other actors to act according to one's preferences' (p. 5). The argument is developed in response to the specific question of why Western states bothered to admit CEECs at all, when the gains from doing so were far from obvious. In this context, the preferences concerning enlargement were shaped by egotistic interests and material environmental conditions of CEECs that expected significant benefits from membership. For most EU and NATO members, however, eastward enlargement was not a rational outcome or an efficient institutional arrangement. In fact, for both organizations, enlargement imposed significant transaction, autonomy, and crowding costs. Furthermore, both had at their disposal more efficient institutional mechanisms to address the issues of new member states – associate membership in the case of the European Union, and the Partnership for Peace in the case of NATO. And while it is true that some EU and NATO member states such as Germany would derive great benefits from enlargement, neither they nor the CEECs had the bargaining power to impose enlargement on a reluctant majority of EU and NATO members. Put differently, the standard arguments advanced by neoliberal institutional analysis do not hold. At the same time, there is little evidence to suggest that the logic of appropriateness trumped material interests or egoistic action among Western states. In fact, a distinctive feature of the enlargement process is the fact that neither member nor applicant states acted in accordance with either rule-based enlargement routines or internalized membership norms. The rules of the community were not taken for granted or interpreted as moral commands by either members or prospective accession states.

What spurred enlargement was the ability of CEEC governments and their Western supporters to invoke rhetorical action in order to overcome an unfavorable constellation of preferences and power inside the European Union and NATO. They based their case for enlargement on the constitutive liberal values and norms of the community of states that both organizations represented, and to which all member states professed to adhere. They emphasized the inconsistency between members' reluctance to enlarge and the organizations' liberal rules of membership, as well as past rhetorical commitments and treatment of outsiders. This proved to be an effective shaming strategy in getting reluctant states to cross over and support enlargement. States opposing enlargement could not afford to veto it, as such an act would have been immensely costly for their credibility and standing in the West. In the end, 'opponents of Eastern enlargement found themselves rhetorically entrapped' (p. 5).

In analyzing the process by which the decision to enlarge came about, Schimmelfennig is self-conscious in comparing the relative significance of four modes of social action. Each elaborates different cognitive mechanisms which can be measured against the null hypothesis of rational action, in which outcomes reflect actors' fixed preferences and bargaining power. *Habitual* modes of action leave the least room for individual agency. Goals and behavior that result from unreflective habit will necessarily conform most closely to collective rules because these already influence social action at the cognitive level. *Normative* action gives more play to individual agency. While an actor's goals are rule-based, the rules reflect the actor's normative reasoning and thus are a matter of reflected choice which may deviate from collective rules. *Communicative* action assumes that actors have conflicting preferences, and that their conflicts cannot be resolved by habit or norms, but only by entering into a rational discourse in which they engage according to standards of true reasoning and rational argumentation. These standards reflect social rules that directly influence actors' behavior, including behavior that contradicts initial preferences. *Rhetorical* action is an argumentative mode of strategic action that is distinguished from communicative action in that it accepts individual and instrumental choice as the starting point of analysis. Actors employ rhetoric that invokes social rules which, in turn, affect their interaction and ultimately influence collective outcomes.

The first two modes of action – habitual and normative – typically form the basis for sociological institutionalist theories of EU and NATO enlargement. These theories do expect enlargement to be the general outcome, but Schimmelfennig's analysis of enlargement preferences and initial enlargement decision making indicates that neither habitual nor normative modes of action trump the rationalist account of actors' preferences and behavior. For example, he finds that 'the enlargement preferences of the member states reflected divergent egoistic calculations of enlargement costs and benefits based on national security and welfare interests and on different degrees of positive and negative interdependence with the CEECs' (p. 191). Schimmelfennig's eclectic analysis thus turns to a complex investigation of the deployment of rhetorical action in understanding the process and decision making of EU and NATO enlargement.

Schimmelfennig's conception of rhetorical action builds on the sociology of Erving Goffman's (1959) classic study on the 'presentation of self in everyday life.' Goffman's conceptualization of actors ranges from a highly socialized construction of 'self,' which features little agency, to the strategic calculation of behavior. His conceptualization of social interactions ranges from structured rituals with prescribed rules, to games in which actors with different capacities and information engage each other. These variations reflect 'a dialectical relationship between strategic action and cultural values and norms' (p. 195). Building on this understanding of self and society, Schimmelfennig's conception of rhetorical action relies on a scale rather than a dichotomy to examine the variable mix of social and rational mechanisms at play in the behavior and interaction of actors operating within the Western community that forms the basis for both the European Union and NATO. Thus, for Schimmelfennig, 'the strategic conception of rules combines the social and ideational ontology of constructivism – in a nonstructuralist, processualist variation – with rationalist instrumentalism' (p. 198) This is a sophisticated and self-conscious use of eclectic reasoning that is applied deftly to the empirics of the processes of EU and NATO enlargement.

In any political environment, rhetorical action is crucial for three reasons. First, political actors operate in a cultural and institutional community environment in which they must pay particular attention to certain core principles thought to define that community. Second, political success in this sort of community environment depends on the legitimacy of actors' choices and actions. And third, to gain, maintain, or increase legitimacy, actors deploy and respond to rhetorical action. Whether or not rhetorical action is effective depends on the availability of formal and informal mechanisms to induce cooperation among opponents. In the processes of EU and NATO enlargement, formal mechanisms such as institutional sanctions and decisions were not as significant as informal mechanisms involving social pressure and social influence. Social influence, in particular, stands out as crucial to the process through which rhetorical action produces collective outcomes. It is most significant when the setting is public, and when rhetorical action conforms to rules perceived as legitimate. Thus, influence ultimately relies on cognitive and emotional reactions that are triggered by social rewards such as popularity and respect for compliance, and punishments such as shaming and shunning for non-compliance. Rhetorical arguments can entrap actors and give rise to the civilizing force of hypocrisy. Even among selfish actors and in the absence of coercive institutional power or egoistic incentives to comply, rule-based collective outcomes are possible as the consequence of rhetorical action. Compliance, from this perspective, becomes the unintended outcome of hypocritical performances and untruthful arguments of uncommitted actors.

This, Schimmelfennig argues, is precisely what occurred in the NATO debate about achieving compliance with complex practical consequences rather than the relatively unproblematic principle of enlargement. At key junctures of the NATO enlargement process, shaming was an important part of the story: for example, when Central European leaders encountered President Clinton at the emotionally charged occasion of the dedication of the US Holocaust Museum; or when Clinton encountered opposition from other NATO members and members of the US Senate. Rhetorical entrapment and shaming were also very much in evidence in the case of the European Union. The rhetorical commitment of the European Union to the founding myth of integrating all European liberal societies, and its unwavering support of this principle since the 1950s, created the basis for an effective shaming strategy throughout the enlargement process.

Schimmelfennig's analysis thus is based on an eclectic mix of constructivist and rationalist thinking. He argues that the constitutive effects of liberal identity have shaped the policies that governed fundamental issues such as membership in regional IOs. However, these collective identities neither correspond to issue-specific interests of states, nor explain the particular process through which actors in organizations may convince their opponents to conform to choices and outcomes that are not in their material interest. In the case of the European Union and NATO, material self-interest and power differentials go a long way in explaining the initial reluctance over eastward expansion among key players. At the same time, rhetorical action was effectively employed by an initially less powerful minority of actors to leverage community rules and to override egotistic interests and instrumental rationality. Without an analysis of rhetorical action, the gap between rule-ignoring individual preferences and rule-conforming collective outcomes could not have been bridged. It is the combination of material interests and power differentials, stressed by rationalists; community rules and norms, stressed by sociological institutionalists; and the strategic deployment of rhetorical action making reference to those rules and norms, which accounts for an outcome that neither rationalist nor sociological accounts can explain fully on their own.

Schimmelfennig's analysis has important implications which deserve to be tested further. It also provides a basis for engaging in practical political action in the international arena without waiting for the conditions that the major international relations paradigms stipulate as necessary for building a viable international order. Rationalism views such an order as epiphenomenal to elusive power- or interest-based international cooperation. Constructivism relies on the equally elusive internalization of norms that are thought to define and encourage 'appropriate' behavior in the international arena. These are high thresholds for the creation of effective forms of governance. For Schimmelfennig, a 'strategic conception of rules and the story of Eastern enlargement draw a more optimistic picture' (p. 287). This is because of the possibilities opened up by rhetorical action even when the constellation of power and interests, or the diffusion of shared norms and conceptions of appropriateness, are not sufficient to enable cooperation. As long as an international community has rules that are considered constitutive, legitimate, and salient, the absence of self-interest or deep socialization does not constitute an insurmountable barrier to

Box 5.4
Frank Schimmelfennig – Eclecticism builds on theoretical ideas from outside the mainstream

When I first started working on *The EU, NATO and European Enlargement* (Schimmelfennig 2003) in the mid-1990s, I was mainly interested in gaining a better understanding of a process of utmost relevance for European international politics. At the same time, I had a hunch that enlargement constituted a puzzle for the rationalist international relations (IR) theories in which I had been trained. But I did not set out to develop an eclectic approach. Rather, my idea was to formulate and apply a (purely) constructivist theory of enlargement, and thus to make a contribution to the major IR debate at the time. It was only when I dug deeper into the subject that I found that neither rationalist nor constructivist institutionalism provided a satisfactory account of both the process and the outcome of EU and NATO enlargement.

My eclectic approach – rhetorical action – was not a result of my empirical work on enlargement. I had come across the idea while reading up on the theory of argumentation, which I needed for my doctoral dissertation, and I had elaborated it to position myself in the German IR debate on Habermas's theory of communicative action. When I did research on enlargement, I again found 'rhetorical action' to be useful to solve the theoretical puzzles I encountered.

I feel that my eclecticism was mostly favorably received. I was lucky that my research was published at a time (early 2000s) when the rationalist–constructivist debate had lasted for a decade and become stale in the eyes of many. At the same time, I was often amused to hear people telling me that it was 'really' a rationalist approach – or that it only worked because it had a constructivist foundation. But most of the debate to this day has been on the substance of the argument, and whether enlargement could not be (better) explained on a purely rationalist or constructivist basis.

My advice follows from my experience: It does not make sense to pursue an eclectic approach as a research goal. Rather, eclecticism is the unintended result of research that seeks to explain specific events as well as possible. Moreover, in order to make a good case for an eclectic approach, you need to start – and try very hard – with pure and parsimonious theories. Finally, eclectic theorizing does not emerge inductively from empirical research. It requires new theoretical ideas, and you are most likely to find those outside the mainstream of disciplinary theorizing.

the construction of international normative order. Rhetorical action and strategies of entrapment provide political substitutes for generating unlikely coalitions that can sustain such an order.

Alice Ba, *[Re]Negotiating East and Southeast Asia* (2009)

The political logic shaping the dynamics of regional organizations varies, as a comparison between Europe and Southeast Asia illustrates. Ba's analysis focuses on how ideas interact with material power in the shaping of a regional integration process that looks quite different from the enlargement of the European Union and NATO. The Association of Southeast Asian Nations (ASEAN) raises intriguing puzzles for analysts of international relations. In that part of the world, states are often divided. Economic interests are often more competitive than complementary. And unilateral action often trumps multilateral cooperation. All of this suggests that a standard realist analysis grounded in the examination of relative capabilities and interests should be perfectly adequate. To the extent that there are diplomatic initiatives centering on ASEAN, they tend to produce little more than meaningless noise – all talk and no action. ASEAN, furthermore, has often been criticized for failing to respond creatively and energetically to a number of recent crises – the financial crisis in 1997, the SARS crisis of 2003, the human rights crisis in Myanmar, and recurrent environmental crises caused by the annual fires in Indonesia.

The problems of policy coordination within ASEAN appear to confirm the skepticism that realists harbor towards regional organizations, and to disappoint the hopes neoliberals generally place in the mutual benefits associated with institutions. While ASEAN states may view the organization as a useful instrument for defending their interests against more powerful countries, they have shunned the pooling of military capabilities that is at the center of balance-of-power theories in world politics. Even military initiatives such as the creation of a Zone of Peace, Freedom, and Neutrality (ZOPFAN) are in the eyes of realists useless, offering little by way of enhanced military capability or deterrent against possible attack. Contractual and neoliberal approaches that are usually more optimistic about the effects of international institutions also see little value in ASEAN. In the face of competing national economic interests, it is striking that ASEAN has virtually none of the formal constraints and binding obligations that are employed to spur political cooperation in organizations such as the European Union and NATO. On all measures of institutional power, ASEAN scores abysmally low in the eyes of rationalist scholars of international relations. At best, it is thought to be a weakly institutionalized 'talking shop.'

Realist and liberal theories can teach us why ASEAN has not done more, but they have difficulty accounting for why ASEAN has not done less. Their perspective reflects the tendency to measure regional cooperation in terms of material benefits and strictly utilitarian terms; but this is only one half of the story. The other half, left curiously under-analyzed and unexplained, concerns the ways in which the dynamics and evolution of ASEAN reflect the dramatic transformation of a once highly volatile, poor, and fragmented region during the last four decades. Specifically, conventional approaches to ASEAN do not suffice to explain what it does do, how it has succeeded in generating a greater degree of cooperation and stability, and what its member states get out of the ASEAN process.

Although ASEAN's regionalism may be weak by some standards, its creation in 1967 provided an important turning point in the history of the region, replacing a confrontational and unstable politics with a cooperative and stable one. It is indeed hard to recall today the fragile political and poor economic conditions that characterized national and regional politics a decade after Southeast Asia had emerged from a deeply divisive colonial rule. Furthermore, during the Cold War Southeast Asia was a pawn in the hands of the great powers, most conspicuously in the Vietnam War. At the regional level the original members of ASEAN – Indonesia, Malaysia, the Philippines, Singapore, and Thailand – were divided by numerous quarrels. Despite weak domestic structures, great power interventions, and serious regional rivalries, for reasons not appreciated in standard realist and liberal accounts, Southeast Asia's regional cooperation has gradually widened and deepened during successive decades. Economic ties have grown, as new regional arrangements have drawn the attention of more powerful and influential regional actors, as in the case of the ASEAN Regional Forum (ARF), the ASEAN Plus Three (APT) meetings, and the East Asia Summit (EAS). Some have gone so far as to refer to these processes as the 'ASEAN-ization' of Southeast and East Asia as well as of Asia-Pacific relations. Arguably ASEAN's most important achievement has been the improvement of relations with China, and the latter's recognition of the value of ASEAN for its evolving regional and global strategy. In the realm of security, it is significant that some longstanding territorial disputes between founding members have been settled or moderated peacefully. In fact, ASEAN's Treaty of Amity and Cooperation (TAC) is now a widely accepted indigenous, political security treaty in a region once accustomed to rivalry and conflict. Furthermore, the domestic structures of ASEAN's member states have become more stable and consolidated, though not always in a democratic form. All of these changes represent 'remarkable and dramatic developments for an organization of lesser states for which conflict, not cooperation, had once dominated so many levels of their politics' (p. 3).

In exploring how and why these changes occurred, Ba finds little help in rationalist styles of analysis. She frames her puzzle on the basis of a baseline that is not constrained by the assumptions and expectations of either realist or liberal-institutionalist theories. The puzzle is cast in the form of four interrelated questions: How did competing states with divergent interests manage to stabilize their relations and deepen cooperation to the point that they now refer to 'One Southeast Asia'? How did ASEAN, which viewed itself as specifically 'Southeast Asian' and as a lesser power in the wider region, become the gravitational center of post-Cold War patterns of cooperation encompassing East Asian and Asia-Pacific regionalisms? What do these expanded regionalisms mean for ASEAN's self-defined identity as a Southeast Asian organization? And how can significant change in the direction of regional cooperation be reconciled with the challenges that continue to be evident in intra-ASEAN coordination? In answering these questions, Ba does not deny the relevance of national power and interest. But her self-consciously eclectic analysis aims also to incorporate ideas and social processes in the disciplined effort to account for both the relative weakness of regional cooperation at any given moment and its surprisingly vibrant evolution during the last four decades.

The center of Ba's analysis focuses on regionalism as a set of ideas and a cumulative social and political process. Ideas, she argues, are necessary for a more diverse and expanded view of the exchanges that take place between actors. And, alongside a more complex view of bargaining processes and material exchanges, they help in explaining both the challenges and the accomplishments of regional integration. Ideas of diversity and diverse interests created the conditions for insecurity and regional rivalry. Over time, these ideas also provided a justification for a regional organization that would mitigate conflict and encourage political cooperation without formal cooperation and centralized coordination. Among these ideas, the continued salience of national sovereignty ranked high, creat- ing normative obstacles to more formalized political coopera- tion and centralized policy coordination. This did not mean that regional cooperation was doomed, only that it would occur through different mechanisms and processes.

In addition, Ba's conceptualization of the problem emphasizes an extended process evolving over a longer period of time. Rather than treating cooperation and coordination as one-shot deals, Ba charac- terizes them as ongoing social processes that involve 'interactive and cumulative social negotiations' (p. 4). Individual initiatives in ASEAN certainly merit attention. Many of them are fraught with difficulties and disappointments, as realist and liberal analyses note. Yet each of these initiatives is also no more than a point along an extended process of social negotiation that can transform social contexts and relationships. In fact, regional elites themselves have tended to view regional cooperation as a relationship-building process rather than as a series of discrete agreements. The social dynamics evident in such a complex process, Ba argues, should be as much an analytical and political concern as the gains and losses, successes and failures associated with each individual initiative. This is why Ba extends her analysis to various forms of regionalism – such as Asia-Pacific Economic Cooperation (APEC), ARF, and APT – that have been influenced or spurred by ASEAN, but are all related, interactive elements of the same cumulative set of dia- logues and practices associated with ASEAN's evolution over time. Material incentives and bargaining are included in this concep- tualization of regional cooperation. But 'the process of cooperation involves not just the negotiation of specific material interests but also social relations, social practices, and indeed social identities' (p. 4).

Central to cumulative processes of social negotiation is the insti- tution of regional dialogue. It is through talk (what Schimmelfennig refers to as rhetorical and communicative action) that ASEAN's diverse states have maintained and pursued agreement and consen- sus on various issues of common concern. And it is their talk that has, over time, generated a regional political culture of restraint, respect, and responsibility that offers a striking contrast to both the conflict-ridden Southeast Asia of the 1960s and the more formal- ized rules and procedures for encouraging political cooperation in European organizations. Traditional writings on ASEAN certainly emphasize the point that ASEAN regionalism involves a lot of talk (as opposed to action). But what these writings miss is the cumulation of substantive, material effects of regional talk over time.

These effects are evident in the production of new norms and the formation of a new regional culture, as expressed in institutionalized practices that stress non-confrontational and inclusive political engagements. Careful attention to the process of dialogue reveals the crystallization of a regional commitment to non-violent resolution of problems, as well as a shared normative belief that ASEAN's member states should work toward regional solutions. This also means that, to the extent that regional stability is a prerequisite for economic growth, ASEAN has created the conditions for an astonishing growth rate for the region and for many of its member states. At the same time, ASEAN's norms and practices are not free of flaws. They are generally state-centric, and often undemocratic. They can also be quite inefficient in generating collective action in response to particular situations. Nevertheless, these norms and practices have proven to be effective in preventing conflicts from escalating – a fact that is widely recognized by political leaders throughout the region, though not sufficiently appreciated in much of the academic literature.

In a nifty analytic move, Ba emphasizes the significance of Southeast Asia's relatively high level of regional diversity as the starting point for regional dialogue. This focus also reveals how closely material and ideational factors are intertwined. Diversity in people, geography, colonial experience, ethnic complexity, and national perspectives is pervasive, making Southeast Asia a much less coherent regional space, comparatively speaking. Realists recast this diversity, quite appropriately, in terms of competing national interests that often spur regional rivalries and political tensions. However, in Ba's formulation, this diversity is not only an objective reality but also an intersubjective fact. It is a strong, shared belief that Southeast Asia is an unusually diverse region, and that this diversity is likely to be a source of division and disunity. This intersubjective component of diversity has made reinterpretation possible over time, as government leaders became more committed to the ASEAN way because of the objective diversity of the region.

Ba argues that, 'alongside beliefs about the dangers of Southeast Asia's diversity and fragility, ASEAN politics are also guided by an important concern for regional unity' (p. 7). This is precisely the story she tells about ASEAN's evolution since its founding in 1967. Elites at the time were fully cognizant of the enormous diversity of the region. In addition, they understood the risks that diversity posed to the political stability and economic growth in which they all had a vital interest. Diversity meant weak national integration and regional divisions. The solution thus was to be found in national integration and regional unity; ASEAN offered a promising path to both. Partial realist accounts of ASEAN's diversity and division are thus augmented on this crucial point by Ba's ideational explanation of ASEAN's astonishingly successful evolution during the last four decades. Concern for the negative effects of diversity spur regional elites to engage in dialogues and to value regional cooperation. Yet because these efforts are motivated by a strong, longstanding, and shared belief in the reality of diversity, there exists also a shared fear of pushing regionalism so far that it may fall apart. Thus, 'concern for regional unity … becomes both driver and constraint on ASEAN regionalism' (p. 7), explaining the accomplishments of ASEAN as well as the difficulties, delays, and limitations of its various initiatives.

A distinctive aspect of Southeast Asian regionalism is the linkage between the evolution of intra-ASEAN relations and broader, extra-regional developments, especially perceived changes in the policies of the United States and other major powers toward the region. This link is a function of the particular dependence of specific Southeast Asian states on the United States for economic and security assistance. The link also depends on the ability of the United States to intervene militarily and otherwise in the region's affairs should it choose to do so. During the last half-century, the Vietnam War was the defining event in the region's history. However, conditional trade, investment, and aid concessions also have figured prominently. US policy changes have thus provided an important catalyst for both intra- and extra-regional relations. For example, Ba notes that ASEAN's creation in 1967 was a response to the US war in Vietnam as well as the retrenchment of the United Kingdom in Southeast Asia in the mid to late 1960s. Similarly, the TAC was a response to the end of the Vietnam War, while ZOPFAN evolved as a reaction to the US–China détente. In the economic realm, a series of preferential trade agreements (PTAs) was largely a reaction to the Nixon shock of 1971 and the subsequent food and oil crises. And, more recently, ARF, AFTA, and ASEAN 10 have all responded to shifts in ASEAN's external relations since the end of the Cold War, while East Asian initiatives such as ASEAN-plus have been spurred by disappointment over the US reaction to the Asian financial crisis of 1997. Changes outside of Southeast Asia, and particularly changes in US policy, thus were deeply intertwined in the ongoing regional evolution of Southeast Asia. The linkage between external environments and intra-ASEAN developments, however, has been consistently mediated by the cumulative social processes accompanying dialogue, whether in the form of argument, information sharing, consensus seeking, or social reinforcement.

Ba's analysis has important implications for both scholarship and practice. In relation to theories of international relations, her study highlights three related dynamics that play an underappreciated role in system change: the long-term roles played by seemingly unimportant events and shocks; evolutionary processes of change that are more gradual and incremental; and the cumulative effects of ideas and processes on thinking and practice. 'Each of these dynamics,' Ba argues, 'is better revealed when we consider cooperation in more process-driven, less outcomes-driven or even events-driven terms' (p. 233). Regarding policy implications, Ba's analysis points to reasons why ASEAN and its most recent initiatives should be taken seriously even if the track record of ASEAN regionalism is not as strong as the European Union's by the measures typically used to analyze regional integration. With ASEAN's forays into the region of 'East Asia' through initiatives such as ARF, APT, and EAS, there are reasons to be cautious about whether the social processes that have generated a common understanding of regional diversity and unity in Southeast Asia can automatically be translated into similar social processes with similar effects in East Asia. What ASEAN's experience does suggest, however, is that 'the future of East Asian regionalism – indeed, East Asian security – hinges on states' ability to strengthen the ideational glue, foundational agreement, and processes that can maintain relations in the face of adversity and division' (p. 242). For Southeast Asia itself, the adoption of a new ASEAN Charter in 2007 reveals the continuing commitment to regional unity through an 'ASEAN Community' based on security, economic, and sociocultural pillars. At the same time, the passing of many of the 'old men of ASEAN' (p. 245), as well as the explicit efforts to ensure participation among new societal groups and transnational networks, point to new challenges in negotiating, or renegotiating, the significance of diversity

Box 5.5
Alice D. Ba – The 'whens' and 'hows' of process

Eclecticism was not explicitly on my mind when I began work on *[Re]Negotiating East and Southeast Asia* (Ba 2009), though it probably was eclectic from the beginning. I was self-conscious about investigating the role played by particular ideas as both focal points and frames for ASEAN cooperation. I was also interested in questions of change and continuity. Those interests then led me down other roads, especially as I tried to pinpoint and answer the theoretical and empirical 'whens' and 'hows'.

For me, 'process' became critical to the project and its ultimate conclusions in more ways than one. Partly, it was the method: The process of tracing ASEAN and particular ideas over time revealed the importance of process in ASEAN and a pattern of ideational-material interactions, both of which became important pieces of my explanation. For example, when I began the project, I knew that the question of power and the question of divergent interests would have to be accounted for (not just because of the ASEAN states' structure of relations with world actors that material accounts emphasize, but also because they have been ongoing preoccupations of the regional discourse on and in Southeast Asia). Process tracing was the method that revealed both the patterns and the different ways in which they mattered.

Similarly, in pursuit of the 'whens' and 'hows' the importance of process – both cooperation as an extended, cumulative process involving ideational, material, and social negotiations, and the specific process by which ASEAN states pursue agreement – came to be as important as my original interest in specific ideas.

If I have advice for others, it is simply to be open to discovery. Perhaps consistent with my own findings on this particular project, one thing that I have learned is that the way in which debates are framed in both international relations and in the existing ASEAN literature have a way of bounding what we are inclined to see and how we see it. This is a constant struggle for one personally and in terms of how one's work is received and interpreted – but it is also a struggle that for me led to greater clarity and new directions. As I conceive it, my project is a project that is not just about both material and ideational factors but also about how, when brought together, they contribute to an explanation that may be more than the sum of its parts.

and the value attached to different aspects of regional unity. While radical changes are likely to be constrained by the founding ideas associated with ASEAN, Ba emphasizes that 'states' willingness – albeit gradual and often reluctant – to discuss contentious and formerly taboo issues' also points to an organization that has matured greatly over the last forty years (p. 248).

Conclusion

The works surveyed in this chapter examine the evolution of diverse institutions of governance, ranging from regional institutions such as the European Union and NATO (Schimmelfennig 2003) and ASEAN (Ba 2009) to global institutions such as the IMF and UNHCR (Barnett and Finnemore 2004), the UN Security Council (Hurd 2007), and the ICC (Schiff 2008). In all of these cases, we find not only that these institutions potentially challenge exclusive claims of state sovereignty, but also that they shape, and evolve in response to, economic and other issues. The evidence suggests that global and regional institutions will generally not prevent powerful states from pursuing their interests. At the same time, it is clear that states frequently join institutions in part because they want to be perceived by the international community as acceding to international norms that have become more salient to them over time. In addition, the studies suggest that in their day-to-day functioning, global and regional institutions discover new sources of influence and encounter unexpected constraints. These are often related to the internal organizational dynamics of the institutions, and cannot be reduced to either their specific mandates or the distribution of power and interests among its members. The ongoing operations of global and regional institutions reflect the complex interplay of power differentials and material interests, on the one hand, and of norms and shared identities, on the other. Denying the existence of one or the other will leave our analysis shortchanged and our practices ill-informed.

All five books exemplify eclectic scholarship. Specifically, they all conform to the three criteria outlined in Chapter 1 (see Table 1.1) for identifying analytic eclecticism in the study of world politics. First, each of the studies characterizes its core research question in a nuanced way that reflects the actual experiences and challenges faced by real institutions or organizations as they attempt to pursue or redefine their mandates in a changing international environment. What motivates each study is not so much the application of an existing paradigm or the desire to fill in a gap in the scholarly literature, but a curiosity about the behavior and evolution of global or regional organizations and the success or failure of IOs' various efforts to influence aspects of world politics.

Second, all of the authors aim at middle-range theories rather than universal laws or highly detailed descriptions. Their causal stories are not idiosyncratic, as they incorporate portable mechanisms that can be found to varying degrees in other international institutions. But explanations of specific outcomes reveal distinctive configurations of mechanisms and processes which makes it impossible to develop a parsimonious model of how international institutions behave. As Schimmelfennig notes (see Box 5.4), not all of the authors set out to be self-consciously eclectic in their respective approaches. In the process of digging more deeply into the evidence, however, they all came to recognize the complex interactions among material and ideational factors, and between the internal and external environments of the organizations and their members.

Finally, all of the works discussed in this chapter reveal a more or less direct interest in issues of practice and policy. They seek not only to understand and explain outcomes, but also to assess, and in some cases improve, the efficacy and legitimacy of collective governance in various contexts. This is evident, for example, in Barnett and Finnemore's and Hurd's concerns for the moral and political authority of the United Nations, as well as in Schiff's and Ba's emphases on the limited accomplishments of the ICC and ASEAN in very challenging environments. These five books thus illustrate how eclectic analyses can meaningfully engage efforts underway in the world of policy and practice to explore new, more representative multilateral institutions and modes of governance.[2]

In their own reflections (Boxes 5.1 to 5.5), the authors discussed in this chapter concur that eclecticism is not an end in itself; but they also reveal that eclecticism can emerge from many different paths, some more self-consciously traveled than others. Barnett and Schiff make clear that they pursued eclectic approaches from the outset because they found paradigm-bound theories to be inadequate. The fact that dominant theories of international relations had so little to say about international institutions made it useful for Barnett and his coauthor, Martha Finnemore, to turn to organization theory as a point of departure. And Schiff is explicit that, instead of being loyal to any particular 'theoretical god,' he saw fit to incorporate selected aspects of realism, liberalism, and constructivism insofar as this procedure helped him to construct 'as broad and complete an understanding of the Court as possible within the confines of a short and readable book.'

Ba, Hurd, and Schimmelfennig, in contrast, did not initially set out to pursue eclecticism. For Schimmelfennig, 'eclecticism is the unintended result of research that seeks to explain specific events as well as possible.' In fact, Schimmelfennig notes that he initially set out 'to formulate a (purely) constructivist theory' to explain the processes of EU and NATO expansion unfolding in the 1990s. It was only when he 'dug deeper into the subject' that it became apparent that he had to adopt a more eclectic strategy that incorporated elements from both rationalist and constructivist works. For Ba and Hurd, attention to the respective processes of social negotiation and legitimation provided the basis for their gradual movement in an eclectic direction. Hurd began with an interest in constructivist theories of international relations alongside organization theory and sociology; along the way he found paradigmatic boundaries too confining for understanding the most interesting aspects of the politics of the Security Council. And Ba notes that tracing the processes of how ASEAN member states pursued agreement is what drew her towards a careful consideration of 'ideational-material interactions.'

The authors' reflections also suggest that departures from dominant theoretical traditions can be driven by both the latter's limitations and the varied insights each tradition provides into related aspects of the complex realities the authors are trying to grasp. However, they emphasize that *which* insights to draw upon and *how* to combine them are crucially important questions that cannot be taken lightly. Barnett and Schimmelfennig join the other authors in rejecting the notion of paradigmatic battles and recognizing the virtues of eclecticism. However, they also insist that the values of simplicity and parsimony should not be tossed aside; before proceeding to eclecticism, it is worth pausing to consider whether less is more. Barnett (see Box 5.1) warns that 'causal complexity can be potentially mistaken for a "garbage can" approach in which everything matters.' He invokes Occam's razor to emphasize the value of exploring the simplest available explanations before proceeding to combine them in more complex causal accounts. Schimmelfennig goes further in pointing out that eclectic theorizing is not entirely an inductive exercise, and requires a search for potentially usable novel theoretical ideas that extends beyond the mainstream. For him, the debates among German international relations scholars over the utility of Habermas's theory of communicative action paved the way for the development of the concept of 'rhetorical action' that would later provide a theoretical core for his eclectic account for EU and NATO enlargement.

For Ba and Schiff, the answers to the questions of which factors matter most and how to combine them emerged from the process of delving into the empirics of their subject matter. Schiff was not interested in exploring each and every possible permutation of factors drawn from different paradigms. But in carefully tracing the ICC's development, it became clear that each approach had heuristic value in accounting for some important aspects of the story. Similarly for Ba, the significance of policy processes *inside* ASEAN became progressively more apparent, setting her on a path to exploring 'cooperation as an extended, cumulative process involving ideational, material, and social negotiations.' In both cases, analytic eclecticism emerged from a careful exploration of the empirics in light of the limitations of existing paradigm-bound theories. At the same time, as Hurd reminds us, eclectic scholarship can neither reconcile nor ignore the differences over epistemology and philosophy that underlie inter-paradigm debates. The pragmatist ethos that permits the eclectic researcher to temporarily set aside these differences to tackle complex realities also imparts 'the obligation to eventually return to these questions and reflect on what the research says about them.' This is perhaps a point with which all of the authors would agree: eclecticism offers a pragmatic way of getting on with the work of understanding the world, but also requires us to reflect back on existing theoretical perspectives and metatheoretical foundations.

The notes struck by the authors we met in Chapters 3 and 4 resonate with these statements. Eclectic research is problem- rather than theory-driven. The nature of the problem, and of the causal account offered, cannot be circumscribed on the basis of immutable theoretical priors derived from paradigmatic assumptions. And intellectual curiosity and individual biography can play a major role in shaping the pathways through which one arrives at eclectic scholarship.

Chapter 6

Conclusion

In this concluding chapter we consider the lessons of the various examples of analytic eclecticism discussed in Chapters 3 to 5. Drawing on only some of these studies for purpose of illustration, we emphasize the similar ways in which authors have posed their problems, developed their arguments, and engaged the issue of practical relevance. We also consider in passing how the substantive issues tackled by some of these authors might be problematized and analyzed in paradigm-bound scholarship. In the second part of the chapter we offer a discussion of the professional risks and trade-offs of eclectic scholarship for individual scholars, acknowledging the difficulties of sustaining eclectic research in an institutional environment in which scholarly assessments and professional advancement frequently require standards to be established on the basis of paradigmatic assumptions and boundaries. Considering the track record of conventional scholarship in generating practically useful knowledge about international affairs (Nye 2009), we emphasize the importance of accepting and encouraging eclectic work alongside paradigm-driven research. Our view is in broad agreement with a proliferation of arguments in favor of eclectic styles of reasoning in other subfields of political science, in other disciplines, and in various historical or practical contexts.

Lessons from eclectic scholarship

Long ago, the British philosopher Michael Oakeshott (1962 [1947], p. 15) noted that 'nobody supposes that the knowledge that belongs to a good cook is confined to what is or may be written down in the cookery book.' The best way to learn a recipe may well be to watch the cook at work in the kitchen. In a similar vein, the best way to discuss how to pursue eclectic research is to consider the common attributes of works that have fruitfully adopted an eclectic approach to generate interesting and useful insights. It is not possible to construct a definitive 'model' or 'guide' for conducting eclectic scholarship. But we can learn from considering what makes these diverse works similarly eclectic, and what sets them apart from conventional paradigm-bound research projects. This takes us back to the three criteria for defining and distinguishing eclectic styles of research outlined in Chapter 1 (Table 1.1): the open-ended formulation of problems; the construction of complex middle-range causal stories; and the facilitation of pragmatic engagement between the academic world and the world of policy and practice. We draw selectively on the books discussed in Chapters 3 to 5 to recapitulate the significance of these criteria and to distinguish eclectic from paradigm-bound research.

Problem formulation

Eclecticism is more than problem-driven research. Any problem can be formulated in a manner that fits closely with the theoretical priors of the researcher (Shapiro 2005; Sil 2004). Thus, paradigm-bound research can also claim to be problem-driven. Eclectic scholarship is distinctive in that it seeks to resist the temptation to articulate problems in a manner that facilitates the application of particular paradigmatic assumptions or pre-given metatheoretical principles. It is thus significant that each of the books discussed in Chapters 3 to 5 is not only problem-driven but formulates research questions in an open-ended manner, highlighting their inherent complexity rather than focusing on selected aspects that are emphasized in existing paradigm-bound theories. In their problem definition, eclectic analyses lay the groundwork for exploring how concepts, logics, mechanisms, and findings associated with various paradigms might be selectively integrated to shed new light on substantive problems that are of interest to both scholars and practitioners.

Realists, for example, have frequently organized their research questions on issues of conflict and security around concepts such as the balance of power, the logic of deterrence, and the significance of offense or defense. Such questions are undeniably important, and have generated path-breaking studies. At the same time, it becomes difficult to recognize, let alone problematize, more complex phenomena where the logics associated with balancing, deterrence, or offensive/defensive postures are fundamentally intertwined with a host of other pertinent logics and unfolding processes. Jervis thus analyzes the relations among the United States and European powers, not only in terms of an alliance formed against a common security threat, but also as a security community encompassing the most powerful and developed states in the international system. This security community is an unprecedented phenomenon that cannot be explained solely by traditional realist arguments. Jervis also problematizes in a variety of contexts the internal dynamics of that community, specifically in relation to the United States as its most powerful member.

The same holds true for Finnemore's study of intervention. Within the framework of realism, the emphasis would rest solely on the power differentials that enable stronger states to intervene in weaker ones. Power differentials matter, of course. However, Finnemore's formulation of the problem is richer, and incorporates an observation that has eluded realist treatments of intervention: over time, the motivations for intervening and the conditions under which interventions are deemed acceptable have changed dramatically.

Relatedly, realism provides useful insights into why states pursue nuclear weapons, and why they are not likely to use them when confronted with the prospect of mutually assured destruction. However, the questions that Solingen and Paul ask – why states that are capable of developing weapons choose not to do so, and why some states have helped to promote a tradition of non-use – are more difficult to articulate within a theoretical framework that assumes the primacy of logics associated with nuclear deterrence or the security dilemma. This is why the title of Solingen's book, *Nuclear Logics* (2007), employs the plural.

On questions of international and global political economy discussed in Chapter 4, neoliberalism has made important advances in developing a systematic and cumulative research program. Beginning with the concept of interdependence, it has effectively employed game theory to clarify the logics through which states, even under conditions of anarchy, manage to cooperate and advance their separate and joint interests. Within such a framework, the architecture of international financial institutions, the coordination of economic liberalization, and processes of regional integration are typically problematized as instances of institutionalized cooperation that reflect the material interests and resources of member states. While this is a useful intellectual move that highlights important aspects of political economy, it often requires us to treat as 'exogenous' vital domestic issues such as the social bases and political coalitions that enhance or constrain a state's ability to act on its preferences.

These are precisely the factors that the authors discussed in Chapter 4 incorporate into the formulation of their research questions. Seabrooke's formulation of his research question, for example, investigates two processes: how various social groups respond to different policies of credit allocation, and how this in turn affects a state's capacity to project financial power in the international arena. The connection between these two processes is normally ignored by paradigmatic research, which takes for granted the causal primacy of states' absolute or relative gains, factor endowments, or international institutions. Similarly, Woll problematizes the ambiguity and fluidity of trade preferences among particular European business groups; she refuses to simply assume that firm interests are fixed or that firms will always oppose deregulation for fear of undermining their privileged positions in non-competitive home markets. Stubbs is also very clear in resisting a paradigm-driven problem formulation. His research question – why high economic growth occurs in sites marked by destructive wars or the threat of war – is located at the intersection of security studies and political economy. Such a question cannot be formulated neatly within the parameters typically associated with either realist or neoliberal research programs.

The questions addressed by the authors we discuss in Chapter 5 are more conducive to eclectic analysis. The study of transnational governance is a relatively new field of scholarship which is not clearly dominated by any one paradigm. Yet it would not take much imagination to reframe these books' questions in narrower terms that seek greater conformity with particular paradigms. For example, questions about the influence and interests of powerful members in international organizations tend to be cast in realist terms, while neoliberals are more likely to focus on the efficiency gains and reduced transaction costs associated with those organizations. Alternatively, constructivist approaches to the emergence or transformation of international organizations might focus on questions relating to the effects of transnational norms or regional identities. All of these formulations would miss the unexpected or self-defeating outcomes on which Barnett and Finnemore thus focus their attention – the interaction of international organizations (IOs), conceived as autonomous bureaucratic organizations, with their member states and international environments.

Questions about persistence or expansion of regional institutions are often cast in paradigmatic research in terms of the utility of institutions for their members. Schimmelfennig views the problem of NATO and EU enlargement as more complex, treating it as a complicated and risky course of action that the member states decided to undertake without any assurance of obvious material gains. Such a phenomenon needs to be problematized in a manner that recognizes the complexity, diversity, and evolution of the various interests and ideals pursued by new and old member states, and this would be difficult to do within the confines of paradigm-bound research.

Complex middle-range causal accounts

Eclectic scholarship is characterized by complex causal stories that are cast at the level of middle-range theory. They lie somewhere between context-sensitive descriptive narratives, and universal theories or models. Typically they include elements – mechanisms and logics – that are portable across a set of comparable contexts, often implicitly defined by a stated problem. However, the particular attributes of a context influence the specific configuration of mechanisms and logics that generate distinctive processes and outcomes (Falleti and Lynch 2009). It is of course possible to employ parsimonious middle-range explanations that are founded on metatheoretical principles associated with specific paradigms, thus emphasizing the operation of some mechanisms while downplaying the effects of others. What distinguishes an *eclectic* middle-range account is the sacrifice of parsimony in favor of an open-ended exploration of a broader range of causal factors, normally analyzed in isolation by contending paradigm-bound theories (Sil and Katzenstein 2010).

While some mechanisms and logics are general enough to be present in every definable context, the fact remains that the particular assortment and configuration of mechanisms and logics in any given context may be idiosyncratic. Hence, eclectic analysis resists overly abstract models or parsimonious universal theories in favor of more modest middle-range causal stories intended to trace and compare the configurations of relevant mechanisms across comparable contexts. Such a view of causality is entirely compatible with the growing acceptance of more extensive endogeneity, and the ubiquity of complex interaction effects in the study of politics (Hall 2003). In the context of contemporary international relations, we assume that eclectic causal stories will typically incorporate elements of at least two and possibly all three of the main contending paradigms: constructivism, liberalism, and realism. We also expect such accounts to feature processes that cut across the analytic divides presumed to exist between levels of analysis and the material and ideational dimensions of social reality (see Figure 1.1).

On questions of security, Jervis offers an eclectic causal account, cast in the form of a 'synthetic interactive explanation,' of the emergence and dynamics of a novel security community encompassing most of the great, developed powers. Jervis is very self-conscious in considering whether, how, and to what extent different causal forces contributed to the general and issue-specific outcomes he addresses. His explanation features material factors (such as the costs of war and the difficulty of conquest) as well as ideational ones (the emergence of a shared identity among great powers that also embrace democratic norms).

Kang's study is also motivated by the presumption that identities, interests, and relative capabilities all influence how East and Southeast Asian states are responding to China's rise. Questioning the falsifiability of realist arguments that stretch unduly the concept of balancing to explain East Asian regional dynamics, Kang presents a complex causal account of how historically shaped configurations and understandings of power, interests, and identities have produced regionally specific interpretations of China's capabilities and policies.

Finally, in relation to the pursuit of nuclear weapons, Solingen's explanation considers not only the regional contexts within which states make the decision on whether to acquire weapons, but also the way in which the domestic political survival of elites influences political calculations. In each of these cases, the causal stories are not as general and parsimonious as those based on realism. At the same time, they offer middle-range explanations of empirical processes that are difficult to capture in a purely realist theoretical framework.

The arguments reviewed in Chapter 4 are similarly complex in seeking to link processes that operate at different levels of analysis, and that straddle the analytic divide presumed to exist between material and ideational factors. This is clearly evident in Seabrooke's analysis of states' financial capacity in the international arena. In adopting a Weberian perspective emphasizing the legitimacy of economic policies among lower-income groups, Seabrooke's book breaks with conventional rationalist or materialist approaches to financial statecraft. At the same time, in contrast to constructivist accounts stressing the primacy of norms and identities, the distribution of credit and the flow of capital are important components of his causal story. Sinclair's analysis is also more complex than more parsimonious accounts that assess the role of rating agencies in terms of efficiency. Such studies typically stress the importance of knowledge and information. Sinclair acknowledges their significance in his book, but he digs deeper to uncover the ways in which the origins and evolution of knowledge networks related to credit rating agencies affect their authority in global financial markets.

Jabko's 'strategic constructivism' also reflects an effort to develop a complex analytic framework to explain the sources and implications of the intensification of European integration processes starting in the 1980s. His account is built on a constructivist foundation, but adds to this a more complicated story about the emergence of a political strategy in which elites self-consciously deployed the 'market' concept to simultaneously promote economic liberalization and strengthen supranational governance. In contrast to straightforward interest-based or identity-based explanations of European integration, Jabko's analysis is able to account for the timing of the deepening of European integration, while also explaining why the same elites could both embrace market-friendly reforms and concentrate decision-making power within European-level institutions.

The scholars discussed in Chapter 5 offer similarly complex accounts of the behavior, efficacy, and transformation of different IOs. Barnett and Finnemore, for example, draw on organization theory to construct an account in which the internal bureaucratic features of international organizations interact with conventionally posited causal factors to produce distinctive outcomes. Some of these results surprise powerful member states, while others can undermine the IO's original mission. Barnett and Finnemore put less emphasis than rationalists might on the role of powerful members in influencing IO behavior, and they do not insist, as constructivists might, on a fixed relationship between the diffusion of international norms and the behavior of IOs in a given sphere of politics.

Schiff's analysis of the ICC is explicit in borrowing from realist, liberal, and constructivist research traditions to explain the emergence and operation of the Court. His complex account weaves together realist elements that help to explain why the Court can play only a limited role; neoliberal elements that specify the extent of overlapping interests in the case of the Court's limited successes; and constructivist elements that stress why states committed themselves to creating an IO that does not appear to advance their material interests.

Hurd's analysis, too, sacrifices parsimony in order to generate a more comprehensive understanding of how and why the UN Security Council operates the way it does. Hurd recognizes that the Council, like sovereign states and some other organizations, is endowed with the right to exercise final authority. However, he emphasizes that international relations consist of different fields within which there exist different sources of ultimate legitimacy. Thus, the very limits to the powers of the Security Council, frustrating to many observers, are for Hurd integral to its legitimacy.

At a minimum, the books discussed in Chapter 5 illustrate how seemingly inexplicable aspects of IO behavior begin to make sense once we extend the scope of causal analysis beyond the theoretical boundaries established by any one paradigm.

Pragmatic engagement with the 'real world'

Finally, eclectic scholarship is partially motivated by a desire to generate useful practical insights that are, at least in principle, responsive to debates that extend beyond the academe. To be sure, paradigm-bound research sometimes claims to offer prescriptions for policy, and eclectic scholarship sometimes leaves implicit the practical significance of its findings. For the most part, however, paradigm-driven research is intended to engage with the world of existing theories, with the aim of either pursuing theory building within a preferred paradigm, or confronting theories constructed within a competing paradigm. The result is a growing gap between theory and policy which, as Nye (2009) notes, many academics view as unproblematic so long as 'better social science theory' emerges in the process. In a similar vein, Craig Calhoun (2009) notes how the dramatic growth of universities and the emphasis on academic professionalism since the Second World War has spurred social scientists to focus their communications on others in the academy, with very little engagement of public issues and audiences.

Analytic eclecticism certainly engages existing social science theories, but with the intention of systematically drawing together elements of diverse theories in ways that can shed new light on real-world issues of policy and practice. Eclectic approaches may yield original findings that are interesting and compelling scholarly contributions in their own right. But analytic eclecticism can do more than this. Because it is not invested in either intra-paradigm progress or inter-paradigm competition, analytic eclecticism can respond to calls for a more 'public social science' (Calhoun 2009).

The authors discussed in Chapters 3 to 5 are not equally explicit about the practical or normative relevance of their scholarship; indeed, on this third criterion there exists the greatest variation among the books we have discussed. Even so, none of the scholars we discuss is attempting to shy away from the messiness and complexity of issues of policy and practice. And all at least partially justify their research in terms of the insights it can generate for contemporary and future debates over policy and practice.

For questions of security, for example, Jervis is quite explicit in spelling out the implications of his analysis for the conduct of US foreign policy. He is naturally concerned with the strengths and weaknesses of paradigm-bound theoretical accounts. But his primary objective is to correct for the fact that the models and protocols guiding US foreign policy have not kept up with important changes in the international environment. Paul is also clear about the relevance of his analysis of the tradition of nuclear non-use for foreign policy. While cautioning against excessive reliance on this tradition for ensuring peace and security, he emphasizes the gains to the United States and other nuclear powers of pursuing self-deterrence given the long-term material and reputational costs of breaking with the tradition of non-use.

Similarly, Solingen sketches out practically useful scenarios that follow from her eclectic analysis: internationally oriented political coalitions will drive policy away from the acquisition of nuclear weapons while inward-oriented coalitions, all other things being equal, are more likely to move toward it. This has important implications for how much emphasis policymakers should place on either international norms or the balance of threats in trying to understand the motivations of particular leaders who opt to either pursue or forgo nuclear weapons. Finnemore's analysis is not framed in terms that directly suggest any specific policy prescriptions; however, it does speak to important and enduring normative concerns about intervention which indirectly bear on policy and practice.

The analyses of political economy discussed in Chapter 4 are also driven to varying degrees by a concern for normative or policy issues. Jabko's analysis of the political strategy behind Europeanization, for example, raises the possibility that different strategic calculations under different circumstances could lead to a weakening of supranational governance. This in turn is important for debates over how much policy makers within and outside of Europe can assume that the power and authority of EU institutions and officials will continue to grow indefinitely. Stubbs acknowledges that his analysis does not have general policy implications for all countries in all regions. However, his approach to East Asian development does have clear practical relevance in that it can alert policymakers to the significance of regionally specific patterns of economic growth, and to the developmental potential that inheres especially in countries that have experienced the threat or impact of war over an extended period of time. Seabrooke's analysis draws attention to the normative and practical significance of the legitimacy accorded to specific social policies by groups normally considered insignificant in the analysis of international financial outcomes. The normative significance rests on the perceived fairness of policies governing the allocation of credit across different strata of society. The practical significance rests on how a greater sense of fairness can help policymakers to draw upon a broader and deeper pool of capital when seeking to shore up a state's financial position in the international arena.

Finally, on questions related to international organizations and supranational governance, the eclectic studies discussed in Chapter 5 lead to more ambivalent appraisals than paradigm-driven scholarship tends to offer. Although they recognize the achievements of some IOs (such as the UNHCR) under challenging circumstances, Barnett and Finnemore highlight the risks that inhere in the undemocratic liberal cosmopolitanism underpinning many IOs. Their case studies suggest that the pursuit of liberal policy goals through impersonal bureaucratic procedures is easily impaired by a lack of political mechanisms assuring accountability. This risk also points to the need for a more nuanced and critical treatment of the normative claims IOs typically advance on their own behalf.

By way of contrast, Ba's and Hurd's books soften the harsh criticisms often leveled at ASEAN and the Security Council. Ba's analysis, for example, suggests to policymakers the need for a more realistic baseline for assessing the performance of regional organizations such as ASEAN. Her emphasis on the question of why ASEAN has not done less stands in stark contrast to conventional rationalist treatments that question ASEAN's value in light of its limited significance for either the security or economic interests of member states. Similarly, Hurd's analysis of the Security Council implies that policymakers would do well to adjust their expectations of what the Council, with its carefully calibrated mandate, can and cannot accomplish.

Although the authors are not equally self-conscious in pursuing each of the three criteria we use to denote analytic eclecticism, they do collectively demonstrate its distinctive features and potential utility. Each has identified an interesting question that either represents an anomaly from prevailing theoretical perspectives, or cuts across the boundaries established by competing paradigms. Each offers causal accounts that constitute original and interesting middle-range explanations, combining mechanisms and logics drawn from at least two contending paradigms. And each offers usable insights that at least implicitly serve to connect scholarly debates within the academe to normative and practical issues of potential interest to both policymakers and the wider public. For those seeking to pursue eclectic scholarship, we regard these as the defining objectives.

The risks, trade-offs, and promise of analytic eclecticism

A commitment to analytic eclecticism is not without risk for individual scholars, particularly those who are relatively junior. Apart from the challenge of incommensurability we addressed in Chapter 1, eclectic researchers face a number of practical challenges. First, precisely because eclectic scholarship incorporates elements of diverse theories embedded in separate paradigms, it risks being subjected to a wider range of scrutiny and criticism, often reflecting the assumptions, standards, and practices associated with all of those paradigms. One of the most important benefits offered by paradigms or research traditions is what Lakatos (1970) referred to as a 'protective belt' of assumptions that can shield scholarly analyses from questions about core theoretical and metatheoretical assumptions. Scholars pursuing eclectic scholarship not only forgo this sort of protection but leave themselves open to challenges from adherents of each of the paradigms they seek to engage.

Second, a scholar adopting an eclectic approach must invest significant energy in guarding against the conceptual muddiness (Johnson 2002) that can emerge when working with multiple analytic perspectives. The pursuit of analytic eclecticism requires enough familiarity with different theoretical languages to ensure that the terms and concepts employed in various paradigm-bound theories are properly redefined and translated in the context of an eclectic analytic framework. Engaging concepts and theories drawn from multiple paradigms requires scholars to develop the facility for 'multilingual' conversations with diverse research communities, each confidently speaking a single theoretical language to which its members have been wedded for much of their careers. This problem is magnified by institutionalized procedures for deciding how to deal with hiring, promotions, grants, and prizes. These procedures tend to work most smoothly when there is consensus on what constitutes 'good' research. This implies that eclectically minded scholars are taking some professional risks that adherents of paradigms can avoid. At the same time, eclecticism promises considerable intellectual and professional rewards, as attested to, for example, by the careers of the 15 authors whose work we have discussed in this book.

Third, there is the fundamental problem of how to evaluate eclectic research. This problem is not unique to eclecticism. In the absence of a stable consensus among philosophers on what distinguishes 'science' from 'non-science' (Jackson 2010), protocols and standards for research vary across paradigms, since each proceeds on the basis of a distinct set of epistemic norms. This suggests that eclectic research should not be judged solely according to the criteria that adherents of any one paradigm employ to determine what constitutes good scholarship. Yet eclectically minded scholars are also not absolved from having the quality of their work evaluated by those not impressed by the benefits of eclecticism.

To begin with, any piece of social scientific research can be minimally assessed in terms of quality of evidence, falsifiability, and generalizability – criteria that are taken seriously by most members of most research traditions. For example, work by eclectic scholars that does not supply adequate empirical evidence to support causal stories, or that offers broad generalizations without careful consideration of the representativeness of cases or specification of scope conditions, will rightly be found wanting. But eclectic researchers can and should try to do more. They can become familiar with the evaluative criteria employed by adherents of various paradigms, and selectively triangulate these criteria to form their own problem-specific sets of 'cross-epistemic judgments' (Schwartz-Shea 2006). These judgments can be based on the deployment of different types of criteria in evaluating each of the individual elements – observations, inferences, interpretations, and conceptual moves – that constitute a given piece of eclectic research.

At its best, eclectic research is explicit at the outset about how it will make a compelling case, both for the overall analysis and for each of its theoretical and empirical components. Such efforts do not generate uniform standards for evaluating all eclectic research. However, by forming and meeting reasonable problem-specific criteria, analytic eclecticism can contribute to methodologically sophisticated conversations across metatheoretical divides, while encouraging all researchers to make the most plausible case possible to the widest possible audience (Pouliot 2010). This abstract formulation is in full agreement with Justice Potter Stuart's chief criterion for identifying pornography. That is, we recognize good eclectic work when we see it.

Even so, the risks and difficulties associated with eclectic scholarship beg the question of whether we should expend resources on eclectic projects in the absence of prior indications of their value to a discipline. Because eclectic scholarship poses novel questions, explores a wider range of possibilities, and may not offer definitive results, Stephen Sanderson (1987, p. 321) has criticized it as a waste of time and energy: 'A better alternative … is to adopt the theoretical tradition that seems at the time most useful and to follow it as intensively as possible.' This observation, however, fails to consider the obvious. Claims made by adherents of a paradigm to theory accumulation and intellectual progress are rarely accepted by adherents of competing paradigms. This is evident, for example, in the radically different assessments of realism offered by Stephen Walt (1997), who sees it as evolving and increasingly sophisticated, and John Vasquez (1997), who sees it as degenerating in the face of a growing number of anomalies that it cannot explain. If two such prominent scholars are capable of producing such different evaluations, then there is no reason that eclectic modes of inquiry should be viewed as any more wasteful or inefficient than paradigm-bound research from the perspective of the field of international relations writ large.

Moreover, whatever successes are claimed by adherents of a given paradigm often require them to exclude or simplify aspects of reality to facilitate the deployment of concepts, mechanisms, and logics typically privileged by adherents of that paradigm. As we noted above, such simplification can be useful in illuminating specific aspects of a complex reality, particularly in connection with phenomena about which little is known. However, this also generates blind spots that may go unrecognized in the absence of challenges from other paradigms or from eclectic research. As Anatol Rapoport (1960) noted long ago, it is not fruitful to apply a single set of intellectual tools to make sense of what he argued were three archetypical types of social situations – fights, games, and debates – that comprise conflict:

> It seems to me that no single framework of thought is adequate for dealing with such a complex class of phenomena as human conflict. But an acquaintance with several frameworks may serve to bring our ignorance to our attention. ... Thus, although none of the approaches here presented is adequate, each can serve as a reminder of what has been left out in the others. (Rapoport 1960, p. 359)

This view parallels Waltz's (1959) contention that prescriptions based on a single image are inadequate because they are based on partial analyses. It also resonates with Moravcsik's (2003) observation that the complexity of most important events in world politics precludes the possibility of unicausal explanations. Without a dose of eclecticism, scholarship based on a single paradigm risks mistaking some trees for the forest. Although this point is compelling and hardly novel (Haas 1990, p. 213), it has not produced any significant changes in scholarly practice in the field of international relations. As the TRIP surveys discussed in Chapter 2 indicate (Jordan et al. 2009; Maliniak et al. 2007), paradigmatic boundaries remain powerful. They are reflected not only in research, but also in teaching, hiring, competition for grants, manuscript reviews, and conference organization. The result is that scholars often speak past one another even when they are addressing related aspects of the same phenomena (Adler and Pouliot 2008). This also has the unfortunate effect of furthering what Ian Shapiro (2005) calls the 'flight from reality,' and undermining contemporary efforts to bridge the widening divide between academic research and problems of policy and practice (Calhoun 2009; Krasner et al. 2009).

In contrast to paradigm-driven scholarship in international relations, analytic eclecticism embraces a pragmatist conception of social inquiry. It thus places a premium on inclusive dialogue among all who are concerned with the consequences of knowledge claims, including decision makers and ordinary actors engaged in their own forms of inquiry, reflection, and persuasion (Flyvbjerg 2001, p. 139; Mazlish 1998, pp. 197–206). This does not, however, mean that analytic eclecticism rejects the idea of a scientific study of international politics. Rather, it follows E. H. Carr, Morgenthau, and other founders of the field whose approach to a 'science' of international politics eschewed overt political partisanship but nonetheless incorporated a strong dose of moral reasoning and normative reflection (Reus-Smit 2008). Fortunately, normative concerns have not disappeared entirely from the academe, as Keohane (2009a, p.363) reminds us:

> We should choose normatively important problems because we care about improving human behavior, we should explain these choices to our students and readers, and we should not apologize for making value-laden choices even as we seek to search unflinchingly for the truth.

Besides questions of theory, analytic eclecticism offers opportunities to enhance our collective ability to communicate across paradigmatic boundaries, and to engage normative and policy issues of interest to a broader public. This dialogical benefit underscores the fact that, far from being dissociated from paradigm-bound scholarship, analytic eclecticism is concerned with the practical relevance of theoretical elements drawn from diverse paradigms. Eclecticism that summarily dismisses existing paradigmatic scholarship risks devolving into ad hoc arguments that may be meaningless to other scholars and will do little to narrow the gap between scholarly debates and the world of policy and practice. At the same time, for intellectual progress to be made in the study and practice of international politics, it is as important to engage the full menu of intellectual possibilities as it is to refine existing theories concerning subsets of those possibilities. Analytic eclecticism is specifically designed to probe those possibilities that elude researchers who work within paradigmatic boundaries and who have come to take those boundaries for granted. By expanding the repertoire of assumptions, concepts, analytic principles, interpretive moves, and inferential logics, analytic eclecticism enables us to add new layers of complexity to phenomena that paradigm-bound research must necessarily oversimplify. The complementary processes of paradigm-driven simplification and eclectic 'recomplexification,' we believe, are the key to expanding the scope and quality of dialogue concerning problems in international life within and beyond the academe. For this reason, it is desirable to gamble at least some of our resources on analytic eclecticism and to accept the risks and trade-offs associated with that gamble.

The case we make for analytic eclecticism in the study of world politics runs parallel to similar arguments across and beyond academe concerning the intellectual and practical benefits of drawing on diverse perspectives. Within political science, for example, the fields of social movements and institutional analysis draw upon elements of a range of approaches that, while not full-blown paradigms, were once considered to be in competition with one another. The study of social movements has historically been characterized by a wide variety of approaches, including relative deprivation theory (Gurr 1970), macro-structuralist analysis (Skocpol 1979), resource mobilization theory (Tilly 1978), rational choice theory (Chong 1991), and ideational approaches related to 'framing' (Benford and Snow 2000).

Although usually presented as competing perspectives, these approaches are, in fact, organized around different though somewhat related questions, each focused on a different segment of the process whereby grievances ultimately lead to a reaffirmation, recalibration, or transformation of the status quo. Recognizing this, leading students of social movements have tried in recent years to build more integrated frameworks with the hope of bridging different perspectives and generating more comprehensive understandings of social movements (McAdam, Tarrow, and Tilly 2001). This intellectual initiative rests on a clear recognition of the multiplicity of processes that connect structural and individual levels, and that combine to convert initial sets of grievances into organized collective action capable of altering the status quo. This does not suggest that earlier approaches were inconsequential or incorrect. Precisely because these earlier studies yielded important insights into particular aspects of social movements, it made sense to explore how, taken together, these insights might contribute to more complex narratives about contentious politics.

Recent moves toward eclecticism are also readily observable in the study of institutions. Generally treated as competing alternatives, economic, historical, and sociological variants of the 'new institutionalism' (Hall and Taylor 1996) have all relaxed their original metatheoretical assumptions in order to expand the range of analytic constructs to be used in institutional analysis. Historical institutionalists have moved away from the emphasis they initially placed on institutional persistence linked to path dependence. They have begun to pay closer attention to more incremental or gradual processes of change, which can either generate novel institutional forms over long time horizons or produce unexpected breakdowns at critical thresholds (Pierson 2004; Thelen 2004). Economic institutionalists go beyond the treatment of institutions as spontaneously emerging, self-enforcing equilibria produced by strategic agents acting on their preferences. Instead, they presume that shifting parameters over iterated games can generate complex effects, and therefore focus on how historically situated systems of rules, beliefs, and norms affect the supply of information and the motivations of actors engaged in different transactions (Greif and Laitin 2004; Greif 2006). Finally, sociological institutionalists have generated more complex understandings of how shared worldviews, cognitive scripts, and normative templates interact with discursive or symbolic practices in the process of shaping institutions and institutional actors (Schmidt 2008). Although the analytic boundaries between the different new institutionalisms may not be as rigid or enduring as those between paradigms in international relations, the theories associated with each of the new institutionalisms have expanded in scope and complexity. This has paved the way for more self-consciously eclectic approaches such as

John Campbell's (2005) analysis of institutional change as a process encompassing a wide range of mechanisms drawn from all three 'new institutionalisms.'[1]

Beyond the efforts to overcome the boundaries separating paradigms or distinct schools within a given field of scholarship, there is the call for 'collaborations across subfields and disciplinary boundaries' (Granato and Scioli 2004, p. 321). Analytic eclecticism does not necessarily privilege interdisciplinary work for its own sake. However, there are instances in which boundaries between subfields and disciplines function in much the same way as those between paradigms: they artificially segment complex phenomena into discrete aspects that are analyzed only with the concepts and methods privileged in a given subfield or discipline (Sil and Doherty 2000). Thus, analytic eclecticism is more drawn to the kind of interdisciplinary scholarship called for in the report of the Gulbenkian Commission, fittingly titled *Open the Social Sciences* (Wallerstein et al. 1996). The report discourages the creation of permanent interdisciplinary programs, and with it, further specialization and fragmentation. At the same time, it calls for the establishment of interdisciplinary research groups that are funded on a temporary basis to explore insights generated by different disciplines and subfields in relation to specific questions or urgent issues. A similarly problem-focused argument for cutting across scholarly divides is evident in James Caporaso's (1997) plea for systematically integrating comparative and international politics. Given that students of comparative politics and international relations are frequently concerned with related facets of the same substantive phenomena – for example, the making of foreign economic policies or the effects of different political institutions – it makes sense to explore more fully the ways in which elements normally studied separately in the two fields might combine to generate interesting outcomes.

In other disciplines too, there have been efforts to promote something akin to analytic eclecticism as a welcome counterweight to separate schools of thought. In the field of economic theory, for example, Sheila Dow (2004) has called for a 'structured pluralism' to complement scholarship being carried out in separate research communities. While a common provisional structure and language is necessary to promote the development of communication *within* separate paradigms or research communities, Dow views pluralism as indispensable for providing useful channels of communication *across* these communities. One excellent example of scholarship that captures and extends this pluralism is Avner Greif's (2006) analysis of medieval commerce. Greif parts ways with conventional economists in emphasizing the necessity of combining general theories and models about politics and markets with historical studies of their institutional foundations in particular contexts. His approach thus depends on 'merging the study of institutions, as conducted in mainstream economics, with the study of cultural and social factors, as conducted in sociology' (Greif 2006, p. xv).

In psychology too, we see efforts to stretch or cut across boundaries in the study of judgment and decision making. Historically, different aspects of choice and judgment have been studied by separate groups of researchers, each with its own distinct metatheoretical frameworks and scientific priorities (Goldstein 2004). The conventional approach to judgment and decision making was originally informed by preferential choice, relying heavily on expected utility theory in conjunction with Bayesian principles for coping with uncertainty. Growing evidence of deviation from those principles in human decision making, however, spurred alternative lines of research. One prominent alternative, social judgment theory (SJT), builds on the pioneering work of Egon Brunswik. It is distinguished by a more probabilistic approach which views judgment and decision-making outcomes as products of the interaction between a more differentiated set of cognitive mechanisms (including intuition and perception) and mechanisms embedded in the external environment (Hammond 1996). Contemporary applications of SJT extend from the analysis of interpersonal conflict and individual learning to the investigation of feedback effects, organizational psychology, and even human values (Doherty and Kurz 1996; Hammond and Stewart 2001). Significantly, although the initial pioneers of SJT were skeptical of non-Brunswikian approaches, many of its contemporary proponents have come to view engagement with multiple research paradigms as useful to understanding the links between judgment, thinking, and decision making in a variety of practical settings (Goldstein and Hogarth 1997; Hammond and Stewart 2001).[2]

Finally, it is worth recognizing that the fundamental intuition behind analytic eclecticism has been articulated in slightly different terms in relation to a number of historical or practical settings. In Chapter 1, we noted how an excessive emphasis on parsimony and steadfast reliance on a single analytic perspective can decrease judgmental accuracy and increase the likelihood and size of errors in forecasting (Hirschman 1970; Tetlock 2005). This basic logic is also evident in arguments about the conditions under which we are more likely to witness surprising achievements among organizations and societies. Scott Page (2007), for example, argues that progress and innovation over the long term are more likely when a group or society depends less on singular solutions offered by brilliant individuals or like-minded experts, and instead pools a broader range of perspectives offered by diverse individuals and groups. Drawing upon evidence from a wide range of settings, from schools and firms to groups and societies, Page (2007, p. xx) proceeds to demonstrate 'how diverse perspectives, heuristics, interpretations, and mental models improve our collective ability to solve problems and make accurate predictions.'

Josiah Ober's (2008) work on Athenian democracy provides an excellent illustration of this point. Ober offers a compelling account of Athens' ability to flourish above and beyond other city-states. From the level of material well-being and the distribution of minted coins to the prominence of Athens in classical Greek literature, it is clear that 'Athens ranks as the preeminent Greek polis by a very substantial margin' (Ober 2008, p. 39). While it is tempting to attribute this success to Athenian democracy, Ober notes that many categories of Athenians were excluded from citizenship and democratic participation. He emphasizes instead the significance of the diverse perspectives that Athens' socially diverse community were encouraged to voice in public debate and discourse. The distinctive Athenian approach to the aggregation, alignment, and codification of useful knowledge allowed Athenians to employ resources deftly by exploiting opportunities and learning from mistakes. The Athenians' capacity to make effective use of knowledge dispersed across a large and diverse population enabled democratic Athens to compete well against non-democratic rivals (Ober 2008, p. 2).

A similar logic is at play when identifying the conditions that facilitate learning and innovation in the contemporary world of business. The most dynamic firms embrace 'collaborative learning,' which depends heavily on the promotion of 'dialogue within and across groups of individuals with proximate knowledge of a particular problem' (Helper, MacDuffie, and Sabel 2000, p. 484). Also worth noting is the difference between firms that rely solely on existing bodies of knowledge that have produced their current capabilities, and those that seek to recombine different types of knowledge in innovative ways to cope with changing market opportunities. The 'information pooling' in which the latter firms engage may not produce the economies of scale of hierarchically structured organizations; but it does deliver 'economies of scope' while reducing the likelihood of 'insular, self-absorbed decisions' that can prove costly in the long term (Helper et al. 2000, p. 470). Sweeping curricular changes in American business schools appear to validate such insights. There is a discernible shift away from standard methods and models taught in specialized departments, and toward greater emphasis on exploring multiple perspectives and paying close attention to cultural contexts (Wallace 2010). These and related developments in other fields underscore the promise that analytic eclecticism holds for the field of international relations.

Edward Wilson (1998, p. 8) insists that the 'fragmentation of knowledge and resulting chaos in philosophy are not reflections of the real world but artifacts of scholarship.' We do not necessarily assume, as Wilson does, that this observation implies a full-blown 'consilience' across all branches of learning in search of unified knowledge. However, we do believe that the boundaries between disciplines and paradigms are constructs that, while practically useful for some purposes, are often reified to the point that they prevent us from recognizing, analyzing, and addressing socially important problems in international life. Analytic eclecticism is intended not as a means to erase those boundaries but as a counterweight to them. It proceeds from a flexible pragmatist ethos to grapple with problems that are not only theoretically interesting but also have normative and practical significance for decision makers and the wider public. Thus, the spirit of analytic eclecticism is very much in keeping with what Aristotle referred to as *phronesis*, practical wisdom (Flyvbjerg 2001; Schram 2005). Whereas the natural sciences may generally fare better when it comes to testing theories and predicting outcomes, the social sciences are in a position to promote vigorously a practical wisdom that recognizes the contingencies, complexities, and uncertainties embedded in various social settings (Schram 2005, pp. 108–10). Alongside, and in dialogue with, paradigm-bound research, analytic eclecticism can serve to improve theoretical and practical knowledge about world politics, and in the process, it can help bridge the gulf between academic scholarship and the world of policy and practice.

Notes

Chapter 1

1   The discussion of analytic eclecticism in this chapter elaborates on earlier treatments of the concept in various articles and chapters, including Katzenstein and Sil (2004, 2008) and Sil and Katzenstein (2010).

2   Throughout this book, we follow Andrew Abbott (2004, pp. 26–30) in dismissing the stark dichotomy between 'explanation' and 'understanding.' Models, theories, narratives, and ethnographies are all 'explanations' in the sense that they all contain causal stories of varying degrees of concreteness.

3   One reason for the fractal nature of these distinctions may be that they represent not dichotomized opposites, but endpoints of an 'epistemological spectrum' along which numerous points of contestation are possible within adjacent segments (Sil 2000b, pp. 162–6).

4   In this regard, O. J. Wisdom (1974) contends that advocates of the incommensurability thesis did not clarify the boundaries of the thesis, allowing a reasonable 'soft' version of the thesis to be treated as a more extreme and less defensible 'hard' one. For evidence, he notes that the Galilean conception of 'length,' though not equivalent to the conception of 'length' in Einstein's work on relativity, is a part of the latter insofar as it captures the length between two points within a frame of reference that is moving within a designated space.

5   This is particularly true in the case of approaches proceeding from pragmatist principles. Pragmatism emphasizes the practical consequences of knowledge claims rather than adherence to rigid metatheoretical postulates. Chapter 2 discusses the relationship between eclecticism and the 'pragmatist turn' in international relations.

Chapter 2

1   In the 2006 survey, for example, nearly 90 percent of scholarship considered to be paradigmatic by respondents consisted of work identified with the realist, liberal, or constructivist traditions (Maliniak et al. 2007, p. 16).

2   Specifically, more than two-thirds of those who said their work did not fall into one of the major paradigms also indicated that they did not rely on paradigms of any kind; the rest chose 'other' over several established paradigmatic alternatives, ranging from realism, liberalism, and constructivism to Marxism, feminism, and the English school (Jordan et al. 2009, p. 33).

3   This figure and some of the accompanying discussion grow out of an earlier overview of the nature and limits of paradigmatic scholarship in the context of East Asian security (Katzenstein and Sil. 2004).

4   Jackson and Nexon (2009, 2004) suggest that current lines of debate in international relations point to four, not three, discrete alternatives: realism, liberalism, realist-constructivism, and liberal-constructivism. We obviously share Jackson and Nexon's (2009, 2004) optimism concerning the possibilities for cutting across paradigmatic fault lines; but it is not clear to us why, in view of their interest in remapping the field around possible areas of complementarity, they do not treat the convergence of realism and liberalism (corner A in our Figure 2.1) as systematically as they do the convergence between realism and constructivism (corner B) or between liberalism and constructivism (corner C).

5   In security studies, for example, articles in each of two leading journals – *Journal of Conflict Resolution* and *International Security* – rarely acknowledge scholarship produced in the other even when addressing the same issues (Bennett, Barth, and Rutherford 2003).

6   The emergence of constructivism may thus be viewed in relation to the path-dependent history of US international relations as a field. Right from the outset, the field was disproportionately influenced by the persistent debate between realists and liberals/idealists, evolving in a way that left important sociological concepts and theories on the margins because they appeared irrelevant to that debate. In this context, constructivist analyses that are not based on a programmatic commitment to a new dominant paradigm may be viewed instead as essentially a long overdue corrective, reconnecting sociology and international relations. This may be why the work of Max Weber, referenced in a number of the studies discussed below (Barnett and Finnemore 2004; Seabrooke 2006; Woll 2008), has become increasingly relevant given its emphasis on the duality of material and ideal interests and on the multiple bases for social action, ranging from instrumentally rational and value-rational to traditional and affectual.

7   This section is adapted from our earlier discussions of the relationship between eclecticism and pragmatism (Katzenstein and Sil 2008; Sil 2009; and Sil and Katzenstein 2010).

8   Empiricism, for example, assigns priority to observation and measurement, and proceeds to generate inferences, with the expectation that the standardized application of replicable methods will generate progressively better inferences of specific phenomena. Logicism is also positivist in its orientation, but proceeds from Hempel's formulation of the deductive–nomological model, with emphasis placed on internally consistent propositions deductively derived from axiomatic covering laws (Shapiro and Wendt 2005).

9   In ethnographic approaches, for example, there is a presumption that there is enough intersubjectivity in social life to permit outside observers to immerse themselves in a particular context in order to extract some

stable understanding of meaningful practices and social relations (Schatz 2009). Subjectivist orientations are also recognizable in interpretive approaches based on hermeneutics, such as the analysis of discourse and everyday practice (Hansen 2006; Pouliot 2010). Critical theorists are more focused on the critique of existing knowledge claims and their political implications, and on a normatively grounded advocacy of political action (Haacke 2005; Price and Reus-Smit 1998).

10 This also suggests a connection between pragmatism, eclecticism, and structurationism (Giddens 1984; Sewell 1992) insofar as all reject a priori postulates concerning the causal primacy of agency or structure, emphasizing instead the need for empirical investigation in specific contexts.

Chapter 3

1 As quoted in *The Los Angeles Times* on February 13, 2009 (see Miller 2009) from the Statement for the Record by Dennis C. Blair, Director of National Intelligence at the Annual Threat Assessment Hearings of the Senate Select Committee on Intelligence, February 12, 2009 <http://www.dni.gov/testimonies.htm> (accessed March 26, 2009).

2 The discussion here of Jervis (2005) expands upon an abridged treatment in Sil and Katzenstein (2010). Also, preliminary accounts of Jervis (2005) and Kang (2007) appeared in Katzenstein and Sil (2008).

3 Tannenwald's (2007) constructivist approach also explicitly recognizes this point.

Chapter 4

1 As quoted in the *Financial Times* (Tett and Gangahar 2007).

2 In a harsh review of one of Soros's earlier books, Robert Solow (1999) glosses over a crucial difference between misperception, which is individually based, and reflexivity, which for Soros has to do with overcoming the interference that results when cognitive dispositions influenced by the external world coexist with manipulative efforts to shape that world. This introduces an element of judgment or bias that is neither reducible to an issue of perception/misperception, nor consistent with the assumptions of individual rationality that inform economics. See also Cassidy (2008) for a balanced and nuanced analysis.

3 Preliminary discussions of Seabrooke (2006) and Sinclair (2005) have appeared in Katzenstein and Sil (2008) and Sil and Katzenstein (2010).

Chapter 5

1 A preliminary version of the discussion of Barnett and Finnemore's (2004) study appears in Sil and Katzenstein (2010).

2   For example, in 2008 the US-based Council of Foreign Relations started a five-year program on international institutions and global governance, premised on the assumption that both existing frameworks of analysis and existing multilateral arrangements cannot cope successfully with rapidly evolving opportunities in and threats to the international system. Although concerned primarily with the role the United States can play in refashioning the architecture of international cooperation, this initiative is motivated by a belief that the diverse ways in which the private sector and a global civil society interact with states require consideration of new modes of governance to replace international institutions that are obsolete, ineffective, and increasingly unrepresentative (Council on Foreign Relations 2008).

Chapter 6

1   Campbell (2005, pp. 29–30) engages in a process of 'bricolage' which involves 'selecting various ideas from different places and combining them in ways that yield something new.' He maps the different configurations of mechanisms – cognitive, normative, diffusion, evolutionary, and others – that drive evolutionary and revolutionary processes of institutional change. In Campbell's open-ended conception of institutional change, path-dependent continuity in some dimensions coexists with processes of change in other dimensions, thus yielding institutional characteristics that are more or less incrementally transformed. This eclectic framework provides the basis for Campbell's substantive investigation of variations in the responses of different tax policy regimes to pressures related to global economic forces.

2   We are grateful to Michael E. Doherty for comments on this discussion of the field of judgment and decision making.

Bibliography

Abbott, Andrew (2004) *Methods of Discovery*. New York: W. W. Norton.

Abdelal, Rawi, Mark Blyth and Craig Parsons (2010) 'Re-Constructing IPE: Some Conclusions Drawn from a Crisis.' In Rawi Abdelal, Mark Blyth, and Craig Parsons, eds., *Constructing the International Economy*. Ithaca, N.Y.: Cornell University Press.

Acharya, Amitav, and Barry Buzan (eds.) (2010) *Non-Western International Relations Theory: Insights From and Beyond Asia*. London and New York: Routledge.

Adler, Emanuel and Vincent Pouliot (2008) 'The Practice Turn in International Relations: Introduction and Framework.' Presented at the Conference on 'The Practice Turn in International Affairs,' Munck Centre for International Affairs, University of Toronto, Canada, 21–22 November.

Alt, James A. and Michael Gilligan (1994) 'The Political Economy of Trading States: Factor Specificity, Collective Action Problems and Domestic Political Institutions.' *Journal of Political Philosophy* 2(2): 165–92.

Amsden, Alice (1989) *Asia's Next Giant: South Korea and Late Industrialization*. New York: Oxford University Press.

Ba, Alice D. (2009) *[Re]Negotiating East and Southeast Asia: Region, Regionalism, and the Association of Southeast Asian Nations*. Stanford, Calif.: Stanford University Press.

Baldwin, David (ed.) (1993) *Neorealism and Neoliberalism: The Contemporary Debate*. New York: Columbia University Press.

Barkin, J. Samuel (2010) *Realist Constructivism: Rethinking International Relations Theory*. New York: Cambridge University Press.

Barkin, J. Samuel (2004) 'Realist Constructivism and Realist-Constructivisms.' *International Studies Review* 6(2) (June): 349–51.

Barkin, J. Samuel (2003) 'Realist Constructivism.' *International Studies Review* 5(3) (September): 325–42.

Barnett, Michael N. (2003) 'Alliances, Balances of Threats, and Neorealism: The Accidental Coup.' In Colin Elman and John A. Vasquez (eds.), *Realism and the Balancing of Power*. Upper Saddle River, N.J.: Prentice Hall, pp. 222–49.

Barnett, Michael N. (1996) 'Identity and Alliances in the Middle East.' In Peter J. Katzenstein, ed., *The Culture of National Security: Norms and Identity in World Politics*. New York: Columbia University Press, pp. 400–47.

Barnett, Michael and Martha Finnemore (2004) *Rules for the World: International Organizations in Global Politics*. Ithaca, N.Y: Cornell University Press.

Bauer, Harry and Elizabeth Brighi (2009a) 'Introducing Pragmatism to International Relations.' In Bauer and Brighi (2009c), pp. 1–8.

Bauer, Harry and Elizabeth Brighi (2009b) 'On the Obstacles and Promises of Pragmatism in International Relations.' In Bauer and Brighi (2009c), pp. 159–66.

Bauer, Harry and Elizabeth Brighi (eds.) (2009c) *Pragmatism in International Relations.* New York: Routledge.

Bauer, Raymond A., Ithiel de Sola Pool, and Lewis Anthony Dexter (1963) *American Business and Public Policy: The Politics of Foreign Trade.* Chicago, Ill.: Aldine.

Beckert, Jens (2002) *Beyond the Market: The Social Foundations of Economic Efficiency.* Princeton, N.J.: Princeton University Press.

Beetham, David (1991) *The Legitimation of Power.* London: Macmillan.

Bendix, Reinhard (1977) *Nation-Building and Citizenship*, 2nd edn. Berkeley, Calif.: University of California Press.

Benford, Robert and David Snow (2000) 'Framing Processes and Social Movements: An Overview and Assessment.' *Annual Review of Sociology* 26: 611–39.

Bennett, Andrew, Aharon Barth, and Kenneth Rutherford (2003) 'Do We Preach What we Practice? A Survey of Methods in Journals and Graduate Curricula.' *PS: Political Science and Politics* 36 (July): 387–9.

Bennett, Andrew and Colin Elman (2006) 'Complex Causal Relations and Case Study Methods: The Example of Path Dependence.' *Political Analysis* 14(3): 250–67.

Bennett, D. Scott and Allan Stam (2003) *The Behavioral Origins of War.* Ann Arbor, Mich.: University of Michigan Press.

Bernstein, Richard (1992) 'The Resurgence of American Pragmatism.' *Social Research* 59 (Winter): 813–40.

Bernstein, Richard (1983) *Beyond Objectivism and Relativism.* Philadelphia, Pa.: University of Pennsylvania Press.

Bernstein, Steven, Richard Ned Lebow, Janice Gross Stein, and Steven Weber (2000) 'God Gave Physics the Easy Problems: Adapting Social Science to an Unpredictable World.' *European Journal of International Relations* 6(1): 43–76.

Betts, Richard K. (2000) 'Universal Deterrence or Conceptual Collapse? Liberal Pessimism and Utopian Realism.' In Victor A. Utgoff, ed., *The Coming Crisis: Nuclear Proliferation, U.S. Interests, and World Order.* Cambridge, Mass.: MIT Press.

Blumer, Herbert (1969) *Symbolic Interactionism: Perspective and Method.* Englewood Cliffs, N.J.: Prentice-Hall.

Blyth, Mark (2006) 'Great Punctuations: Prediction, Randomness, and the Evolution of Comparative Political Science.' *American Political Science Review* 100(4): 493–8.

Bohman, James (1999) 'Democracy as Inquiry, Inquiry as Democratic: Pragmatism, Social Science and the Cognitive Division of Labour.' *American Journal of Political Science* 43(2): 590–607.

Brady, Henry and David Collier (eds.) (2004) *Rethinking Social Inquiry: Diverse Tools, Shared Standards.* Lanham, Md.: Rowman & Littlefield.

Broder, John M. (2009) 'Climate Change Seen as Threat to U.S. Security.' *New York Times* (August 9): A1, A4.

Brunkhorst, Hauke (2002) 'Globalising Democracy Without a State: Weak Public, Strong Public, Global Constitutionalism.' *Millennium,* Special Issue on 'Pragmatism and International Relations Theory,' 31(3): 675–90.

Brzezinski, Zbigniew (2004) *The Choice: Global Domination or Global Leadership.* New York: Basic Books.

Buchanan, Allen and Robert O. Keohane (2006) 'The Legitimacy of Global Governance Institutions.' *Ethics & International Affairs* 20(4): 405–37.

Buzan, Barry and Ole Wæver (2003) *Regions and Power: The Structure of International Security.* Cambridge, UK: Cambridge University Press.

Calhoun, Craig (2009) 'Social Science For Public Knowledge.' Social Science Research Council [online] http://publicsphere.ssrc.org/calhoun-social-science-or-public-knowledge/ (accessed December 4, 2009).

Campbell, John (2005) *Institutional Change and Globalization.* Princeton, N.J.: Princeton University Press.

Capoccia, Giovanni (2006) 'Mixed Method Research in Comparative Politics: A Discussion of Basic Assumptions.' Paper presented at the annual meeting of the American Political Science Association, Philadelphia, Pa.

Caporaso, James (1997) 'Across the Great Divide: Integrating Comparative and International Politics.' *International Studies Quarterly* 41: 563–92.

Cassidy, John (2008) 'He Foresaw the End of an Era.' *New York Review of Books* 55(16) (October 23) [online] http://www.nybooks.com/articles/21934 (accessed July 28, 2009).

Checkel, Jeffrey (2006) 'Constructivist Approaches to European Integration.' In K. E. Joergensen, M. Pollack, and B. Rosamond, eds., *Handbook of European Union Politics.* London: Sage, pp. 57–76.

Checkel, Jeffrey (2004) 'Social Constructivisms in Global and European Politics: A Review Essay.' *Review of International Studies* 30(2): 229–44.

Checkel, Jeffrey T. (1998) 'The Constructivist Turn in International Relations Theory.' *World Politics* 50(2) (January): 324–48.

Chernoff, Fred (2007) *Theory and Metatheory in International Relations.* New York: Palgrave.

Chong, Dennis (1991) *Collective Action and the Civil Rights Movement.* Princeton, N.J.: Princeton University Press.

Cochran, Molly. 2002. 'Deweyan Pragmatism and Post-Positivist Social Science in IR.' *Millennium,* Special Issue on 'Pragmatism and International Relations Theory,' 31(3): 525–48.

Cohen, Benjamin J. (2008a) *International Political Economy: An Intellectual History.* Princeton, N.J.: Princeton University Press.

Cohen, Benjamin J. (2008b) 'The Transatlantic Divide: A Rejoinder.' *Review of International Political Economy* 15(1) (February): 30–4.

Cohen, Benjamin J. (2007) 'The Transatlantic Divide: Why are American and British IPE So Different?' *Review of International Political Economy* 14(2) (May): 197–219.

Council on Foreign Relations (2008) 'International Institutions and Global Governance Program – World Order in the 21st Century' (May 1) [online] http://www.cfr.org/project/1369/international_institutions_and_global_governance.html (accessed May 20, 2010).

Davidson, Donald (1974) 'On the Very Idea of a Conceptual Scheme.' *Proceedings and Addresses of the American Philosophical Association* 47: 5–20.

Dessler, David (1999) 'Constructivism within a Positivist Social Science.' *Review of International Studies* 25 (January): 123–37.

Deutsch, Karl W. (1957) *Political Community and the North-Atlantic Area.* Princeton, N.J.: Princeton University Press.

Dewey, John (1916) *Democracy and Education: An Introduction to the Philosophy of Education.* New York: Free Press.

Doherty, Michael E. and Elke M. Kurz (1996) 'Social Judgment Theory.' *Thinking and Reasoning* 2(2/3): 109–40.

Dow, Sheila C. (2004) 'Structured Pluralism.' *Journal of Economic Methodology* 11(3) (September): 275–90.

Duhem, Pierre (1954 [1906]) *The Aim and Structure of Physical Theory.* Princeton, N. J.: Princeton University Press.

Elman, Colin (1996) 'Horses for Courses: Why not Neorealist Theories of Foreign Policy?' *Security Studies* 6(1) (Autumn): 7–53.

Elman, Colin and Miriam Fendius Elman (2003) 'Lessons From Lakatos.' In C. Elman and M. F. Elman, eds., *Progress in International Relations Theory: Metrics and Methods of Scientific Change.* Cambridge, Mass.: MIT Press, pp. 21–68.

Evans, Peter (1995a) Contribution to 'The Role of Theory in Comparative Politics: A Symposium.' *World Politics* 48(1): 1–49.

Evans, Peter (1995b) *Embedded Autonomy: States and Industrial Transformation.* Princeton, N.J.: Princeton University Press.

Falleti, Tulia G. and Julia F. Lynch (2009) 'Context and Causal Mechanisms in Political Analysis.' *Comparative Political Studies* 42(9) (September): 1143–66.

Ferguson, Niall (2004a) *Colossus: The Price of America's Empire.* New York: Penguin.

Ferguson, Niall (2004b) *Empire: The Rise and Demise of the British World Order and the Lessons for Global Power.* New York: Basic Books.

Festenstein, Matthew (1997) *Pragmatism and Political Theory: From Dewey to Rorty.* Chicago, Ill.: University of Chicago Press.

Feyerabend, Paul (1962) 'Explanation, Reduction and Empiricism.' In Herbert Feigl and Grover Maxwell, eds., *Minnesota Studies in the Philosophy of Science Vol. 3.* Minneapolis, Minn.: University of Minnesota Press, pp. 28–97.

Finel, Bernard (2001/02) 'Black Box or Pandora's Box: State Level Variables and Progressivity in Realist Research Programs.' *Security Studies* 11(2) (Winter): 187–227.

Finnemore, Martha (2003) *The Purpose of Intervention Changing Beliefs about the Use of Force.* Ithaca, N.Y.: Cornell University Press.

Flyvbjerg, Bent (2001) *Making Social Science Matter: Why Social Inquiry Fails and How it Can Succeed Again.* New York: Cambridge University Press.

Frankel, Benjamin (ed.) (1996) *Realism: Restatements and Renewal.* London: Frank Cass.

Friedberg, Aaron (1993/94) 'Ripe for Rivalry: Prospects for Peace in Multipolar Asia.' *International Security* 18(3) (Winter): 5–33.

Frieden, Jeffrey (1991) *Debt, Democracy, and Development.* Princeton, N.J.: Princeton University Press.

Frieden, Jeffrey and Lisa Martin (2002) 'International Political Economy: The State of the Sub-Discipline.' In Ira Katznelson and Helen Milner, eds., *Political Science: The State of the Discipline.* New York: Norton, pp. 118–46.

Friedrichs, Jörg and Friedrich Kratochwil (2009) 'On Acting and Knowing: How Pragmatism Can Advance International Relations Theory and Methodology.' *International Organization* 63(4) (Fall): 701–31.

Giddens, Anthony (1984) *The Constitution of Society: Outline of the Theory of Structuration.* London: Polity.

Gilpin, Robert (2001) *Global Political Economy.* Princeton, N.J.: Princeton University Press.

Gilpin, Robert (1987) *The Political Economy of International Relations.* Princeton, N.J.: Princeton University Press.

Gilpin, Robert (1981) *War and Change in World Politics.* New York: Cambridge University Press.

Gilpin, Robert (1975) *U.S. Power and the Multinational Corporation: The Political Economy of Foreign Direct Investment.* New York: Basic Books.

Goffman, Erving (1963) *Behavior in Public Places: Notes on the Social Organization of Gatherings.* New York: Free Press.

Goffman, Erving (1959) *The Presentation of Self in Everyday Life.* Garden City, N.Y.: Doubleday Anchor.

Goldstein, Judith and Robert O. Keohane (eds.) (1993) *Ideas and Foreign Policy: Beliefs, Institutions and Political Change.* Ithaca, N.Y.: Cornell University Press.

Goldstein, William (2004) 'Social Judgment Theory: Applying and Extending Brunswik's Probabilistic Functionalism.' In Derek Koehler and Nigel Harvey, eds., *Blackwell Handbook of Judgment and Decision-Making.* Malden, Mass.: Blackwell, pp. 37–61.

Goldstein, William and Robin Hogarth (eds.) (1997) *Research on Judgment and Decision Making: Currents, Connections, and Controversies.* Cambridge, UK: Cambridge University Press, pp. 3–65.

Gould, Harry and Nicolas Onuf (2009) 'Pragmatism, Legal Realism, and Constructivism.' In Bauer and Brighi (2009c), pp. 25–43.

Granato, Jim and Frank Scioli (2004) 'Puzzles, Proverbs, and Omega Matrices: The Scientific and Social Significance of Empirical Implications of Theoretical Models (EITM).' *Perspectives on Politics* 2(2) (June): 313–23.

Granovetter, Mark (1985) 'Economic Action and Social Structure: The Problem of Embeddedness.' *American Journal of Sociology* 91(3): 481–510.

Gray, Colin S. (2000) 'To Confuse Ourselves: Nuclear Fallacies.' In John Baylis and Robert O'Neill, eds., *Alternative Nuclear Futures*. Oxford: Oxford University Press, pp. 4–30.

Greif, Avner (2006) *Institutions and the Path to the Modern Economy*. New York: Cambridge University Press.

Greif, Avner and David Laitin (2004) 'A Theory of Endogenous Institutional Change.' *American Political Science Review* 98(4): 14–48.

Gruber, Lloyd (2000) *Ruling the World: Power Politics and the Rise of Supranational Institutions*. Princeton, N.J.: Princeton University Press.

Gurr, Ted (1970) *Why Men Rebel*. Princeton, N.J.: Princeton University Press.

Gusterson, Hugh (1995) 'Reading International Security after the Cold War.' Paper prepared for the second workshop on Culture and the Production of Security/Insecurity, Kent State University, April 28–30.

Haack, Susan (2004) 'Pragmatism, Old and New.' *Contemporary Pragmatism* 1(1): 3–41.

Haacke, Jürgen (2005) 'The Frankfurt School and International Relations: On the Centrality of Recognition.' *Review of International Studies* 31(1): 181–94.

Haas, Ernst B. (2001) 'Does Constructivism Subsume Neo-functionalism?' In Thomas Christiansen, Knud Erik Jørgensen, and Antje Wiener, eds., *The Social Construction of Europe*. London: Sage, pp. 22–31.

Haas, Ernst B. (1990) 'Reason and Change in International Life: Justifying a Hypothesis.' *Journal of International Affairs* 44 (Spring/Summer): 209–40.

Haas, Ernst B. (1964) *Beyond the Nation-State: Functionalism and International Organization*. Stanford, Calif.: Stanford University Press.

Haas, Ernst B. (1958) *The Uniting of Europe: Political, Social and Economic Forces, 1950–1957*. Stanford, Calif.: Stanford University Press.

Haas, Ernst B. and Peter M. Haas (2009) 'Pragmatic Constructivism and the Study of International Institutions.' In Bauer and Brighi (2009c), pp. 101–21.

Haas, Peter M. (1992) 'Introduction: Epistemic Communities and International Policy Coordination.' *International Organization* 46(1) (Winter): 1–35.

Haftendorn, Helga, Robert O. Keohane and Celeste A. Wallander (eds.) (1999) *Imperfect Unions. Security Institutions over Time and Space*. New York: Oxford University Press.

Hall, Peter A. (2003) 'Adapting Methodology to Ontology in Comparative Politics.' In James Mahoney and Dietrich Rueschemeyer, eds., *Comparative Historical Analysis in the Social Sciences*. New York: Cambridge University Press, pp. 373–404.

Hall, Peter and Rosemary Taylor (1996) 'Political Science and the Three New Institutionalisms.' *Political Studies* 44(5): 936–57.

Hammond, Kenneth R. (1996) *Human Judgment and Social Policy: Irreducible Uncertainty, Inevitable Error, Unavoidable Injustice*. New York: Oxford University Press.

Hammond, Kennet R. and Thomas R. Stewart (2001) *The Essential Brunswik: Beginnings, Explorations, Applications*. New York: Oxford University Press.

Hansen, Lene (2006) *Security as Practice: Discourse Analysis and the Bosnian War*. London: Routledge.

Hardt, Michael, and Antonio Negri (2000) *Empire*. Cambridge, Mass.: Harvard University Press.

Harvey, Frank and Joel Cobb (2003) 'Multiple Dialogues, Layered Syntheses, and the Limits of Expansive Cumulation.' In G. Hellman, ed., 'The Forum: Are Dialogue and Synthesis Possible in International Relations?' *International Studies Review* 5(1) (March): 144–7.

Hattiangadi, Jagdish N. (1977) 'The Crisis in Methodology: Feyerabend.' *Philosophy of the Social Sciences* 7: 289–302.

Hellmann, Gunther (2003) 'In Conclusion: Dialogue and Synthesis in Individual Scholarship and Collective Inquiry.' In G. Hellmann, ed., 'The Forum: Are Dialogue and Synthesis Possible in International Relations?' *International Studies Review* 5(1) (March): 123–53.

Helper, Susan, John Paul MacDuffie, and Charles Sabel (2000) 'Pragmatic Collaborations: Advancing Knowledge While Controlling Opportunism.' *Industrial & Corporate Change* 9(3): 443–88.

Higgott, Richard and Matthew Watson (2008) 'All at Sea in a Barbed Wire Canoe: Professor Cohen's Transatlantic Voyage in IPE.' *Review of International Political Economy* 15(1) (February): 1–17.

Hirschman, Albert O. (1970) 'The Search for Paradigms as a Hindrance to Understanding.' *World Politics* 22(3) (April): 329–43.

Hoffmann, Stanley (2006) *Chaos and Violence: What Globalization, Failed States, and Terrorism Mean for U.S. Foreign Policy*. Lanham, Md.: Rowman & Littlefield.

Hoffmann, Stanley (2000) *World Disorders: Troubled Peace in the Post-Cold War Era*, Updated ed. Lanham, Md.: Rowman & Littlefield.

Hoffmann, Stanley (1995) 'The Crisis of Liberal Internationalism.' *Foreign Policy* (Spring): 159–77.

Hoffmann, Stanley (1986) 'Hedley Bull and His Contribution to International Relations.' *International Affairs* 62(2) (Spring): 179–95.

Hoffmann, Stanley (1966) 'Obstinate or Obsolete? The Fate of the Nation-State and the Case of Western Europe.' *Daedalus* (Summer): 862–915.

Hopf, Ted (2009) 'The Logic of Habit in IR.' Paper presented at the Annual Meeting of the International Studies Association, New York (February 14–18).

Hopf, Ted (1998) 'The Promise of Constructivism in International Relations Theory.' *International Security* 23(1) (Summer): 171–200.

Hurd, Ian (2007) *After Anarchy: Legitimacy and Power in the United Nations Security Council.* Princeton, N.J.: Princeton University Press.

Ikenberry, G. John and Anne-Marie Slaughter (2006) *Forging a World of Liberty Under Law: U.S. National Security in the Twenty First Century.* Final Paper of the Princeton Project on National Security. Princeton, N.J.: Woodrow Wilson School of Public and International Affairs, Princeton University.

Isacoff, Jonathan B. (2009) 'Pragmatism, History and International Relations.' In Bauer and Brighi 2009c, pp. 63–80.

Jabko, Nicolas (2006) *Playing the Market: A Political Strategy for Uniting Europe, 1985–2005.* Ithaca, N.Y.: Cornell University Press.

Jackson, Patrick T. (2010) *The Conduct of Inquiry in International Relations: Philosophy of Science and Its Implications for the Study of World Politics.* New York: Routledge.

Jackson, Patrick T. (2009) 'Situated Creativity, or, the Cash Value of a Pragmatist Wager for IR.' *International Studies Review* 11(3) (September): 656–9.

Jackson, Patrick T. and Daniel H. Nexon (2009) 'Paradigmatic Faults in International Relations Theory.' *International Studies Quarterly* 53(4): 907–30.

Jackson, Patrick T. and Daniel H. Nexon (2004) 'Constructivist Realism or Realist-Constructivism?' *International Studies Review* 6(2) (June): 337–41.

James, William (1997) 'What Pragmatism Means.' In Louis Menand, ed., *Pragmatism: A Reader.* New York: Vintage Books, pp. 93–111.

Jervis, Robert (2005) *American Foreign Policy in a New Era.* New York: Routledge.

Jick, Todd D. (1979) 'Mixing Qualitative and Quantitative Methods: Triangulation in Action.' *Administrative Science Quarterly* 24(4): 602–11.

Joas, Hans (1993) *Pragmatism and Social Theory.* Chicago: University of Chicago Press.

Johnson, James (2002) 'How Conceptual Problems Migrate: Rational Choice, Interpretation and the Hazards of Pluralism.' *Annual Review of Political Science* 5: 223–48.

Johnston, Alastair Iain (2001) 'Treating International Institutions as Social Environments.' *International Studies Quarterly* 45(4): 487–501.

Johnston, Alastair Iain (1998) *Cultural Realism: Strategic Culture and Grand Strategy in Chinese History.* Princeton, N.J.: Princeton University Press.

Jordan, Richard, Daniel Maliniak, Amy Oakes, Susan Peterson, and Michael J. Tierney (2009) *One Discipline or Many? TRIP Survey of International Relations Faculty in Ten Countries.* Williamsburg, Va.: Program on the

Theory, Research and Practice of International Relations, College of William and Mary.

Kaag, John Jacob (2009) 'Pragmatism and the Lessons of Experience.' *Daedalus* (Spring): 63–72.

Kagan, Jerome (2009) *The Three Cultures: Natural Sciences, Social Sciences, and the Humanities in the 21st Century*. New York: Cambridge University Press.

Kang, David C. (2007) *China Rising: Peace, Power, and Order in East Asia*. New York: Columbia University Press.

Katzenstein, Peter J. (2009) 'Mid-Atlantic: Sitting on the Knife's Sharp Edge.' *Review of International Political Economy* 16(1) (February): 122–35.

Katzenstein, Peter J. (2005) *A World of Regions: Asia and Europe in the American Imperium*. Ithaca, N.Y.: Cornell University Press.

Katzenstein, Peter J. (ed.) (1996) *The Culture of National Security*. New York: Columbia University Press.

Katzenstein, Peter J., Robert O. Keohane, and Stephen D. Krasner (eds.) (1999) *Exploration and Contestation in the Study of World Politics*. Cambridge, Mass.: MIT Press.

Katzenstein, Peter J. and Rudra Sil (2008) 'Eclectic Theorizing in the Study and Practice of International Relations.' In Christian Reus-Smit and Duncan Snidal, eds., *The Oxford Handbook of International Relations*. New York: Oxford University Press, pp. 109–30.

Katzenstein, Peter J. and Rudra Sil (2004) 'Rethinking Security in East Asia: A Case for Analytic Eclecticism.' In J. J. Suh, Peter Katzenstein, and Allen Carlson, eds., *Rethinking Security in East Asia: Identity, Power and Efficiency*. Stanford, Calif.: Stanford University Press, pp. 1–33.

Keohane, Robert O. (2009a) 'Political Science as a Vocation.' *PS: Political Science and Politics* 42(2) (April): 359–63.

Keohane, Robert O. (2009b) 'The Old IPE and the New.' *Review of International Political Economy* 16(1) (February): 34–46.

Keohane, Robert O. (1989) *International Institutions and State Power*. Boulder, Colo.: Westview.

Keohane, Robert O. (1986) 'Theory of World Politics: Structural Realism and Beyond.' In R. Keohane, ed., *Neorealism and its Critics*. New York: Columbia University Press, pp.158–203.

Keohane, Robert O. (1984) *After Hegemony: Cooperation and Discord in the World Political Economy*. Princeton, N.J.: Princeton University Press.

Keohane, Robert O. and Lisa Martin (1995) 'The Promise of Institutionalist Theory.' *International Security* 20(1) (Summer): 39–51.

Keohane, Robert O. and Joseph Nye (1977) *Power and Interdependence: World Politics in Transition*. Boston, Mass.: Little, Brown.

Kirshner, Jonathan (2007) *Appeasing Bankers: Financial Caution on the Road to War*. Princeton, N.J.: Princeton University Press.

Knight, Jack and James Johnson (1999) 'Inquiry into Democracy: What Might a Pragmatist Make of Rational Choice Theories?' *American Journal of Political Science* 43(2): 566–89.

Krasner, Stephen D. (ed.) (1983) *International Regimes*. Ithaca, N.Y.: Cornell University Press.

Krasner, Stephen D., Joseph S. Nye Jr., Janice Gross Stein, and Robert O. Keohane (2009) 'Autobiographical Reflections on Bridging the Policy-–Academy Divide.' *Cambridge Review of International Affairs* 22(1) (March): 111–28.

Kratochwil, Friedrich V. (1989) *Rules, Norms and Decisions on the Conditions of Practical and Legal Reasoning in International Relations and Affairs*. New York: Cambridge University Press.

Kuhn, Thomas (1962) *The Structure of Scientific Revolutions*. Chicago, Ill.: University of Chicago Press.

Lakatos, Imre (1970) 'Falsification, and the Methodology of Scientific Research Programmes.' In Imre Lakatos and Alan Musgrave, eds., *Criticism and the Growth of Knowledge*. New York: Cambridge University Press, pp. 91–196.

Lake, David (2009) 'Open Economy Politics: A Critical Review.' *Review of International Political Economy* 4(3) (September): 219–44.

Laudan, Larry (1996) *Beyond Positivism and Relativism: Theory, Method, and Evidence*. Boulder, Colo.: Westview.

Laudan, Larry (1977) *Progress and its Problems: Toward a Theory of Scientific Growth*. Berkeley, Calif.: University of California Press.

Lemke, Douglas (2003) 'African Lessons for International Relations Research.' *World Politics* 56 (October): 114–38.

Lepgold, Joseph and Alan Lamborn (2001) 'Locating Bridges: Connecting Research Agendas on Cognition and Strategic Choice.' *International Studies Review* 3(3): 3–30.

Lewis, Martin and Kären E. Wigen (1997) *The Myth of Continents: A Critique of Metageography*. Berkeley, Calif.: University of California Press.

Lichbach, Mark (2007) 'Theory and Evidence.' In Richard Ned Lebow and Mark Lichbach, eds., *Theory and Evidence in Comparative Politics and International Relations*. New York: Palgrave Macmillan, pp. 261–80.

Lichbach, Mark (2003) *Is Rational Choice All of Social Science?* Ann Arbor, Mich.: University of Michigan Press.

Lieberman, Evan (2005) 'Nested Analysis as a Mixed-Method Strategy for Comparative Research.' *American Political Science Review* 99(3): 435–52.

Lindblom, Charles and David Cohen (1979) *Usable Knowledge: Social Science and Social Problem Solving*. New Haven, Conn.: Yale University Press.

Lobell, Steven, Norrin Ripsman, and Jeffrey Taliaferro (2009) 'Introduction: Neoclassical Realism, the State, and Foreign Policy.' In S. Lobell, N. Ripsman and J. Taliaferro, eds., *Neoclassical Realism, the State, and Foreign Policy*. New York: Cambridge University Press, pp. 1–41.

MacFarlane, S. Neil and Yuen Foong Khong (2006) *Human Security and the UN: A Critical History*. Bloomington and Indianapolis, Ind.: Indiana University Press.

Maier, Charles S. (2006) *Among Empires: American Ascendancy and Its Predecessors*. Cambridge, Mass.: Harvard University Press.

Maliniak, Daniel, Amy Oakes, Susan Peterson, and Michael J. Tierney (2007) *The View From the Ivory Tower: TRIP Survey of International Relations Faculty in the United States and Canada*. Williamsburg, Va.: Program on the Theory, Research and Practice of International Relations, College of William and Mary.

Maliniak, Daniel and Michael J. Tierney (2009) 'The American school of IPE.' *Review of International Political Economy* 16(1): 6–33.

Mansfield, Edward D. and Etel Solingen (2010) 'Regionalism.' *Annual Review of Political Science* 13 (May).

March, James G. and Johann P. Olsen (1998) 'The Institutional Dynamics of International Political Orders.' *International Organization* 52(4) (Autumn): 943–69.

Martin, Lisa (1992) *Coercive Cooperation: Explaining Multilateral Economic Sanctions*. Princeton, N.J.: Princeton University Press.

Martin, Susan (2004) 'Realism and Weapons of Mass Destruction: A Consequentialist Analysis.' In S. H. Hashmi and S. P. Lee, eds., *Ethics and Weapons of Mass Destruction*. New York: Cambridge University Press, pp. 96–110.

Mayntz, Renate and Fritz W. Scharpf (eds.) (1995) *Gesellschaftliche Selbstregelung und politische Steuerung*. Frankfurt, Germany: Campus.

Mazlish, Bruce (1998) *The Uncertain Sciences*. New Haven, Conn.: Yale University Press.

McAdam, James, Sidney Tarrow, and Charles Tilly (2001) *Dynamics of Contention*. New York: Cambridge University Press.

Mead, George Herbert (1934) *Mind, Self and Society From the Standpoint of a Social Behaviorist*. Chicago, Ill.: University of Chicago Press.

Mearsheimer, John J. (2001) *The Tragedy of Great Power Politics*. New York: W. W. Norton.

Mearsheimer, John J. (1994/95) 'The False Promise of International Institutions.' *International Security* 19(3) (Winter): 5–49.

Menand, Louis (1997) 'An Introduction to Pragmatism.' In L. Menand, ed., *Pragmatism: A Reader*. New York: Vintage Books.

Merton, Robert (1968) *Social Theory and Social Structure*. New York: Free Press.

Miller, Greg (2009) 'Global Economic Crisis Called Biggest U.S. Security Threat.' *Los Angeles Times*, February 13, 2009 [online] http://articles.latimes.com/2009/feb/13/nation/na-security-threat13 (accessed August 18, 2009).

Milner, Helen (1988) *Resisting Protectionism: Global Industries and the Politics of International Trade*. Princeton, N.J.: Princeton University Press.

Moravcsik, Andrew (2008) 'The New Liberalism.' In Christian Reus-Smit and Duncan Snidal, eds., *The Oxford Handbook of International Relations*. New York: Oxford University Press, pp. 234–54.

Moravcsik, Andrew (2003) 'Theory Synthesis in International Relations: Real Not Metaphysical.' Contribution to Gunter Hellman ed., 'Forum: are Dialogue and Synthesis Possible in International Relations?' *International Studies Review* 5(1) (March): 131–6.

Moravcsik, Andrew (1997) 'Taking Preferences Seriously: A Liberal Theory of International Politics.' *International Organization* 51(4) (Autumn): 513–53.

Morgenthau, Hans J. (1970) 'Common Sense and Theories.' In H. J. Morgenthau, ed., *Truth and Power: Essays of a Decade 1960–1970*. New York: Praeger, pp. 241–8.

Münkler, Herfried (2007) *Empires: The Logic of World Domination from Ancient Rome to the United States*. Malden, Mass.: Polity.

Nau, Henry (2002) *At Home Abroad: Identity and Power in American Foreign Policy*. Ithaca, N.Y.: Cornell University Press.

Norton, Anne (2004) 'Political Science As a Vocation.' In Ian Shapiro, Rogers M. Smith, and Tarek E. Masoud, eds., *Problems and Methods in the Study of Politics*. New York: Cambridge University Press, pp. 67–82.

Nye, Joseph (2009) 'Scholars on the Sidelines.' *Washington Post* (April 13): A15.

Oakeshott, Michael (1962 [1947]) 'Rationalism in Politics.' In M. Oakeshott, *Rationalism in Politics, and Other Essays*. London: Methuen, pp. 5–42.

Ober, Josiah (2008) *Democracy and Knowledge: Innovation and Learning in Athens*. Princeton, N.J.: Princeton University Press.

Oberheim, Eric (2006) *Feyerabend's Philosophy*. Berlin and New York: W. de Gruyter.

Onuf, Nicholas (1989) *World of Our Making: Rules and Rule in Social Theory and International Relations*. Columbia, S.C.: University of South Carolina Press.

Owen, David (2002) 'Re-orienting International Relations: On Pragmatism, Pluralism and Practical Reasoning.' *Millennium*, Special Issue on 'Pragmatism and International Relations Theory,' 31(3): 653–73.

Page, Scott (2007) *The Difference: How the Power of Diversity Creates Better Groups, Firms, Schools and Societies*. Princeton, N.J.: Princeton University Press.

Parsons, Craig (2007) *How to Map Arguments in Political Science*. New York: Oxford University Press.

Paul, T. V. (2009) *The Tradition of Non-Use of Nuclear Weapons*. Stanford, Calif.: Stanford University Press.

Paul, T. V. (2007) *Power versus Prudence: Why Nations Forgo Nuclear Weapons*. Montreal, Canada: McGill-Queen's University Press.

Pierson, Paul (2004) *Politics in Time: History, Institutions and Social Analysis*. Princeton, N.J.: Princeton University Press.

Popper, Karl (1959) *The Logic of Scientific Discovery*. London: Hutchinson.

Porter, Bruce (1994) *War and the Rise of the State: The Military Foundations of Modern Politics*. New York: Free Press.

Potter William C. and Gaukhar Mukhatzhanova (2008) 'Divining Nuclear Intentions: A Review Essay.' *International Security* 33(1) (Summer): 139–69.

Pouliot, Vincent (2010) *International Security in Practice: The Politics of NATO-Russia Diplomacy* New York: Cambridge University Press.

Price, Richard, and Christian Reus-Smit (1998) 'Dangerous Liaisons? Critical International Theory and Constructivism.' *European Journal of International Relations* 4(3): 259–94.

Price, Richard and Nina Tannenwald (1996) 'Norms and Deterrence: The Nuclear and Chemical Weapons Taboo.' In Peter J. Katzenstein, ed., *The Culture of National Security.* New York: Columbia University Press, pp. 114–52.

Putnam, Hilary (2002) *The Collapse of the Fact/Value Dichotomy and Other Essays.* Cambridge, Mass.: Harvard University Press.

Putnam, Hilary (1981) *Reason, Truth and History.* New York: Cambridge University Press.

Putnam, Robert D. (1988) 'Diplomacy and Domestic Politics: The Logic of Two-Level Games.' *International Organization* 42 (Summer): 427–60.

Rapoport, Anatol (1960) *Fights, Games and Debates.* Ann Arbor, Mich.: University of Michigan Press.

Ravenhill, John (2008) 'In Search of the Missing Middle.' *Review of International Political Economy* 15(1) (February): 18–29.

Resende-Santos, Joao (2007) *Neorealism, States, and the Modern Mass Army,* New York: Cambridge University Press.

Reus-Smit, Christian (2008) 'Constructivism and the Structure of Ethical Reasoning.' In Richard Price, ed., *Moral Limit and Possibility in World Politics.* New York: Cambridge University Press, pp. 53–82.

Reus-Smit, Christian (2001) 'Human Rights and the Social Construction of Sovereignty.' *Review of International Studies* 27(4): 519–38.

Review of International Political Economy (2009) 'Not so Quiet on the Western Front: The American School of IPE.' Special Issue, 16(1) (February): 1–143.

Rorty, Richard (1999) *Philosophy and Social Hope.* Harmondsworth, UK: Penguin.

Rorty, Richard (1982) *Consequences of Pragmatism.* Minneapolis, Minn.: University of Minnesota Press.

Rose, Gideon (1998) 'Neoclassical Realism and Theories of Foreign Policy.' *World Politics* 51(1): 144–72.

Ruggie, John G. (1998) *Constructing the World Polity: Essays on International Institutionalization.* New York: Routledge.

Ruggie, John G. (1986) 'Continuity and Transformation in the World Polity: Toward a Neorealist Synthesis.' In Robert Keohane, ed., *Neorealism and Its Critics.* New York: Columbia University Press.

Rule, James B. (1997) *Theory and Progress in Social Science.* Cambridge: Cambridge University Press.

Sagan, Scott (2004) 'Realist Perspectives on Ethical Norms and Weapons of Mass Destruction.' In S. H. Hashmi and S. P. Lee, eds., *Ethics and Weapons of Mass Destruction*. New York: Cambridge University Press, pp. 73–95.

Sanderson, Stephen (1987) 'Eclecticism and Its Alternatives.' *Current Perspectives in Social Theory* 8: 313–45.

Sartori, Giovanni (1970) 'Concept Misinformation in Comparative Politics.' *American Political Science Review* 64(4) (December): 1033–53.

Scharpf, Fritz W. (1997) *Games Real Actors Play: Actor-Centered Institutionalism in Policy Research*. Boulder, Colo.: Westview Press.

Schatz, Edward, (ed.) (2009) *Political Ethnography: What Immersion Contributes to the Study of Power*. Chicago, Ill.: University of Chicago Press.

Schiff, Benjamin N. (2008) *Building the International Criminal Court*. New York: Cambridge University Press.

Schimmelfennig, Frank (2003) *The EU, NATO and Integration of Europe: Rules and Rhetoric*. New York: Cambridge University Press.

Schmidt, Vivien (2008) 'Discursive Institutionalism: The Explanatory Power of Ideas and Discourse.' *Annual Review of Political Science* 11: 303–26.

Schram, Sanford (2005) 'A Return to Politics: Perestroika, Phronesis, and Post-Paradigmatic Political Science.' In Kristen Renwick Monroe, ed., *Perestroika: The Raucous Rebellion in Political Science*. New Haven, Conn.: Yale University Press.

Schwartz-Shea, Peregrine (2006) 'Judging Quality: Evaluative Criteria and Epistemic Communities.' In Dvora Yanow and Schwartz-Shea, eds., *Interpretation and Method: Empirical Research Methods and the Interpretive Turn*. Armonk, N.Y.: M. E. Sharpe, pp. 89–113.

Schweller, Randall (2006) *Unanswered Threats: Political Constraints on the Balance of Power*. Princeton, N.J.: Princeton University Press.

Scott, James (1995) Contribution to 'The Role of Theory in Comparative Politics: A Symposium.' *World Politics* 48(1) (October): 1–49.

Seabrooke, Leonard (2006) *The Social Sources of Financial Power: Domestic Legitimacy and International Financial Orders*. Ithaca, N.Y.: Cornell University Press.

Sewell, William (1992) 'A Theory of Structure: Duality, Agency and Transformation.' *American Journal of Sociology* 98(1) (July): 1–29.

Shapiro, Ian (2005) *The Flight From Reality in the Human Sciences*. Princeton, N.J.: Princeton University Press.

Shapiro, Ian and Alexander Wendt (2005) 'The Difference That Realism Makes: Social Science and the Politics of Consent.' In Shapiro 2005.

Sil, Rudra (2009) 'Simplifying Pragmatism: From Social Theory to Problem-Driven Eclecticism.' Contribution to 'The Forum: Pragmatism and International Relations.' *International Studies Review* 11(3) (September): 648–52.

Sil, Rudra (2004) 'Problems Chasing Methods or Methods Chasing Problems? Research Communities, Constrained Pluralism, and the Role of

Eclecticism.' In Ian Shapiro, Rogers Smith, and Tarek Masoud, eds., *Problems and Methods in the Study of Politics.* New York: Cambridge University Press, pp. 307–31.

Sil, Rudra (2000a) 'The Foundations of Eclecticism: The Epistemological Status of Agency, Culture, and Structure in Social Theory.' *Journal of Theoretical Politics* 12(3): 353–87.

Sil, Rudra (2000b) 'Against Epistemological Absolutism: Towards a Pragmatic Center?' In Sil and Doherty 2000, pp. 145–75.

Sil, Rudra and Eileen M. Doherty (eds.) (2000) *Beyond Boundaries? Disciplines, Paradigms and Theoretical Integration in International Studies.* Albany, N.Y.: State University of New York Press.

Sil, Rudra and Peter J. Katzenstein (2010) 'Analytic Eclecticism in the Study of World Politics: Reconfiguring Problems and Mechanisms Across Research Traditions.' *Perspectives on Politics* 8(2) (June): 411–31.

Sinclair, Timothy J. (2005) *The New Masters of Capital: American Bond Rating Agencies and the Politics of Creditworthiness.* Ithaca, N.Y.: Cornell University Press.

Simpson, Gerry (2008) 'The Ethics of the New Liberalism.' In Christian Reus-Smit and Duncan Snidal, eds., *The Oxford Handbook of International Relations.* New York: Oxford University Press, pp. 255–66.

Skocpol, Theda (1979) *States and Social Revolutions.* New York: Cambridge University Press.

Snyder, Jack (2002) 'Anarchy and Culture: Insights from the Anthropology of War.' *International Organization* 56(1) (Winter): 7–45.

Solingen, Etel (2007) *Nuclear Logics: Contrasting Paths in East Asia and the Middle East.* Princeton, N.J.: Princeton University Press.

Solingen, Etel (1998) *Regional Order at Century's Dawn: Global and Domestic Influences on Grand Strategy.* Princeton, N.J.: Princeton University Press.

Solow, Robert M. (1999) 'The Amateur.' *The New Republic* (February 8).

Soros, George (2008) *The New Paradigm for Financial Markets: The Credit Crisis of 2008 and What it Means.* New York: Public Affairs.

Soros, George (1998) *The Crisis of Global Capitalism: Open Society Endangered.* New York: Public Affairs.

Soros, George (1987) *The Alchemy of Finance.* Hoboken, N.J.: Wiley.

Steele, Brent J. (2007) 'Liberal-Idealism: A Constructivist Critique.' *International Studies Review* 9(1) (Spring): 23–52.

Sterling-Folker, Jennifer (2002) *Theories of International Cooperation and the Primacy of Anarchy.* Albany, N.Y.: State University of New York Press.

Sterling-Folker, Jennifer (2000) 'Competing Paradigms or Birds of a Feather? Constructivism and Neoliberalism Compared.' *International Studies Quarterly* 44(1) (March): 97–119.

Stubbs, Richard (2005) *Rethinking Asia's Economic Miracle.* New York: Palgrave.

Tannenwald, Nina (2007) *The Nuclear Taboo.* New York: Cambridge University Press.

Tannenwald, Nina (2005) 'Ideas and Explanation: Advancing the Theoretical Agenda.' *Journal of Cold War Studies* 7(2) (Spring): 13–42.

Tarrow, Sidney (1995) 'Bridging the Quantitative–Qualitative Divide in Political Science.' *American Political Science Review* 89(2) (June): 471–4.

Tetlock, Philip (2005) *Expert Political Judgment: How Good Is It? How Can We Know?* Princeton, N.J.: Princeton University Press.

Tett, Gillian and Anuj Gangahar (2007) 'Limitations of Computer Models.' *Financial Times* (August 14) [online] http://www.ft.com/cms/s/0/b54f3ea8–4a91–11dc-95b5–0000779fd2ac.html (accessed August 14, 2009).

Thelen, Kathleen (2004) *How Institutions Evolve.* New York: Cambridge University Press.

Therborn, Göran (2005) 'In Lieu of Conclusion: More Questions.' In E. Carroll and L. Erickson, eds., *Welfare Politics Cross-Examined: Eclecticist Analytical Perspectives on Sweden and the Developed World from the 1980s to the 2000s.* Amsterdam: Aksant, pp. 321–32.

Tickner, Arlene B. (2003) 'Seeing IR Differently: Notes from the Third World.' *Millennium* 32(2): 295–324.

Tickner, Arlene and Ole Waever (eds.) (2009) *International Relations Scholarship Around the World.* London: Routledge.

Tilly, Charles (1978) *From Mobilization to Revolution.* New York: McGraw-Hill.

Triana, Pablo (2009) *Lecturing Birds on Flying: Can Mathematical Theories Destroy the Financial Markets?* Hoboken, N.J.: John Wiley.

Vasquez, John A. (2003) 'Kuhn versus Lakatos? The Case for Multiple Frames in Appraising International Relations Theory.' In Colin Elman and Miriam Fendius Elman, eds., *Progress in International Relations Theory: Metrics and Methods of Scientific Change.* Cambridge, Mass.: MIT Press, pp. 419–54.

Vasquez, John A. (1997) 'The Realist Paradigm and Progressive versus Degenerative Research Programs.' *American Political Science Review* 91(4): 899–912.

Vasquez, John A. and Colin Elman (eds.) (2003) *Realism and the Balancing of Power: A New Debate.* Upper Saddle River, N.J.: Prentice-Hall.

Vaughan, Diane (1996) *The Challenger Launch Decision: Risky Technology, Culture, and Deviance at NASA.* Chicago, Ill.: University of Chicago Press.

Waever, Ole (1996) 'The Rise and Fall of the Inter-Paradigm Debate.' In Steve Smith, Ken Booth, and Marysia Zalewski, eds., *International Theory: Positivism and Beyond.* Cambridge, UK: Cambridge University Press, pp. 149–85.

Wallace, Lane (2010) 'Multicultural Critical Theory. At B-School?' *New York Times* (January 9) [online] http://www.nytimes.com/2010/01/10/business/10mba.html (accessed January 11, 2010).

Wallace, William (1996) 'Truth and Power, Monks and Technocrats: Theory and Practice in International Relations.' *Review of International Studies* 22: 301–21.

Wallerstein, Immanuel et al. (1996) *Open the Social Sciences: Report of the Gulbenkian Commission on the Restructuring of the Social Sciences.* Stanford, Calif.: Stanford University Press.

Walt, Stephen M. (2003) 'The Progressive Power of Realism.' In Colin Elman and John A. Vasquez, eds., *Realism and the Balancing of Power.* Upper Saddle River, N.J.: Prentice-Hall, pp. 58–67.

Walt, Stephen M. (1997) 'The Progressive Power of Realism.' *American Political Science Review* 91(4): 931–5.

Walt, Stephen M. (1987) *The Origins of Alliances.* Ithaca: Cornell University Press.

Waltz, Kenneth N. (1999) 'Globalization and Governance.' *PS Online* (December).

Waltz, Kenneth N. (1996) 'International Politics is not Foreign Policy.' *International Security* 6(1) (Autumn): 54–7.

Waltz, Kenneth N. (1979) *Theory of International Politics.* Reading, Mass.: Addison-Wesley.

Waltz, Kenneth N. (1967) *Foreign Policy and Democratic Politics: The American and British Experience.* New York: Little, Brown.

Waltz, Kenneth N. (1959) *Man, the State and War.* New York: Columbia University Press.

Weaver, Catherine (2009) 'Reflections on the American School: An IPE of Our Own Making.' *Review of International Political Economy* 16(1) (February): 1–5.

Weeks, Jessica (2008) 'Autocratic Audience Costs: Regime Type and Signaling Resolve.' *International Organization* 62(1) (January): 35–64.

Wendt, Alexander (1999) *Social Theory of International Politics.* New York: Cambridge University Press.

Wendt, Alexander (1992) 'Anarchy is What States Make of It: The Social Construction of Power Politics.' *International Organization* 46 (Spring): 391–425.

Wilson, Edward O. (1998) *Consilience: The Unity of Knowledge.* New York: Alfred Knopf.

Wisdom, O. J. (1974) 'The Incommensurability Thesis.' *Philosophical Studies* 25: 299–301.

Woll, Cornelia (2008) *Firm Interests: How Governments Shape Business Lobbying on Global Trade.* Ithaca, N.Y.: Cornell University Press.

World Bank (1993) *An East Asian Renaissance: Ideas for Growth.* Washington D.C.: World Bank.

Yanow, Dvora (2006) 'Thinking Interpretively: Philosophical Presuppositions and the Human Sciences.' In Dvora Yanow and Peregrine Schwartz-Shea, eds., *Interpretation and Method: Empirical Research Methods and the Interpretive Turn.* Armonk, N.Y.: M.E. Sharpe, pp. 5–26.

Index